# CAMPUS HATE
# SPEECH ON TRIAL

# ONE WEEK LOAN

# CAMPUS HATE SPEECH ON TRIAL

## Second Edition, Revised

Timothy C. Shiell

UNIVERSITY PRESS OF KANSAS

Published by the University Press of Kansas (Lawrence, Kansas 66045), which was organized by the Kansas Board of Regents and is operated and funded by Emporia State University, Fort Hays State University, Kansas State University, Pittsburg State University, the University of Kansas, and Wichita State University

Library of Congress Cataloging-in-Publication Data

Shiell, Timothy C.
Campus hate speech on trial / Timothy C. Shiell. — 2nd ed.
    p. cm.
  Includes bibliographical references and index.
  ISBN 978-0-7006-1647-3 (cloth : alk. paper) — ISBN 978-0-7006-1648-0 (pbk. : alk. paper)
1. Freedom of speech — United States. 2. Hate speech — United States. 3. Discrimination in higher education — Law and legislation — United States. I. Title.
  KF4772.S445 2009
  342.7308'53 — dc22
                                                                                            2008054899

British Library Cataloguing-in-Publication Data is available.

Printed in the United States of America

10 9 8 7 6 5 4 3 2 1

The paper used in this publication is recycled and contains 30 percent postconsumer waste. It is acid free and meets the minimum requirements of the American National Standard for Permanence of Paper for Printed Library Materials Z39.48-1992.

To Mackenzie and Ethan

# CONTENTS

# PREFACE TO
# THE SECOND EDITION

As I write this preface, ten years after publication of the first edition of *Campus Hate Speech on Trial*, restrictions on faculty and student speech on college campuses continue to be hotly contested in the mainstream media; on the Internet; in the journals of academic disciplines; in courtrooms, classrooms, and chat rooms; and elsewhere. In order to educate interested readers about the most significant developments in the controversy arising post–first edition, the University Press of Kansas and I undertook this updated edition. The prominent developments concern the Deterrence Argument, the hostile environment approach, new judicial decisions, and the International Argument. Rather than rewrite chapters 1 through 7, the most direct and logical way to address these developments was to add a new chapter, Chapter 8, "The Debate: 1998–2008."

I wish to point out that although these developments raise some new questions and new theses and provide additional material for reflection and debate, none of them warrant (in my opinion) any substantive changes in the major "lessons" I offered in Chapter 7, "And the Verdict Is . . ."; specifically, that (1) hostile environment theory was and is the most plausible legal basis for regulating hate speech on American campuses; (2) problems in this approach and the special nature of universities require us to apply it with extreme caution to college students and faculty; (3) those who administer campus speech codes too often are not qualified to do so; (4) universities are best advised to emphasize an educational, proactive approach rather than a punitive, reactionary speech code; and (5) universities ought to enforce punitive speech restrictions only in cases in which one or more specific individuals were targeted in a captive-audience context, the speech was intended to cause harm to the victim(s), was unrelated to any legitimate academic purpose, and was egregious (in a single case), pervasive (in a series of incidents), or done in conjunction with illegal conduct. I contend that by and large the new developments support these lessons too.

In addition to the new chapter, this second edition has a significantly expanded bibliography and list of legal decisions. Both now include many of the pre-1998 items that were not included in the 1998 edition as well as over two hundred post-1998 items, the most significant of which are addressed in the new chapter. While the addition of these items does not exhaust the vast literature on the subject, the new bibliography offers the reader the most comprehensive and up-to-date list of resources currently available.

Finally, I have a brief list of thanks to extend. First, I want to thank the readers of the first edition as well as the audiences at my speaking engagements on campus hate speech for their insightful comments and questions. I hope this second edition elicits even more reader response, whether favorable or critical, and is even more helpful to individuals who are contemplating the pros and cons of hate speech codes, the victims of hate speech, administrators of speech codes, and those who face or have faced enforcement of a campus speech code. Second, I want to thank editor in chief Michael Briggs and the University Press of Kansas for publishing this second edition. Given the immense literature on the subject, it is our hope that this revised second edition will strengthen the status of *Campus Hate Speech on Trial* as a uniquely valuable resource on the topic. I must also report that developing and delivering this second edition was as smooth and pleasurable as the first edition, for which I also am very thankful to Susan McRory. Last but not least, I want to thank my wife, Carolyn, daughter, Mackenzie, and son, Ethan, for their support of my scholarly work, not the least of which includes their listening to my ideas, their comments on ideas and drafts, and their patience with my working at the dinner table all day and many a night for many months. All thanks and support aside, I, of course, remain solely responsible for any mistaken claims or other errors contained herein.

# PREFACE TO
# THE FIRST EDITION

When I began my research into campus hate speech in 1991–1992, it was my suspicion that a university was legally and morally justified (given certain qualifications) in restricting campus hate speech on hostile environment harassment grounds. In a classic case of finding evidence that supports one's prejudgments, my initial research supported my suspicion, and I defended this approach in a series of papers presented at the 1993 Wisconsin Philosophical Association Meeting, the 1994 Central Division Meeting of the American Philosophical Association, and the 1994 Minnesota Philosophical Society Meeting. Joseph Ellin, as guest editor, invited me to submit and then published a short version of my argument in 92 *APA Newsletter on Philosophy and Law* 64 (1993). Most of the participants in these sessions and several respondents to the published paper supported my position, but (to my good fortune) several critics raised questions that forced me to reconsider some of my proposals and justifications. In time, I discovered several legal scholars were making similar arguments, but as I read more deeply into the arguments on both sides and investigated free speech and hostile environment harassment doctrines and cases, I began to back off from my original proposals. For reasons that shall become clear in the book, I ultimately came to believe that the critics have the stronger position for the most part and that American universities and colleges should adopt and enforce only very narrow speech restrictions. Yet I hope my presentation of the arguments adequately reflects my own personal struggle with the arguments on both sides of the issue.

I have many people and organizations to thank for their support. My travel to many conferences to present or to hear papers on this topic was underwritten by the UW-Stout English and Philosophy Department; Gerhane Dougherty, dean of the UW-Stout College of Arts and Sciences; and a UW-Stout Faculty Research Initiative Grant. I thank John Arthur and Don Scheid in particular for their critical comments on papers I delivered at those conferences. My arguments and exposition matured greatly as a result of a 1994 National Endowment for the Humanities Summer Study Grant and a 1996–1997 UW-Stout Faculty Research Initiative Grant. In obtaining both of these grants, I received valuable support and advice from Ted Knous and Sue Foxwell from the UW-Stout Research and Promotion office. As I worked on details in the final chapter during 1996, I held two department "roundtables" and want to thank Sue Bridwell Beckham, Dick Gardner, Janet Polansky, Bob Schuler, and Virginia Wolf for their considered judgments shared during those discussions. I owe a great debt of gratitude to my colleagues Alan Block and Clark Leeson as well as my wife, Carolyn, and my brother Doug for their valuable insights and willingness to serve as sounding boards for my ideas all through the years this manuscript was in progress. I thank Sam Walker, Thomas Grey, Charles Calleros, Don Lively, and Bob Ladenson for their useful comments and suggestions on various aspects of my project, and Andrew Altman for making several major suggestions for improving the final chapter. And, last but certainly not least, my thanks go to the good people at the University Press of Kansas, especially Nancy Scott Jackson, who judged that this book was worth publishing and helped fix several problems in Chapter 7, and Rebecca Knight Giusti, whose production work was inspired. I am solely responsible for any remaining defects.

# CAMPUS HATE
# SPEECH ON TRIAL

# 1
# Introduction

*It is an unfortunate fact of our constitutional system that the ideals of freedom and equality are often in conflict. The difficult and sometimes painful task of our political and legal institutions is to mediate the appropriate balance between these competing values.*

JUDGE AVERN COHN, *Doe v. University of Michigan*

## FREEDOM AND EQUALITY

In 1989 Judge Avern Cohn faced the decision of whether or not to uphold an antidiscrimination speech code at the University of Michigan at Ann Arbor that a graduate student, "John Doe" (a conventional court pseudonym used to keep one's real identity anonymous), had filed suit against. An easy case? Well, the judge might have thought that the university was obviously correct and dismissed Doe's complaint in deference to a public university's legal and moral obligation to provide equal educational opportunity to all students. On the other hand, he might have thought that the university was obviously wrong and happily struck down the code in order to ensure that the university's legal and moral obligation to provide freedom of expression to all students was met. (Doe wanted to be free to discuss in class and other academic forums "controversial theories positing biologically-based differences between sexes and races," which he was afraid might be perceived as sexist and racist and thereby punished under the policy.) But Judge Cohn did not find this an easy case: he found it "unfortunate," "difficult," even "painful." He had to decide for somebody, but clearly he was torn.

Judge Cohn is not alone. In my years of researching hate speech, I have found that this issue and the real-life cases it involves leave most people unsettled: they think that there are egregious cases that deserve sanctions, yet they also recognize that regulatory policies are often vague and can be arbitrarily or otherwise wrongly enforced. They want the guilty to be punished and the innocent to be left alone. Would that we had a policy that worked so neatly! But of course we don't, and what is more, we can't. If this book accomplishes nothing else, it should make clear that any policy, no matter how sophisticated, no matter how well-grounded in history or law or philosophy or politics, will leave something to be desired. Still, we are in the position of Judge Cohn: we have to decide *something*, we have to set some kind of policy on hate speech (even if only in the somewhat awkwardly put sense of having a policy not to have a policy).

You may wonder why people make such a fuss about campus hate speech. Is it really a problem that warrants the spilling of so much ink (literally thousands of articles and dozens of chapters in books) or the expense and effort of analyzing and arguing over legal technicalities (literally thousands of hours)? How often does hate speech really occur? How seriously does it hurt anyone? Is it just a matter of some oversensitive students and faculty overreacting?

Judge for yourself. You will find instances of hate speech at many American campuses. It might be a racial or sexual insult or epithet, a threat, a demeaning joke, or a degrading stereotype. It might be posted on a dormitory bulletin board or scratched into a bathroom stall or overheard in the hall. You might read it in the campus newspaper or access it through a computer terminal or have it mysteriously "spammed" onto your screen. Students, professors, staff, administrators: they use hate speech, sometimes intentionally, sometimes unwittingly, and there is no safe haven. According to one study, serious hate speech incidents have occurred on more than 250 American campuses and involve between eight hundred thousand and one million students each year.[1] This same report found that one-fifth of minority students experience hate speech during an academic year and that one-fourth of the victims face it more than once. Advocates of speech codes, whose arguments we examine in detail in Chapters 2 and 5, offer compelling evidence of the serious harms and heavy burdens that hate speech can and does impose on its victims. Study after study has shown that hate speech can cause fear in the gut, difficulty in breathing, nightmares, posttraumatic stress disorder, hypertension, even psychosis and suicide.[2] As Richard Delgado and Mari Matsuda have so aptly put it, hate speech can be "words that wound." These words (often combined with illegal actions such as vandalism, theft, and battery) have caused people to quit jobs, leave school, move to a new neighborhood, and avoid public places.

The seriousness of these harms has led many people to believe that hate speech, at least under certain conditions, violates the guarantees of equal protection under the law provided for by the Fourteenth Amendment to the U.S. Constitution and by various pieces of federal legislation (such as the Civil Rights Acts of 1964 and 1990). That is, some people believe that hate speech affecting faculty and students (not to mention administrators and staff) can be so severe as to constitute a denial of equality under the law and equal opportunity in employment and education. Since these equality rights are essential to our modern conception of a just political and legal order (and were obtained only through a long and sometimes bloody struggle), many educators and legal scholars have come to believe that even though free speech is an important moral and political value, hate speech should not be tolerated on college campuses. As Charles R. Lawrence III writes:

> We must eschew abstractions of first amendment theory that proceed without attention to the dysfunction in the marketplace of ideas created by the racism and unequal access to that market. We must think hard about how best to launch legal attacks against the most indefensible forms of hate speech. Good lawyers can create exceptions and narrow interpretations limiting the harm of hate speech without opening the floodgates of censorship. We must weigh carefully and critically the competing constitutional values expressed in the first and fourteenth amendments.[3]

Following this logic, a nationwide push for campus hate speech regulations began in 1987, when leading American institutions like Stanford University and the University of Michigan adopted hate speech regulations as part of a response to growing problems of bigotry and prejudice on their campuses. The movement was widely embraced on U.S. campuses, and by 1992 more than three hundred universities had similar codes.[4] Many of the original codes were directed only at students, but as we shall see, present codes typically regulate faculty and staff too.

To be sure, the phenomenon of campus hate speech and the burdens it imposes on some students, faculty, and administrators are not new. After all, hate speech has been used in the United States as long as—well, as long as there has been a United States. These jokes, these stereotypes, these derogatory terms are part of our history and our present and may seem natural, inevitable, the way it is, and thus hardly an appropriate subject of media and scholarly attention. Thus, some observers want to dismiss out of hand any attempt to deal with hate speech as doomed to fail. I recently saw this kind of attitude expressed in a slogan on a student's T-shirt: "End racism. Kill everyone." As if racism couldn't be dealt with in any other way, as if we must simply accept it because it seems inevitable.

Advocates of speech codes see things differently. They see speech codes as one tool to help minorities and women attain equal access to and equal opportunity within higher education. Advocates typically viewed the increase in hate speech on college campuses in the late 1980s and early 1990s as a reaction to increased diversity on campus, a kind of lashing out to protect old ways and old privileges that benefited white males. In view of these factors, advocates urge action now because the problem has taken on increased importance—hate speech should no longer be considered just another fact of life to be accepted. It is to be dealt with, directly and effectively.

Despite this widespread push by advocates, many other people maintain that campus hate speech regulations violate the First Amendment's guarantee of free speech. Critics of campus speech codes typically acknowledge the offensiveness and harm of hate speech, yet they still argue against campus speech regulations. They recognize the moral and political value of equality but believe that equality should not come at the expense of another one of our most fundamental political values, namely, freedom of speech and press. They worry that these codes are too sweeping in their regulation and that overzealous enforcers will abuse their authority. Reasoning in this way, some universities, such as Yale, decided not to enforce existing regulations that punished offensive speech,[5] while others, such as the University of Pennsylvania, decided to drop their speech regulations after a short period.[6] Perhaps more important, some who oppose speech codes believe that racial and sexual equality are enhanced through free speech, not at the expense of free speech. As Nadine Strossen, president of the American Civil Liberties Union from 1991 to 2008, writes in a direct response to Professor Lawrence in a *Duke Law Journal* debate:

> Because civil libertarians have learned that free speech is an indispensable instrument for the promotion of other rights and freedoms—including racial equality—we fear that the movement to regulate campus expression will undermine equality, as well as free speech. Combating racial discrimination and protecting free speech should be viewed as mutually reinforcing, rather than antagonistic, goals. . . . Those who frame the debate in terms of this false dichotomy simply drive artificial wedges between would-be allies in what should be a common effort to promote civil rights and civil liberties.[7]

Strossen's point is that those who argue for their rights—including those who argue for equal rights—are often minority dissenters, outsiders, social critics whose speech may not be protected if government is allowed to silence those who offend the majority. Suffragettes offended many men. Civil rights marchers offended white segregationists. Vietnam War dissidents offended war supporters. The list goes on and on.

The debate between the two sides—advocates who champion college hate speech codes and critics who oppose them—hit the public eye in a big way from 1989 to 1992 as literally hundreds of articles appeared in national and local newspapers and magazines, academic newsletters and journals, publications of professional organizations, law reviews, alumni newsletters, and other places. The attention given to these codes brought hate speech back into the national spotlight in a way it hadn't been since a group of Nazis proposed to march in the substantially Jewish Chicago suburb of Skokie in 1977.[8] The collision of these points of view has, in effect, put hate speech "on trial," in some cases figuratively and in others quite literally, as in *Doe v. University of Michigan*. This trial raises crucial questions we must answer candidly and carefully: Should universities allow full freedom of expression, including hateful and harassing speech concerning race, ethnic origin, gender, and the like? If a regulatory code is adopted, what should it prohibit? And why? What exactly are we hoping to accomplish through such a code? How effective will codes be in attaining their goals? Are there more effective ways to promote and attain these goals? Will adoption of such codes open the door to self-righteous censors who simply want to silence their opponents? Will hate speech codes wrongfully impinge on student and faculty academic freedom?

These questions are important for many reasons, some of which are explored in this book, but many people simply don't understand very clearly what really happened in the hate speech debate, why it happened, what was at stake, and what important developments have taken place since the debate fell out of the popular media spotlight. In view of this, a major aim of this book is to bring people up to speed on what the current situation is and how we got here, through a comprehensive and up-to-date analysis of hate speech on college campuses—to provide a singularly useful resource for those interested in this specific debate or in public policy issues in general. However, my aim in this book is not merely to help the reader understand what happened and why, but also to "move the dialectic," so to speak, to provide the single most cogent and comprehensive argument and offer a constructive proposal on this uniquely American dilemma in the final two chapters.[9] Thus, in addition to describing and analyzing historical, political, legal, and philosophical dimensions of the debate, I will draw several conclusions from my study and defend a proposal for how universities might best deal with campus hate speech. Before we put hate speech on trial, however, a few cautionary points are in order.

## SOME CAUTIONARY NOTES

The task of analyzing the campus hate speech debate and defending one's opinion on the issue (whether one advocates or objects to speech codes) is a daunting one. It is, in effect, to attempt to draw a line between individual liberty and state regulatory authority, and this is one of the perennial problems of politics, law, and philosophy. How free should we be? Within our constitutional democracy, when does my conduct and speech go so far as to require government intervention? Assuming words can cause harm, is it within the proper purposes and competency of government to protect citizens from such harms? If the government can punish me for hate speech, can it also punish me for sexually explicit speech or vulgar expressions lampooning politicians or government policies? It is to join a debate whose roots are in ancient political philosophy (remember Plato's thoughts about the education of the guardians and philosopher-kings and his attack on the poets in *The Republic*?[10]), and whose drama has been played out on the American scene at least since Justice Oliver Wendell Holmes Jr., in powerfully written dissents in the aftermath of World War I, began defending the citizen's right to assert speech offensive to other citizens, even a majority of other citizens.[11] Samuel Walker, an authority on the history of hate speech in America, has described how Americans wrestled with the issue of how "tolerant" we should be of the "intolerant" (those who wish to force an opinion or lifestyle on others) in cases involving Jehovah's Witnesses and Nazis in the 1930s, Communists and racists in the 1940s and 1950s, and Vietnam War dissidents in the 1960s and 1970s, long before we got concerned about college hate speech codes in the 1980s and 1990s.[12] Should people be free to assert "fighting words"? What are fighting words, anyway? Should citizens be punished for using racist epithets or promoting a racist ideology? Can we identity and punish "bad" speech without chilling "good" speech? Should citizens be punished for proclaiming politically unpopular, even "un-American," speech? It also is to join a continuing debate over two fundamental American values, equal opportunity and free speech, values that cannot both be fully realized in this situation, but only balanced to a greater or lesser degree; for even if equality and free speech are mutually supporting in many ways, as Strossen maintains, they do not support each other in all ways.

In light of such complexities, one is tempted to simplify, to propose a kind of one-dimensional litmus test. Many critics of college hate speech codes have done so by arguing that all hate speech codes are mere billy clubs in the hands of the politically correct liberal thought police. Edward J. Cleary, for example, a self-professed liberal and the lawyer who defended Robert Viktora's right to express his racism in the 1992 Supreme Court case challenging a St. Paul hate crimes ordinance, suggests this in his book *Beyond the Burning Cross*.[13] So do a host of politically conservative critics of speech codes, including the nationally syndicated columnist George Will and the academic critic Dinesh D'Souza.[14] Let us call this the "political correctness objection" (or "p.c. objection," for short).

I want to caution against a simplistic understanding of the p.c. objection for several reasons. We ought not preemptively reject all arguments for college hate speech codes on the grounds that they all are attempts by ideologically bound feminazis or thought police to silence their political opponents. Why? First, because it is simply not true that all advocates of campus speech codes are ideologues bent on silencing political opponents. Although some defenders of speech codes may be out to silence political opponents, some defenders of speech codes have no such intention. Not all hate speech code advocates endorse "broad" hate speech codes banning single uses of epithets or racist speech by whites but not blacks; some advocates of college speech codes defend "narrow" codes whose point is not to "privilege" anyone's discourse or change balances of power, but rather to provide a mechanism for the protection of individual rights guaranteed by law. In fact, critics of speech codes often cryptically suggest their own speech codes.[15] In other words, the p.c. objection falsely imputes evil intentions to all of its opponents (they're all ideological thought police bent on destroying freethinkers), when the intention of many defenders of speech codes is to design a public policy sensitive to the requirements of both free speech and equal opportunity, not to silence political opponents (whoever exactly those might be).

The p.c. objection also fails because it is essentially made ad hominem, an attack on the person making the argument, not the argument itself. To reject a public policy because of the circumstances or intentions of its proponent without refuting the arguments for the public policy is a logical fallacy, a piece of "pseudo-reasoning," as some logicians put it, because it seems to be offering a reason for a belief when it really is not.[16] If an advocate's (or critic's) position is to be rejected, it must be because he or she has failed to offer logically compelling arguments for the position, not because you disapprove of or dislike the arguer or suspect bad motives.

Finally, the p.c. objection should be put aside because it forces the debate to move to its lowest level—the level of crass, narrowly self-interested partisan politics—and abandons the moral and political high ground: the level of our shared political ideals embodied in the U.S. Constitution and federal legislation. The debate will leave us talking past one another if conducted at the level of ideologically driven agendas and will join us in genuine dialogue only if engaged in at the level of shared democratic values. This is not to say that we should ignore people's motives or agendas when they seek greater power and legal authority to punish others, it is only to say that we must also look beyond that and determine whether the arguments for the proposals pass our shared tests of sound public policy.

The danger inherent in the p.c. objection is that it is too often used to try to preempt careful reflection about the issues by reducing one's opponents to the level of a caricature. It's a time-honored tactic in our political life, of course, because it is often a rhetorically effective one. But we must separate the rhetoric from the reality. In this case, the accusation of "political correctness" is purely rhetorical (in the sense of illogical persuasion), a kind of "horse laugh" that people would be foolish to fall for. Even if the arguments for hate speech codes ultimately fail (as I shall argue), they are worth listening to because they help us understand our common political values and history as well as our different visions of what America ought to be today and in the future.

I also want to caution against accepting another kind of overly simple pre-emptory strike that critics of speech codes may employ, namely, the claim that no argument for speech codes is worth taking seriously because the debate is over: judges have refused to enforce broad hate speech codes. In *Doe v. University of Michigan*, 721 F. Supp. 852 (E.D. Mich. 1989), a federal court struck down the university's code when an anonymous graduate student in psychology, represented by the ACLU, argued that the code violated his First Amendment right to discuss in the classroom controversial theories positing biologically based differences between sexes and races. In *UWM-Post v. Board of Regents of the University of Wisconsin*, 774 F. Supp. 1163 (E.D. Wis. 1991), a federal court struck down the UW System's code when a student newspaper that feared prosecution under the UW System hate speech code and an anonymous student who had been punished for a violation of the code challenged it on First Amendment grounds. In *Iota Xi Chapter of Sigma Chi Fraternity v. George Mason University*, 773 F. Supp. 792 (E.D. Va. 1991), a federal court upheld a fraternity's free speech rights in striking down the university's disciplinary action against the fraternity's members for dressing as "ugly women" in a "Dress a Sig" event during Derby Days. In *R.A.V. v. City of St. Paul*, 505 U.S. 377 (1992), the U.S. Supreme Court struck down a municipal hate crimes ordinance. In *Dambrot v. Central Michigan University*, 839 F. Supp. 477 (E.D. Mich. 1993), a federal court struck down the university's ban on "verbal harassment" when challenged by a coach and several students on First Amendment grounds. And in *Robert Corry et al. v. Leland Stanford Junior University*, County of Santa Clara Superior Court, Case no. 740309, February 27, 1995, the court struck down Stanford's speech code when it was challenged by nine students who argued that the code "permanently damages the quality of education" by "artificially chilling open discussion of important issues." In Chapter 8, I will address several more recent cases arriving at the same conclusion.

The critic might claim that the courts' refusal to enforce speech codes in all of these cases was inevitable, given landmark free speech decisions permitting a man to wear in a courthouse a jacket with the words "Fuck the Draft" written on the back, *Cohen v. California*, 403 U.S. 15 (1971); a neo-Nazi group to march in a predominantly Jewish community, *Collin v. Smith*, 578 F.2d 1197 (7th Cir.), *cert. denied*, 439 U.S. 916 (1978); publishers to print violent pornography, *American Bookseller's Association v. Hudnut*, 475 U.S. 1001 (1986), and lampoon a religious figure by portraying him having sex with his drunken mother in an outhouse, *Hustler v. Falwell*, 485 U.S. 46 (1988); and a protestor against the U.S. government to burn the American flag, *Texas v. Johnson*, 491 U.S. 397 (1989). The courts protected free speech in all of these cases; they will certainly see their way to protecting freedom of speech against an assault by public universities.

This attempt to preempt arguments for speech codes is mistaken in several respects. First, the court decisions on campus hate speech codes, and the other examples typically listed, were not inevitable. Any serious student of free speech knows that what was once protected may not be in the future, and that what was once unprotected may well become protected at some future point. The words the Supreme Court punished in *Chaplinsky v. New Hampshire*, 315 U.S. 568 (1942), would not be punished today. Words the court is unconcerned with in peacetime become subject to close scrutiny in wartime. A politically conservative majority in the Supreme Court would undoubtedly uphold greater restrictions on speech than a politically liberal majority. As free speech historian Samuel Walker notes:

> There was nothing inevitable about the outcome [of precedent-setting free speech cases]. My central argument is that the strong tradition of free speech resulted from a series of choices. These choices have been not only Supreme Court decisions but also choices by advocacy groups that brought major cases before the court and choices by American society.[17]

Second, in saying the debate is over, the critic fails to recognize the new battleground on which the debate is now being fought, namely, the law of hostile environment. Beginning with *Rogers v. EEOC*, 454 F.2d 234 (5th Cir. 1971), *cert. denied*, 406 U.S. 957 (1972), courts have been holding employers and educators liable for damages when employees or students suffer from a hostile environment materially altering the employment or educational conditions of members of groups protected under Titles VII and IX of the Civil Rights Act of 1964. Since hostile environment harassment based on race, color, sex, religion, or ethnicity has been ruled illegal by the U.S. Supreme Court in *Meritor Savings Bank, FSB v. Vinson*, 477 U.S. 57 (1986), and upheld in *Harris v. Forklift Systems*, 114 S. Ct. 367 (1993), most analysts of hate speech codes, myself included, have left fighting words and group defamation/libel arguments to the side and focus on the relationship of hate speech and hostile environments. (This argument is discussed in detail in Chapters 5 and 8.) Thus, even if courts struck down earlier hate speech codes relying on some free speech doctrines, we shall see how they have left open the door to the development of Title VII–like harassment-based codes.

To be sure, there are critics (whose arguments will be heard in Chapters 6 and 8) who maintain that the hostile environment approach should fare no better than the fighting words or group libel or emotional distress approaches in spite of its acceptance by the Supreme Court, because hate speech codes employing it will violate the First Amendment on exactly the same grounds of overbreadth, vagueness, and overzealous enforcement as codes employing the fighting words, group libel, and emotional distress approaches. But in taking this line of argument, these critics recognize not only that the debate is not over and that its outcome is unsettled, but also that the ideals pitted against one another are shared, not merely held by the "politically correct," for even these critics concede the legality of punishing quid pro quo harassment in view of the value of equality.[18] Numerous issues concerning campus speech codes remain hotly contested, and whatever other objections may face arguments for campus speech codes (and there are many to be considered), one cannot dismiss every proposed campus speech code as being foreclosed by present court decisions.

Finally, even if it were true that present legal doctrine is inconsistent with every proposed campus speech code, it would still be wrong to assume that the law is static. The law—whether the law of contracts, torts, or free speech—changes constantly. This is a fact of all legal systems, and perhaps especially true of U.S. constitutional law, including First Amendment law, in the twentieth and twenty-first centuries. For better or worse, the law evolves in response to social and political pressures as well as technological innovations. As the former chief justice, William Rehnquist, has put it, the Constitution is a "living document."[19] Moreover, the law must be sensitive to contexts, and it is not a settled conclusion that all forms of offensive speech should be tolerated.

First Amendment expert Rodney Smolla points out in his book *Free Speech in an Open Society*:

> Flag-burning and race-baiting are both forms of offensive speech. But race-baiting is much worse. To burn the flag is to attack the polity as a

whole. The attack may be fierce, but a nation brave enough to embark on the experiment of a truly open culture is big enough to endure it. To attack another because of his or her racial, ethnic, religious, or sexual identity, however, is not to engage in mere dissent against the whole. Such an attack is rather to separate out certain members of the whole and make them targets, degrade them, strip them of their humanity, and set others against them.[20]

Nor is it a foregone conclusion that the law of the street or sidewalk should be exactly the same as law for the dormitory or classroom, since there are considerations of privacy that arise in the dorm and disruption in the classroom. Even Nadine Strossen, generally a critic of university speech codes, concedes that

> in weighing the constitutional concerns of free speech, equality and privacy that hate speech regulation implicates, decisionmakers must take into account the particular context within the university in which the speech occurs. For example, the Court's generalization about the heightened protection due free speech in the academic world certainly is applicable to some campus areas, such as parks, malls, or other traditional gathering places. The generalization, however, may not be applicable to other areas, such as students' dormitory rooms.[21]

Thus, we should not fall for simplistic attempts to preempt debate on the topic of hate speech codes. We ought not dismiss codes as mere stabs at enforcing political correctness, nor casually dismiss them as inconsistent with current court holdings. We must look carefully at the political and moral values at stake, the facts of enforcement and administration, the most plausible arguments on each side, and not merely the anecdotal evidence of a newspaper editorial or the exaggerated and one-sided arguments of ideologues.

## THE IMPACT OF HATE SPEECH REGULATION

The University of Massachusetts at Amherst proposed a "sweeping" new code regulating the speech of all students, faculty, and staff members in 1995.[22] The code would have banned "verbal or physical conduct that a reasonable person, with the same characteristics as the targeted individual or group of individuals, would find discriminatorily alters" their conditions of employment or education on the basis of "race, color, national or ethnic origin, gender, sexual orientation, age, religion, marital status, veteran status, or disability" (to which the graduate students added: citizenship, culture, HIV status, language, parental status, political affiliation or belief, and pregnancy status). The policy banned everything from epithets to "ritual and unspoken behaviors." Supporters said the policy was needed even if courts have struck down other policies as unconstitutional. Opponents regarded the proposal as "disconnected from the world at large" and maintained that "reverting to an old-fashioned speech-code is not helpful." Who is right? When does hate speech go too far? Will a code like this achieve its goals? Cornell University was torn over the James B. Maas sexual harassment case in 1995.[23] Maas, a longtime popular psychology professor at Cornell (he had been named best professor at Cornell in a student survey in 1994), was accused by four former students of sexual harassment and convicted by a faculty panel. He sued the university for $1.5 million for violating his due process rights. Some faculty and students feel the investigation was proper and accuse him of trying to divert attention away from the charges. Others, including the American Association of University Professors, share his due process concerns. Maas's counsel, law professor Fausto Rossi, compared the situation to "a Massachusetts witch trial," and Jeremy Rafkin, a professor of government, believes Maas is guilty of nothing more than "rudeness." How should a university conduct an investigation into hate speech or harassment charges? What exactly constitutes "hate speech" or "harassment"?

Our answers to the questions raised by campus hate speech regulation should come closer to the mark if we examine the hate speech and hostile environment harassment issues systematically—looking at their many historical and political dimensions; relevant court decisions outlining the contours of free speech, academic freedom, and government authority; and the many implications (both philosophical and nonphilosophical) of our public policy decisions. This should result in a better understanding not only of the whos, whats, and whys of the hate speech debate, but also of our individual and collective goals. Edward Cleary writes, "Part of the constitutional birthright in America is the right to dissent. It is how we respond to situations such as that in *R.A.V. v. St. Paul* which define us as a nation."[24]

How we respond to hate speech, on and off campus, helps define us as a nation. Free speech in the United States has a unique history and offers unique protections (a point we shall consider more fully in Chapter 8).[25] But if some advocates of campus hate speech codes are correct, government would be able to punish speech currently protected. For example, if Catharine MacKinnon is right, all "hard" and "soft" pornography (on or off campus) would be punishable too on grounds that it violates equality rights.[26] Again, if Richard Delgado is right, all use of racial and gender epithets (on or off campus) would be punishable on grounds that they cause harm.[27] On the other hand, if some critics of campus hate speech codes are correct, government will be prevented from punishing speech currently sanctioned. For example, if Kingsley Browne is correct, all racist and sexist speech (on or off campus) would be protected, even if it creates a hostile environment.[28] Because of the doctrines and principles involved in the campus hate speech debate, what we say about it will have important ramifications for speech in other areas.

The issues are more complicated than many commentators let on. Especially in newspaper and magazine articles, both defenders and critics of campus hate speech codes often omit or weakly state arguments from the other side of the debate, offer only examples that confirm their own position, and substitute slanted rhetoric for rational argument. The discussions are generally much better in the academic and legal journals, but there also, defenders too heavily rely on descriptions of the most horrific cases (which always involve illegal conduct and not just offensive words) to score their points, while critics too often merely repeat the free speech mantra ("it is our first freedom," etc.). We will have to analyze important doctrines and concepts involved in the debate: what "harm" under the law is; what "fighting words" and "group libel" and "hostile environments" are; what "academic freedom" is; what "overbreadth" and "undue vagueness" and "arbitrary enforcement" are; and so on. We will have to analyze important assumptions underpinning the doctrines and arguments: what the relevant moral principles are; what the "marketplace of ideas" really is; what the consequences of our policy decisions are likely to be on individuals, institutions, and our constitutional democracy; and the like. A study of this depth and breadth is needed, but has not been undertaken.

Before concluding this introduction, I should note that the focus of this book is on public policy analysis in First Amendment contexts (that is, situations involving a government agency or authorized agent or publicly funded program) rather than non–First Amendment contexts. I focus on First Amendment contexts for three main reasons. First, that is the context for virtually all of the work on the subject in the debate I am addressing. As we shall see in Chapters 2 and 5, those who seek to establish campus speech codes spend considerable effort showing how their regulations are compatible with the First Amendment. Second, speech policies set by public universities are legally governed by First Amendment doctrines. Non–First Amendment contexts are, in effect, matters of private morality. And third, even private universities are subject to First Amendment doctrines in various ways, for example, by state laws incorporating First Amendment guarantees (such as California's so-called Leonard Law, which is discussed in Chapter 4); by official or unofficial institutional acceptance of the moral, not merely legal, force of the First Amendment (such as at Yale University, which is discussed in Chapter 3); and by the guidelines of related organizations or institutions (such as when the AAUP censures an institution for violating speech rights of a faculty member). Non–First Amendment contexts are surely as important as First Amendment contexts, but to address them is to address a different debate and to write another book.

Even with this qualification, it is easy to see that if free speech and equality are really as important as we think they are, we must get beyond oversimplifications and distortions and analyze the issues in a more systematic fashion. Decisions affecting the speech of so many people should not be reached behind closed doors or be made by self-righteous speech czars or be hastily adopted in the heat of the moment. When we examine the issues in depth, we will see that the harms of hate speech are real and that the goal of educational equality is an important one, but we will also see that the dangers to free speech that campus speech codes represent are very real and that our goal of equality may be best attained by restricting campus speech only in the most egregious cases.

Despite the book's depth and breadth, I do not suppose that my arguments will end the debate over hate speech. Our country's indecision (and changes in decisions) about whether and how we should deal with hate speech is not likely to end soon. The free speech–equality rift at issue in the campus hate speech trial is but one in a long, continuous series of free speech controversies that began with the founding of our country.[29] Still, I may convince a few others of the strength of my proposal, and I should be happy with that, for my aim is not so much to end the debate as to make a contribution to it, to help novices see what the issues are and why they are so important, and to push experts in the field to the next level in the debate. In the end, the value of this book lies, I hope, in its deepening our appreciation of both free speech and equality and adding to our understanding of how to balance them properly. Though the task be daunting, and, indeed, never completed, it is always worth undertaking—with our hearts and a passion for justice, not just our minds. When we put hate speech on trial, when we try to balance freedom and equality, the stakes are high: no less than social justice and our national identity. How we deal with dissent, with intolerance, with threats, with offensive ideas, helps define who we are. Let us begin to consider the arguments.

# 2
# Ban It! The Initial Arguments for Campus Speech Codes

*Universities are special places, charged with pedagogy, and duty-bound to a constituency with special vulnerabilities. Many of the new adults who come to live and study at the major universities are away from home for the first time, and at a vulnerable stage of psychological development. Students are particularly dependent upon the university for community, for intellectual development, and for self-definition. Official tolerance of racist speech in this setting is more harmful than generalized tolerance in the community-at-large.*

MARI MATSUDA, "Public Response to Racist Speech"

## THE HARMS OF HATE SPEECH

Mari Matsuda's article has had a powerful impact on the hate speech debate. Judge Cohn, finding the conflict between equality and freedom "unfortunate," "difficult," even "painful," still had to make a decision, and, in the event, held for Doe (for reasons we shall address in Chapter 4). Yet he acknowledges in a somewhat cryptic fashion at the end of his decision that had he had the opportunity to read Matsuda's piece, his decision might have been different.[1] Why should the honorable judge point this out? What does Matsuda—or any other advocate of hate speech codes—say that would undermine judicial confidence in broad freedom of speech? Did Judge Cohn suspect the university had good reasons to adopt a hate speech code but think they just inadequately made their case in the courtroom? What exactly is Matsuda's argument? What legal and moral reasons are behind the push for campus speech codes?

It is a legal fact that every U.S. citizen is entitled to equal opportunity in education and employment, regardless of race, sex, religion, or ethnic origin. This legal guarantee, embodied most prominently in the Civil Rights Acts of 1964 and 1990, is rooted in a moral conviction that certain forms of discrimination ought not be tolerated. At the same time, it is a legal fact that every U.S. citizen is guaranteed freedom of expression by the First Amendment to the U.S. Constitution. This too is rooted in a moral conviction, the pre-Revolutionary belief that a government and its agencies ought not to control the speech of citizens. The trouble, of course, is that some expressions (e.g., words that severely intimidate or threaten or harass) seem to deny equal individual opportunity.

Consider the following examples (based upon real incidents): A white male student ritually shouts whenever and wherever he sees a particular black female student, "My parents own you people." Fliers are distributed on a campus declaring "open season" on blacks, who are referred to as "saucer lips, porch monkeys, and jigaboos." Outside dormitories, white students spit on and taunt Asian-American students. When a small group of women walk across the floor at halftime at a university basketball game, two thousand students stand up and repeatedly yell, "JAP, JAP, JAP." ("JAP" here is short for Jewish American Princess, not Japanese, and in this context is highly derogatory.) Signs at a college fair booth declare, "Make her prove she's not a JAP, make her swallow." A poster exhorts the reader to "Stick rusty nails up the asses of heterosexual men." Another tells the reader, "Preppies, bimbos, men without chest hair, and homos should be shot on sight." A white student tells an Asian American student, "It's people like you—that's the reason this country is screwed up" and "You don't belong here." A Jewish Student Center receives a bomb threat. A student sends an e-mail message to a faculty member: "Death to all Arabs! Die Islamic scumbags." Do such expressions deny members of the academic community equal educational and employment opportunities? Do they materially alter their academic conditions? Should such words receive First Amendment protection? The difficulty in answering these questions is magnified by the fact that the list of such cases—racial and sexual epithets; degrading caricatures; threats of violence; portrayals of groups as subhumans deserving humiliation, torture, even death; physical violence; theft; and other hate crimes—fills volumes.[2]

I believe, as the quote from Matsuda suggests, that it is an awareness of the severity and frequency of hate speech incidents and of the special responsibility of a university to foster student growth and well-being that (primarily) grounds the view that hate speech should be banned from campuses. Highly regarded First Amendment scholar Kent Greenawalt points out in his book *Fighting Words* (1995) that universities, and society at large, have a strong interest in assuring decent conditions of living and learning for all students.[3] If so, the rest of the advocate's argument is primarily clarification or strategy. This is borne out, I think, in an examination of two universities whose situations formed the centerpiece of the campus speech code debate and the arguments of leading advocates of campus speech codes.

## HOW A HATE SPEECH CODE COMES TO BE

Every campus that has adopted a hate speech code has its own story to tell, and I cannot tell them all; but the two stories I do relate in this section come from the University of Michigan at Ann Arbor and the University of Wisconsin System, in particular the main campus in Madison. Their stories are useful places to begin our study because they vividly illustrate important aspects of the hate speech debate, ended in judicial decisions that we address in Chapter 4, and contain events addressed throughout the literature.

*The University of Michigan.* On January 27, 1987, a group of black female students found a pile of handbills in a dormitory lounge declaring "open hunting season" on all blacks (whom it referred to as "saucer lips, porch monkeys, and jigaboos"). Shortly thereafter—on February 4, 1987—a disc jockey for the campus radio station encouraged listeners to call in and tell racist jokes on the air. Word about the incidents quickly spread around campus, and a group of students gathered in an open area to express their opposition to hate speech. Their anger heightened when someone displayed a Ku Klux Klan uniform from a nearby dormitory window in view of the gathered students. Tensions on campus soon increased even more when a computerized file containing racist jokes and a second racist handbill were discovered. This second handbill even included a statement that blacks should be "hanging from trees" rather than attending college. To top off the series of events, vandals repeatedly damaged and destroyed shanties constructed in an open campus ground to protest South African apartheid.

In response to the incidents, the university closed down the computer file and punished those responsible in the two cases in which the perpetrator was identified. The nineteen-year-old white student who admitted to distributing the first handbill was evicted from his dorm and barred from university housing, and the disc jockey who encouraged the racist call-ins was dismissed from his job at the radio station. The president of the university also issued a statement on February 19 condemning the racist acts and reaffirming the university's commitment to a racially, culturally, and ethnically diverse campus.

Others responded too. The chairperson of the state's House of Representatives Appropriation Subcommittee on Higher Education held a public hearing in Ann Arbor on the problem of racism. Forty-eight speakers, who consistently criticized the university for not doing enough to combat racism on campus, addressed the subcommittee and an audience of six hundred; the chairperson even suggested that the subcommittee might withhold funds from the university if further action was not taken by the university.[4] After the hearing, the United Coalition Against Racism, a campus antidiscrimination group, announced its intention to file a class-action civil rights suit against the university "for not maintaining or creating a non-racist, non-violent atmosphere" on campus.

Trying to take the upper hand, university administration in March 1987 met with a national civil rights leader and adopted a six-point plan to remedy the racial problems on campus, including an anti–racial harassment policy, with appropriate punishments, as one part of the university's rules and regulations. However, as events unfolded over the next fall, the university president resigned and an acting president was chosen. After meeting with the Board of Regents on January 15, 1988, the acting president appointed the director of the university Office of Affirmative Action to draft the harassment policy. In consultation with a lawyer in the Office of University Counsel and several University of Michigan Law School professors, the proposed policy went through twelve drafts before it was published in the February 1988 issue of the student newspaper with an invitation to the public to comment. On March 16 a public hearing was held and several speakers suggested various refinements in the policy. The next day, the acting president presented the policy to the Board of Regents, several of whom expressed free speech concerns about the policy. In response to those concerns, the policy was rewritten once again and an interpretive guide added. At the April 14 meeting of the Board of Regents, the policy was unanimously adopted, to be effective May 31, 1988, to December 31, 1989.

The policy identified three "tiers" of speech whereby the degree of regulation depended on the location of the conduct. One tier, composed of the two student newspapers, was exempt from the policy. A second tier, the "public" parts of the university, was subject only to regulations regarding physical violence or destruction of property. The third tier, composed of "educational and academic centers, such as classroom buildings, libraries, research laboratories, recreation and study centers" were subject to discipline for

1. Any behavior, verbal or physical, that stigmatizes or victimizes an individual on the basis of race, ethnicity, religion, sex, sexual orientation, creed, national origin, ancestry, age, marital status, handicap or Vietnam-era veteran status, and that:
   a. Involves an express or implied threat to an individual's academic efforts, employment, participation in University sponsored extracurricular activities or personal safety; or
   b. Has the purpose or effect of interfering with an individual's academic efforts, employment, participation in University sponsored extra-curricular activities or personal safety; or

    c. Creates an intimidating, hostile, or demeaning environment for educational pursuits, employment or participation in university sponsored extra-curricular activities.

2. Sexual advances, requests for sexual favors, and verbal or physical conduct that stigmatizes or victimizes an individual on the basis of sex or sexual orientation where such behavior:

    a. Involves an express or implied threat to an individual's academic efforts, employment, participation in University sponsored extracurricular activities or personal safety; or

    b. Has the purpose or reasonably foreseeable effect of interfering with an individual's academic efforts, employment, participation in University sponsored extra-curricular activities or personal safety; or

    c. Creates an intimidating, hostile, or demeaning environment for educational pursuits, employment, or participation in University sponsored extra-curricular activities.

The policy did recognize that some speech which might be considered in violation may not be sanctionable, stating: "The Office of the General Counsel will rule on any claim that conduct which is the subject of a formal hearing is constitutionally protected by the first amendment." The policy also provided for hearing procedures, privacy in maintaining records, informal as well as formal procedures for resolving disputes, and different sanctions according to the severity of the violation.

The interpretive guide supplementing the policy provided examples of sanctionable conduct. According to court records, these included:

- A flyer containing racist threats distributed in a residence hall.
- Racist graffiti written on the door of an Asian student's study carrel.
- A male remarking in class that "women just aren't as good in this field as men."
- A floor party is held inviting everyone except a student believed to be a lesbian.
- A black student is racially insulted by white students in the cafeteria.
- Male students leave pornographic pictures and jokes on a female student's desk.

The interpretive guide also had a section titled, "You are a harasser when . . . ," which included the following examples, also from court records:

- You exclude someone from a study group because of race, sex, or ethnic origin.
- You tell jokes about gay men and lesbian women.
- Your student organization sponsors a speaker who slurs Hispanics.
- You display a Confederate flag on your dorm room wall.
- You laugh at a joke about someone in your class who stutters.
- You make obscene telephone calls or send racist computer messages.
- You comment in a derogatory way about someone's physical appearance or sexual orientation, or their cultural origin, or their religious beliefs.

Of the complaints that were filed under the policy, three resulted in informal or formal sanctions. First, in a graduate research class in social work, a student stated his belief that homosexuality was a disease and that he intended to develop a counseling plan for changing gay clients into "straight" ones. The student apparently had already been counseling some of his gay patients in this way and had several heated discussions with other students about the validity and morality of his theory and program. A complaint was filed on December 7, 1988, and the policy administrator informed him on January 11, 1989, that there was sufficient evidence to warrant a formal hearing on charges of sex and sexual orientation harassment. The hearing panel, conducted on January 28, unanimously found him guilty of sexual harassment but not of harassing on the basis of sexual orientation.

Second, on September 28, 1988, a complaint was filed against a student in an entrepreneurship class in the School of Business Administration for reading a limerick during a scheduled class public-speaking exercise in which he ridiculed a well-known athlete for his presumed sexual orientation. The policy administrator persuaded the perpetrator to attend an educational "gay rap session," write a letter of apology to be published in the student newspaper, and apologize to his class.

In the third case, a professor teaching a class commonly thought to be the most difficult for second-year dentistry students broke up the class into small groups to discuss the anticipated problems about the class, in the hopes that this might ease their fears. During the discussion a student said he had heard (from his roommate, a black former dentistry student) that minorities had a hard time in the class and were not treated fairly. The minority professor teaching the class filed a complaint alleging that the comment was unfair and hurt her chances of tenure. The student was "counseled" about the policy and agreed to write a letter of apology for making the comment without adequately verifying the allegation.

*The University of Wisconsin System.* In May 1987, Phi Gamma Delta fraternity members staged an annual "Fiji Island" party. Among other things, they paraded in blackface and tropical garb with a fifteen-foot-high plywood carica-ture of a black man with a bone in his nose. Black students picketed the house, and fraternity members took down the caricature. It was, however, put up again the next day; this sparked further demonstrations, which were intensified when the fraternity president apologized by saying the caricature was meant to be a Fijian, not a black person (a comment that then offended Asian students). The demonstrations continued until the university suspended the fraternity and ordered its members to undergo sensitivity training. This decision was reached after a closed-door meeting with black student leaders, who felt the university's original plan to write only a condemnation of the display was not a strong enough response.

The next fall, only one week after Phi Gamma Delta was reinstated, the pre-dominantly Jewish fraternity Zeta Beta Tau held a closed party. Phi Gamma Delta members crashed the party and started a fight by making racial and ethnic slurs. The university immediately re-suspended Phi Gamma Delta; and although Phi Gamma Delta officers denied any racial bias and characterized the event as "just another after-bars fight," five members responsible for the fight were sus-pended by the fraternity. In January 1988, the acting chancellor lifted the group's suspension and apologized after an independent investigator recommended reversal on the grounds that the suspension was probably a violation of due process rights, there having been no determination of whether the behavior was in an individual or representative capacity. And one month later, the university concluded that although the racist remarks were "reprehensible," they were not in violation of any student code and were protected by the First Amendment.

Case closed?

Hardly, for Jewish and black students were outraged.

In an attempt to take the high ground, in that same month, February 1988, Chancellor Donna Shalala unveiled the Madison Plan, a comprehensive uni-versity program aimed at improving recruitment and retention of minorities of color and setting specific targets: double the number of minority students in five years and add over two hundred new minority faculty within three years. It also provided for a new ethnic studies course requirement, a multicultural center, and an outreach program to neighboring schools.

But in April 1988, as Professor Harold Scheub was giving an exam for his African Storyteller course, six men entered the room, shouted obscenities for ten minutes, and left an examination book filled with pornography. Two hours later, Professor Linda Hunter's African Languages classroom was interrupted by six men, who set off a stink bomb and then fled. The six men, later found to be mostly members of the University of Illinois chapter of the Acacia fraternity, were judged to have acted with racial motives and the complicity of the local chapter. As punishment, the local chapter was suspended for one year (which means they lost affiliation with the university, access to student facilities and mailing labels, participation in intramural sports, and membership in the Interfraternity Council). A number of the intruders pleaded no contest to criminal charges of disorderly conduct and unauthorized presence (all were sentenced to write an essay on the incident or on black history or literature, and four were required to donate fifty dollars to charity and perform one hundred hours of community service). The Illinois chapter was suspended by the University of Illinois administration.

Continuing the attempt to gain the high ground, the next month, May 1988, the Board of Regents for the whole University of Wisconsin System adopted Design for Diversity, a program that—like Shalala's Madison Plan—aimed at improving recruitment and retention of minorities and increasing tolerance of multiculturalism and diversity. The board also established a working group to draft supplements to the student conduct code, UWS Chapter 17 (UW-17), to implement its policy systemwide. A policy was created with the help of law professors Gordon Baldwin, Richard Delgado, and Ted Finman.

The next fall, during October 1988, Zeta Beta Tau, the same Jewish fraternity that had been victimized by intruders and racist insults the year before, put on a "slave auction" fund-raiser in a private residence. In one of the skits, pledges in blackface and "afro" wigs lip-synched Michael Jackson songs. In another skit, a pledge impersonated Oprah Winfrey while two others taunted him sexually. When word of the event got out, a complaint was filed, but a student committee determined that the fraternity had violated no campus rule and that the skits were protected speech. Two hundred demonstrators then occupied the administration building in a "day of rage." To end the siege, Chancellor Shalala agreed to establish a committee to study Wisconsin's long-term goal for minority retention and reexamine the future of fraternities on the campus, but she refused to expel the fraternity members on the ground that their actions were constitutionally protected. Once again, demonstrators took to the streets. Moreover, the Wisconsin student association stripped the student committee of authority over complaints about racism and sexism, and the Interfraternity Council suspended Zeta Beta Tau for five years.

The next spring, at its April 1989 meeting, the Board of Regents voted down a proposal to adopt the rewritten UW-17 on an emergency basis, deciding to advance the proposal through regular channels. On June 8, 1989, a public hearing was held to allow public response, and the next day the board adopted the rule by a 12 to 5 vote.

According to the new rule, sanctions were authorized:

(2)(a) For racist or discriminatory comments, epithets, or other expressive behavior directed at an individual or on separate occasions at different individuals, or for physical conduct, if such comments, epithets, or other expressive conduct intentionally:

  1. Demean the race, sex, religion, color, creed, disability, sexual orientation, national origin, ancestry or age of the individual or individuals; and
  2. Create an intimidating, hostile or demeaning environment for education, university-related work, or other university authorized activity.

  (b) Whether the intent required under par. (a) is present shall be determined by consideration of all relevant circumstances.
  (c) In order to illustrate the types of conduct which this subsection is designed to cover, these examples are set forth. These examples are not meant to illustrate the only situations or types of conduct intended to be covered.

  1. A student would be in violation if:
      (a) He or she intentionally made demeaning remarks to an individual based on that person's ethnicity, such as name calling, racial slurs, or "jokes"; and
      (b) His or her purpose in uttering the remarks was to make the educational environment hostile for the person to whom the demeaning remark was addressed.
  2. A student would be in violation if:
      (a) He or she intentionally placed visual or written material demeaning the race or sex of an individual in that person's university living quarters or work area; and
      (b) His or her purpose was to make the educational environment hostile for the person in whose quarters or work area the material was placed.
  3. A student would be in violation if he or she seriously damaged or destroyed private property of any member of the university community or guest because of that person's race, sex, religion, color, creed, disability, sexual orientation, national origin, ancestry, or age.
  4. A student would not be in violation if, during class discussion, he or she expressed a derogatory opinion concerning a racial or ethnic group. There is no violation, since the student's

remark was addressed to the class as a whole, not to a specific individual. Moreover, on the facts as stated, there seems no evidence that the student's purpose was to create a hostile environment.

Thus, for the expressive behavior to be sanctioned, it must

(1) Be racist or discriminatory;
(2) Be directed at an individual;
(3) Demean the race, sex, religion, color, creed, disability, sexual orientation, national origin, ancestry, or age of the individual addressed; and
(4) Create an intimidating, hostile or demeaning environment for education, university-related work, or other university-authorized activity.

In addition to the rule itself and its examples, the university issued a brochure explaining the scope and application of the rule through these additional cases:

*Question 1.* In a class discussion concerning women in the workplace, a male student expresses his belief that women are by nature better equipped to be mothers than executives, and thus should not be employed in upper level management positions. Is this statement actionable under proposed UWS 17.06(2)?

*Answer.* No. The statement is an expression of opinion, contains no epithets, is not directed to a particular individual, and does not, standing alone, evince the requisite intent to demean or create a hostile environment.

*Question 2.* A student living in the University dormitory continually calls a black student living on his floor "nigger" whenever they pass in the hallway. May the university take action against the name-caller?

*Answer.* Yes. The word "nigger" is an epithet, and is directed specifically at an individual. Its use and continuous repetition demonstrate the required intent on the part of the speaker to demean the individual and create a hostile living environment for him.

*Question 3.* Two university students become involved in an altercation at an off-campus bar. During the fight one student uses a racial epithet to prolong the dispute. May the university invoke a disciplinary action?

*Answer.* Perhaps. Use of the epithet, and its direction to an individual suggests a potential violation of proposed s. UWS 17.06(2); however, because the episode occurred off campus, the intent to create a hostile environment for university-authorized activities would be difficult to demonstrate. Additional facts would have to be developed if disciplinary action were to be pursued.

*Question 4.* A group of students disrupts a university class shouting discriminatory epithets. Are they subject to disciplinary action under the provisions related to regulation of expressive behavior?

*Answer.* Perhaps. It is clear that the subjects are subject to disciplinary action for disrupting a class under existing s. UWS 17.06(1)(c)3. The question is whether they also violated the newly created provision concerning expressive behavior, because they shouted epithets while in the course of misconduct. If the epithets were directed to individuals within the class, and were intended to demean them and create a hostile environment, then the behavior might also be in violation of the provision concerning expressive conduct.

*Question 5.* A faculty member, in a genetics class discussion, suggests that certain racial groups seem to be genetically predisposed to alcoholism. Is this statement subject to discipline under Chapter UW 17?

*Answer.* No. A faculty member is in no case subject to discipline under Chapter UWS 17, since that chapter applies only to students. This situation would not warrant disciplinary action under any other policy either, since it is protected expression of an idea.

In a 1991 issue of the *Wayne State Law Review* devoted to articles on campus hate speech codes, Patricia Hodulik, senior legal counsel for the UW-System at the time, defended the policy as an effective balance between freedom and equality, that is, a speech policy that was enforced in a way that didn't threaten protected speech.[5] She points out that of the thirty-two complaints that were filed under the policy in its eighteen months, only ten resulted in sanctions, and each of these complaints involved egregious speech. On the one side, protected speech included an art display in a campus gallery of work offensive to Catholics; a student's reference to a group of student senators as "rednecks"; a statement by a Libyan to a Zionist that Libya would ultimately destroy Zionism; and a cartoon on abortion in a student newspaper that some Christians found offensive. On the other side, speech that faced sanctions included the following incidents.

At UW–Parkside, a student entered another student's bedroom area as an uninvited guest and used inappropriate language, including the term "Shakazulu" (a mocking reference to an African king), which led to a confrontation between the student and the residents of the apartment. The student was placed on probation and required to consult with an alcohol abuse counselor and to "plan a project in conjunction with the Center for Education in Cultural Enhancement to help sensitize [himself] to the issues of diversity."

At UW–Eau Claire, a student yelled epithets at a woman for approximately ten minutes, calling her a "fucking bitch" and "fucking cunt" in response to a letter she had written to the university newspaper criticizing the athletic department. The student was placed on probation for a semester and required to perform twenty hours of community service at a shelter for abused women. In a separate case, a student sent an e-mail stating, "Death to all Arabs! Die Islamic scumbags!" on the university computer system to an Iranian faculty member. The university placed him on probation for the remainder of the semester.

At UW–Oshkosh, a student angrily told an Asian American student, "It's people like you—that's the reason this country is screwed up," and "You don't belong here." He also stated, "Whites are always getting screwed by minorities and some day the Whites will take over." The university put him on probation for several months and required him to participate in alcohol abuse assessment and treatment. In a separate case, a female student referred to a black female student as a "fat-ass nigger" during an argument. The student, who was already on disciplinary probation for a non-race-related incident, was required to view a video on racism and write an essay and letter of apology and was reassigned to a different residence hall.

At UW–River Falls, a male student yelled at a female student in public, "You've got nice tits!" The university placed the student on probation for the remainder of his enrollment at the university and required him to apologize to the female student, to refrain from any further contact with her, and to obtain psychological counseling.

At UW–Stevens Point, a student impersonated an immigration official and harassed a Turkish American by demanding to see immigration documents. The student signed a "no contest agreement" admitting violations of the rule as well as of UWS 17.06(4) (conduct obstructing a university official) and his university housing contract. The student was placed on probation for eight months. In a separate case, a student stole his dorm roommate's debit card and access number. The student acknowledged that he had twice intercepted and opened the Japanese student's correspondence from the bank and successfully withdrawn sixty dollars from the Japanese student's bank account. Moreover, he admitted that he was motivated by racial bias. The student signed a no-contest agreement acknowledging violations of several UWS rules. The student was required to make restitution and take a course in ethics or East Asian history and was placed on probation.

At UW–Stout, a student involved in a physical altercation with two residence hall staff called one of them a "piece of shit nigger" and the other a

"South American immigrant." He was charged with violating the expressive rule as well as UWS 17.06(1) (endangering personal safety) and 17.06(4) (obstructing a university official). The student waived a formal hearing and accepted a seven-month suspension.

According to Hodulik, the low number of complaints, the high number of dismissals, and the egregious nature of the sanctioned speech indicates that there was "no widespread 'chilling' of campus speech activities or threat to first amendment values."[6]

*Conclusion*. At both Michigan and Wisconsin, a series of highly emotional, highly publicized race- and ethnicity-related incidents led to (primarily) minority student demands for university intervention. The intense pressure they were able to bring to bear was accommodated by administrators and faculty through development and implementation of a broad speech code punishing a variety of student expression. The total number of complaints filed under the policies was not high, and both universities had a screening mechanism to sort out legitimate and illegitimate complaints. However, both policies were written and applied in controversial ways (which we shall address in Chapters 3 and 4) and closely monitored by the ACLU. (In fact, it was with legal counsel from the ACLU that the Michigan policy was challenged on First Amendment grounds.)

But why exactly did Michigan and Wisconsin adopt codes? After all, there were people on and off campus who spoke against the codes, and many universities around the country decided to forgo such a code. Why was a speech code accepted as the solution in these cases (and other cases like them)? If administrators in Wisconsin (and other universities around the country) were aware of the outcome of the Michigan case, why did they think their code would fare any better in a court of law?

Samuel Walker, a professor of criminal justice at the University of Nebraska at Omaha and an expert on the history of free speech and hate speech, claims that the main reason hate speech rules were adopted on so many campuses (not just these two, remember, but the hundreds of other campuses that followed suit) was that there existed no effectively organized campus opposition.[7] At one level of analysis, I do not disagree with Walker: surely the Michigan and Wisconsin cases suggest that the success of advocates in getting a code established was due in large measure to their ability to marshal large numbers of vocal supporters and threaten the universities with legal action or withdrawal from the university; while, on the other side, critics of the proposed policies stood pretty much alone. But we should not forget other factors that played a significant role in these cases, including the highly publicized nature of the incidents; students', faculty's, and administrators' beliefs about equality and the worthlessness of hate speech; the (loaded) processes by which the Michigan and Wisconsin policies were developed and adopted; and the interest administrators have in protecting themselves against lawsuits of the sort threatened by the student group in Michigan.

Such considerations may largely answer the causal question of adoption, but we must not forget that what we are ultimately interested in is the legal and moral question of speech restrictions. Should such codes be adopted? Are universities rationally and morally justified in enacting these (or any other) speech codes? Identifying the psychological, sociological, political, or economic causes of adoption does not answer the normative question, although they may in some cases bear on the answer. For example, some public policy experts warn that it is exactly circumstances like these (highly publicized and politicized events producing a new rule) that lead to bad policy. In the famous Pentagon Papers case, *New York Times v. United States*, 403 U.S. 713 (1971), Justice Harry Blackmun recalled words used by Justice Holmes nearly seventy years earlier: "Great cases like hard cases make bad law. For great cases are called great, not by reason of their real importance in shaping the law of the future, but because of some accident of immediate overwhelming interest, which appeals to the feelings and distorts the judgment. These immediate interests exercise a kind of hydraulic pressure."[8] Thus, whatever the cause of the adoption of a speech code on a campus is or was, we must examine the justification offered for the policy. One cannot morally justify a campus policy merely by saying the administration faced organized opposition or legal threats. Nor can we morally justify a campus policy merely by saying the issue is highly publicized. So, how can one justify a speech code? What moral and legal principles support a ban on hate speech? Why, normatively speaking, ought hate speech be banned from campus? Is adoption of a speech code really the best way to respond to such incidents? In the rest of this chapter we examine three main arguments used in tandem to justify campus hate speech codes.

## THE DETERRENCE ARGUMENT

In order to justify a campus speech code, universities needed to be able to show, first, that the affected speech caused serious harms that should be addressed by an explicit university policy and punished and deterred by university sanctions. In its generic form, then, the deterrence argument is this:

1. Campus hate speech causes serious harms that constitute a violation of the Fourteenth Amendment's equal rights guarantee.

2. Serious violations of the Fourteenth Amendment's equal rights guarantee should be punished and deterred by punitive sanctions in accordance with a university policy or "speech code." Thus
3. Campus hate speech codes designed to prevent and punish hate speech are justified.

Stated in such abstract terms the argument raises many questions. What serious harms does hate speech cause? How do these harms constitute a violation of equal rights? Will a speech code actually deter bigots? What exactly is going to count as hate speech under the terms of the policy? In order to answer these questions, let us examine each premise and the conclusion in more detail.

*Premise (1): Hate speech causes serious harms that constitute a violation of the Fourteenth Amendment's guarantee of equal rights.* Proponents of the deterrence argument typically focus on the harmful consequences of hate speech rather than the act itself, pointing out that hate speech is most often directed at members of historically disadvantaged groups in ways in which the victims are relatively powerless to respond. As Mari Matsuda notes in her influential law review article, "Tolerance of hate speech is not tolerance borne by the community at large. Rather it is a psychic tax imposed on those least able to pay."[9] This theme is sounded by many other campus speech code advocates and is a strong one because it represents a direct response to the argument for freedom of speech that maintains we should tolerate even bad speech in order to ensure protection of good speech. This tolerance is unacceptable because it comes at a high cost to only some citizens, women and minorities, who are typically less able to overcome such burdens successfully. In its effect, it imposes a serious inequality in the opportunities of women and minorities to successfully compete for the good things in life.

To back up the point, Matsuda and Richard Delgado extensively discuss the harms of hate speech, outlining not only the specific negative effects of hate speech but also its general power, within a society like ours, with its long history of prejudice and violence, to destroy, to denigrate, to shape our attitudes and actions. In his groundbreaking law review article in 1982, Delgado writes:

American society remains deeply afflicted by racism. Long before slavery became the mainstay of the plantation society of the antebellum South, Anglo-Saxon attitudes of racial superiority left their stamp on the developing culture of colonial America. Today, over a century after the abolition of slavery, many citizens suffer from discriminatory attitudes and practices, infecting our economic system, our cultural and political institutions, and the daily interactions of individuals. The idea that color is a badge of inferiority and a justification for the denial of opportunity and equal treatment is deeply ingrained.[10]

Professor Delgado goes on to list harmful effects on the individual victims and society, focusing on the psychological, physical, and pecuniary harms to the individual.[11] He cites a number of studies indicating that hate speech causes feelings of humiliation, isolation, self-hatred, even mental illness, and points out that these effects, which do not necessarily decrease with socioeconomic status, can alter parenting practices and perpetuate failure.[12] He claims that repeated exposure to hate speech may lead to heightened blood pressure and higher rates of mortality due to hypertension. Moreover, racial stigmatization may be responsible for pecuniary damages, since minorities are "programmed" to fail and face institutional and individual racism in schools, hiring decisions, and other educational and employment settings. The social harm of hate speech includes its violation of the "cornerstone" of the American moral and political system, the belief that all men are created equal, and perpetuates socioeconomic inequality through a racial class of "outsiders." It should be noted that Delgado's concern in this 1982 article was not with campus hate speech codes per se—rather, it was with hate speech throughout society and how it ought to be addressed through a tort action for racial stigmatization. However, his early analysis set the context for his later articles, which do specifically advocate campus speech codes,[13] and for Matsuda's article defending a broad restriction on campus speech seven years later.

Professor Matsuda both follows and builds upon Delgado's 1982 paper in her discussion of the historical and institutional background in which hate speech occurs and the specific negative effects it has on individuals and society.[14] For example, Matsuda cites studies indicating that hate speech can cause "physiological symptoms and emotional distress ranging from fear in the gut, rapid pulse rate and difficulty in breathing, nightmares, posttraumatic stress disorder, hypertension, psychosis, and suicide."[15] She notes that in order to avoid hate speech, some victims quit jobs, leave college, move away, avoid public places, and otherwise alter their behavior. She points out that when society protects hate speech, victims get the message that they are outsiders not worthy of protection by the government; nontarget group members also can have their liberty restricted (since associating with a target group member can lead to hate directed at the nongroup member) and suffer emotional costs (due to their sympathy for the plight of victims, but also from a guilt-ridden feeling of relief that they are not the direct targets of the hate). She maintains that the message of hate is so widely repeated in our society that even those most opposed to it can have a racist response triggered "the next time we sit next to one of 'those people.'" Finally, Matsuda claims that the perpetrators of hate speech harm themselves "in that it is a lesson in getting-away-with-it that will have lifelong repercussions."[16]

Matsuda also goes beyond Delgado's earlier work by pointing out that the international community has banned racist hate propaganda.[17] Two key points emerge from her discussion. First, the United States stands virtually alone in thinking that hate speech ought to be legal. Both in ratifying Article 4 of the International Convention on the Elimination of All Forms of Racial Discrimination and in enacting laws at the national level, the international community is virtually united in declaring the value of equality over liberty in the context of hate speech. Second, these laws do not ban all forms of offensive speech; rather, they target only particularly egregious forms of expression. She writes, "What the emerging global standard prohibits is the kind of expression that interferes with the rights of subordinated-group members to participate equally in society, maintaining their basic sense of security and worth as human beings."[18] Even Canada, our closest kin, permits state regulation of hate speech in ways our judiciary has rejected.[19] Matsuda's point about the uniqueness of the American response to racism has significant rhetorical force because it appears to put the burden on the opponent of speech codes. If no one else in the world, our European and North American allies included, has a problem regulating hate speech, why should we? If everyone else in the world sees that equality outweighs freedom in this limited sphere of cases, why don't we?

If we combine Delgado's and Matsuda's arguments about the harms of hate speech, we have a powerful set of reasons to regulate campus hate speech, even if we note (as we should) that hate speech does not always cause such harms to occur. It is difficult to believe that a student is getting an equal educational opportunity when he faces such intense harassment by virtue of his color that he is effectively forced to withdraw from school. It is difficult to believe that a student gets an equal educational opportunity when she is afraid to go to class because the guy who sits next to her taunts her with graphic sexual banter. It is difficult to believe that a student gets an equal educational opportunity when her religion and ethnicity are daily targets of ridicule and threats from others in her dormitory.

I suggest that this premise can be strengthened if we look at the act of hate speech itself, and not just its consequences, as Delgado and Matsuda do. As ethicists would put it, their consequentialist, or utilitarian, analysis (judging the act in view of its effect on human happiness and unhappiness) can be supplemented by a nonconsequentialist, or nonutilitarian, analysis (judging the act in and of itself). One way of examining the morality of the act itself, rather than its consequences, is provided by the famous eighteenth-century German philosopher Immanuel Kant, who defended the categorical imperative—a "souped-up" version of the Golden Rule—as the general principle by which we should judge the morality of actions.[20]

Kant stated his categorical imperative in several ways (which he thought conceptually equivalent), but I shall leave aside the details in order to emphasize the two of his main points that are most relevant to our present concerns. First, Kant maintained that an action is wrong if its maxim (i.e., its rationale, or the rule in accordance with which the act is done) cannot be universalized.[21] That is, if I think it's okay for me to do X to you, but not okay for you to do X to me, then I am hypocritical (wrong) to do X. My maxim is not a universal law; it is a law particular to me. To be morally right, an act must be universalizable, that is, it must be okay for anyone to do. To use one of Kant's own examples, the immorality of telling a lie is made clear through the inconsistency in the will of the liar (who wants to lie to others, yet wants others to be truthful with him or her) and the contradiction of the purpose of communication that a lie represents. (If everyone were a liar, then communication would be pointless, for no one could be believed.) What Kant is suggesting is that independently of the consequences, we can determine that telling a lie is wrong because of the nature of the act itself.

Second, Kant maintained that an action is wrong if it treats anyone as a mere means.[22] Believing that all human beings have intrinsic worth (i.e., have value in and of themselves just by virtue of being rational agents) and do not exist merely to suit the purposes of other people, Kant held that in all of our actions we should treat others as ends in themselves and not as mere means to our own ends.

In saying this he did not mean that we should never "use" each other as a means; our daily interactions require that we use one another as means to various ends that we have, whether we are students and teachers, buyers and sellers, or parents and children. What Kant meant was that we should never use each other as mere means.

To be sure, drawing a sharp line between use as a means and use as a mere means is no easy task, and both Kant and his followers labor mightily to clarify this distinction. I suggest, however, that these areas of refinement are beyond our present concerns and that we can use the rough and ready idea of agreement that Kant suggests to make the distinction: namely, a person is used as a mere means when one would not agree to the action if rational, fully informed, and uncoerced. For example, a customer uses a bank teller as a means to withdraw money from an account, but a thief uses a bank teller as a mere means to withdraw money from the savings accounts of other people.

Thus, within certain limitations we can usefully employ Kant's ideas to test the morality of the act of hate speech itself and not just its consequences. Can hate speech, like telling the truth, be universalized? Or is it, like telling a lie, not universalizable? Does hate speech, like the customer withdrawing her own money, show respect for others as ends in themselves even while it involves treating another as a means? Or does it, like the act of the thief, treat others as mere means?

Hate speech clearly fails both tests. We should do unto others as we would have them do unto us: who wants others to target hate speech at them? Hate speech—the use of words to wound, to injure, to silence—undermines the basic norms of civility necessary for reasoned discourse. It is an invitation to fisticuffs, not to dialogue. To be sure, some thick-skinned people may have a greater tolerance for truly abusive speech hurled at them, but they do not seek it out or agree to their victim status when made targets of such abuse. And it seems absurd that we should require everyone to have a thick skin or agree to be a target for abuse. One can repeat in one's head "sticks and stones may break my bones but names will never hurt me" only so many times, and there are many expressions of hate that seem closer to "sticks and stones" than mere "name calling"— for example, targeted, repeated, and intentionally harmful hate speech. Consider this instance: a professor habitually calling a female student "honey" and "dear" despite her objections, repeatedly asking her for sexual contact she does not desire and then, when rebuffed, excluding her from class discussions, refusing to help her learn material, calling her "bitch" and "cunt" in public places, refusing to write a letter of recommendation for her graduate school application despite her strong work for him for a year as a teaching assistant, and so on.

To think that anyone would agree to such treatment if rational, fully informed, and uncoerced is beyond the pale.

Hate speech also fails to show respect for others as ends in themselves. Victims have done nothing to deserve these attacks. Bigots do not take into account the goals and ambitions of their targets. They simply aim to silence their targets, to hurt them, to use them as mere objects upon which to vent their hostility, aggression, frustration, and rage, to reduce rational human beings to subhuman status because of their own irrational and bigoted fears. In many instances—for example, the Michigan dormitory flyer—this aim is quite transparent, and it is inconsistent with the basic human norm of respect. As Charles Lawrence writes, "A minority student should not have to risk becoming the target of ridiculing speech every time he or she chooses to walk across campus."[23]

The categorical imperative and its basic norm of equal respect are not just fanciful philosophical inventions of an eighteenth-century Prussian Pietist academic. The Golden Rule, its closest kin in our ordinary moral consciousness, is found in virtually all cultures.[24] It is seen by Ronald Dworkin, one of the leading Anglo-American liberal political and legal commentators of the past thirty years, as the basis of justice. He writes, "Justice as fairness rests on the assumption of a natural right of men and women to equality of concern and respect, a right they possess not by virtue of birth or character or merit or excellence but simply as human beings."[25]

From a different tradition and culture, Molefi Kete Asante, chair and professor of African-American Studies at Temple University, writes, "Civility means that if you speak to or with someone in an effort to express your thoughts or articulate your feelings, you do so in a manner that recognizes the other person's humanity."[26] According to Asante, civility is the basis of the social contract, and hate speech amounts to the dissolution of a social compact, a kind of disintegration of speech that foretells the disintegration of society.

Even mainstream journalists who frequently criticize campus speech codes, like John Leo of *U.S. News and World Report*, accept minimum standards of respect and civility. When addressing the Douglas Hann case at Brown University (in which Hann was expelled for a drunken tirade in which he directed offensive speech at a number of people and had to be restrained from starting a fight), Leo criticizes "speech police" but agrees that Hann's behavior was unacceptable: "The case could have been made that as a repeat offender on probation, the student had failed to observe minimum community standards of decency."[27] Thus, people from many different points on the political and cultural spectrum recognize that hate speech can cross the line and undermine our whole social union, not merely cause harm to individuals—just as lying undermines the whole institution of promise keeping rather than merely causing harm to individuals.

Some speech code advocates believe this distinction between the consequences (harms) of hate speech and the wrongness of the act itself is crucial to understanding the justification for campus speech codes. Andrew Altman, a philosopher of law at George Washington University, argues that it is not the perlocutionary effects of an utterance (its consequences, such as infuriating or frightening a person) that justify speech restrictions, it is its illocutionary force (the subordinating nature of the speech act itself).[28] The "crime" of hate speech is not that it causes harm; rather, hate speech is a certain kind of wrong, namely, violation of equal respect, and it is that which justifies its regulation. Hate speech treats its victims "in a way that takes their interests to be intrinsically less important, and their lives inherently less valuable, than the interests and lives of those who belong to some reference group."[29]

Together, the consequentialist and nonconsequentialist analyses of hate speech offer so strong a case that even those who oppose campus hate speech codes generally concede the immorality of hate speech. Their opposition is not that they think this "bad speech" is actually "good speech"; rather, as Gerald Gunther argues in his response to Charles Lawrence in a *Stanford Lawyer* debate,[30] their opposition is due to fears that government will go too far in regulating speech or that legally enforceable definitions of hate speech are too hard to come by. At most, some opponents of hate speech codes have argued that tolerance of hate speech has moral value (an argument we shall address in Chapters 3 and 6). But even this argument assumes hate speech is wrong in itself; that is why it must be tolerated, not celebrated or encouraged. But once the serious immorality of hate speech is acknowledged, it becomes difficult to give compelling reasons why it should be tolerated. We don't tolerate slander. We don't tolerate breaking contracts. We don't tolerate child pornography. Why not take steps to punish hate speech?

*Premise (2): Serious violations of the Fourteenth Amendment's equal rights guarantee should be punished and deterred by punitive sanctions in accordance with a university policy or "speech code."* Even if it is true that hate speech is so immoral as to threaten equality under the law, it doesn't necessarily follow that it ought to be sanctioned by universities. After all, some other forms of speech are highly immoral and can cause serious personal harms but are not illegal. For example, presidential candidates are permitted to engage in the most blatant forms of negative and deceptive advertising and campaigning, and a person who broke off an engagement with a false confession of sexual infidelity would deserve strong moral condemnation, but no legal punishment. Thus, advocates of campus speech codes must demonstrate why this particular speech deserves regulation. The typical strategy here is to call attention to the frequency of the harm and how it will not abate without university intervention.

Delgado points out that the incidence of hate speech is not limited to the "celebrated" cases that receive national press attention, cases like those he describes in his "Campus Antiracism Rules" article that occurred at The Citadel, Dartmouth, Columbia, the University of California–Berkeley, Stanford, the University of Massachusetts at Amherst, the University of Michigan, and the University of Wisconsin at Madison.[31] It also occurs at the University of Connecticut, the University of Pennsylvania, Brown, the University of Mississippi, Temple, Farleigh Dickenson University, Southern Connecticut, Rutgers, Yale, Smith College, Hastings College, Arizona State, Hamilton College, and Oberlin College. Robin Hulshizer adds cases at St. Cloud State University (Minnesota), the State University of New York (SUNY)–Buffalo, the University of Iowa, and the University of Arkansas.[32] Hundreds more schools could be listed: Charles Jones points out that the National Institute Against Prejudice and Violence reported that between 1986 and 1990, incidents of ethnoviolence occurred at more than 250 campuses and that between eight hundred thousand and one million students are involved each year in such incidents.[33] The Institute estimates that approximately 20 percent of minority students experience some form of ethnic or racial attack during an academic year and that one-fourth are victimized more than once. Moreover, bigots do not merely speak their hate, they too often act it out, destroying and defacing property, committing physical assaults, even killing.[34] Advocates of campus hate speech codes believe that hate speech has gotten so out of hand that we can no longer be tolerant of the intolerant. "The situation on college campuses is such a cause of concern that we have to try something," says Nancy Murray of the Massachusetts Civil Liberties Union.[35]

Advocates believe that the harms of hate speech stand in special need of regulation because the increase in incidents seems caused in large measure by the increasing diversity on American campuses. Charles Jones points out that as universities seek to increase the participation of women and minorities in higher education to ensure equal opportunity, the language and action of hate is adopted by some white males to lash out to defend their privilege and power.[36] Advocates fear that in the absence of university-approved sanctions, bigots may get the message that the university approves of hate speech, thus encouraging the bigots to air their filth and undertake more drastic demonstrations of their beliefs. These events, in turn, will encourage and incite other bigots to express their hate and to grow bolder in demonstrating their beliefs. But this is wrong, not only because these incidents cause psychological and pecuniary harm to the direct victims, but also because they help to ingrain in minorities and women in general the perception of inferiority and outsider status.

Charles Lawrence appeals to *Brown v. Board of Education*, 347 U.S. 483 (1954), to support his opinion that the harms of campus hate speech should be considered unlawful: "*Brown v. Board of Education* is a useful case for our analysis. *Brown* is useful because it articulates the nature of the injury inflicted by the racist message of segregation. When one considers the injuries identified in the Brown decision, it is clear that racist speech causes tangible injury, and it is the kind of injury for which common law provides, and even requires, redress."[37] According to Lawrence, *Brown* speaks to the psychic injury caused by racist speech in noting that the symbolic message of segregation can affect black children "in a way unlikely ever to be undone." It also speaks to reputational injury in maintaining that racism is a form of subordination that achieves its purposes through group defamation. And it speaks to the denial of equal educational opportunity in rejecting the idea that black schoolkids should have to bear the additional burdens of humiliation and psychic assault that accompany segregation. Citing reports prepared at the University of Texas and the University of Massachusetts, he concludes, "The testimony of non-white students about the detrimental effects of racial harassment on their academic performance and social integration in the college community is overwhelming."[38]

Critics of speech codes respond that "hate speech should be condemned wherever it's encountered. But by banning it, we risk opening the floodgate to censors, self-righteous moralists, and other enemies of freedom"[39] and that "the essence of an education system that matters and counts is that people must be free to express ideas, even wrong ideas. . . . The answer is more education, not regulation."[40]

Advocates counterreply that education, counterspeech, and enforcement of purely "conduct"-related regulations will not be enough to protect students' right to equal educational opportunity. After all, these incidents occur at universities across the country with regularity. Hodulik, senior legal counsel for the UW-System, writes:

> While it may be possible to address many situations involving hate speech because they involve other student conduct violations, it is more useful and effective to have an additional provision dealing specifically with hate speech. As the Wisconsin experience demonstrates, there have been, and likely will continue to be, instances of discriminatory harassment which could not be addressed without a separate rule limiting discriminatory expressive behavior. Even if these situations are few in number, their very existence justifies a separate regulatory response.[41]

And James E. Sulton, special assistant to the UW president for minority affairs, writes:

> It is convenient to ignore the pain of students who suffer the ignominy or humiliation due to their color alone. When pressed on this issue, most critics of the student conduct code [UW-17] reply that education is the answer. Now, talk about being vague and overly broad! There you have it. Nothing specific. Just let it be. All things in time and people will learn. Well, in the meantime, people suffer.[42]

*Conclusion (3): Campus hate speech codes designed to prevent and punish hate speech are justified.* Advocates see a hate speech code as an essential component in the fight against discrimination, a mechanism protecting a minimal level of equal opportunity for the historically disadvantaged in education and employment; and they conclude that hate speech codes are justified. One of the functions of law and administrative rules is to protect citizens against injury caused by other citizens. Though not every such form of injury is or should be illegal, when a harm inflicted on campus violates a constitutional right, universities should do what they can to curb further incidents through legal means available to them. We have, in the words of Richard Delgado, two constitutional "narratives" in collision, and the best compromise is a code that punishes "verbal vilifications" but permits robust academic discourse. Since at least some cases of hate speech cause so much harm as to deny individuals the equality guaranteed to them by the Fourteenth Amendment, universities are justified in adopting hate speech codes as a means to punish and deter such rights violations.

If there were no other relevant considerations, the deterrence argument would seem to justify university bans on hate speech. However, even the leading advocates of hate speech codes recognized that there is another relevant consideration, namely, the First Amendment's guarantee of free speech. Thus, all the advocates of hate speech codes produce a second argument, one attempting to show that the restrictions on pure speech that would be part of a campus hate speech regulation do not violate the free speech clause.

## THE FIRST AMENDMENT ARGUMENT

Are hate speech codes consonant with the constitutional right to free speech? Advocates think so, arguing that hate speech, properly defined, has little or no First Amendment value and therefore does not deserve protection under free speech doctrines. In this chapter, I shall focus on the two most popular legal models or approaches popular during the 1987–1992 period, one of which appeals to the "fighting words" doctrine, the other to "group libel" or "group defamation" doctrine.[43]

*The Fighting Words Model.* The fighting words approach has been defended most notably by Charles R. Lawrence III and Thomas C. Grey, both law professors at Stanford University, but it has been endorsed by many others, including prominent First Amendment scholars Cass Sunstein of the University of Chicago Law School[44] and Kent Greenawalt of the Columbia University School of Law.[45] This model appeals to the so-called fighting words doctrine first announced in *Chaplinsky v. New Hampshire*, 315 U.S. 568 (1942), which upheld a state ban on words "which by their very utterance inflict injury or tend to incite an immediate breach of the peace" since "such utterances are no essential part of any exposition of ideas, and are of such slight social value as a step to the truth that any benefit that may be derived from them is clearly outweighed by the social interest in order and morality."

What happened was this: Chaplinsky, a Jehovah's Witness, was proselytizing in a small New Hampshire town with his brethren. Their activities led to a confrontation with local authorities, and when a police officer warned Chaplinsky to "go slow," Chaplinsky called the officer a "God-damned racketeer" and "damned Fascist" and the whole government of Rochester a bunch of fascists. Chaplinsky's choice of epithets was probably deliberate: Jehovah's Witnesses commonly used "racketeer" to refer to leaders of other religions and "fascists" to refer to state authorities who they believed persecuted them as Jews were persecuted by Nazis in Germany.[46] Chaplinsky was then arrested for violating a New Hampshire statute prohibiting "any offensive, derisive, or annoying word to any other person . . . [or] call[ing] him by any offensive or derisive name." Chaplinsky was convicted, but appealed all the way to the U.S. Supreme Court. The Court upheld the conviction by creating the fighting words doctrine: Chaplinsky was not protected by the First Amendment because his words did not contribute to the discussion of public issues but rather contributed to public disorder because they were likely to cause the average person to fight.

Since *Chaplinsky* has never been overruled, advocates of this model maintain that universities are justified in prohibiting fighting words when they are used in effect to deny students equal educational and employment opportunities. Their logic is straightforward:

1. The First Amendment does not protect fighting words.
2. Some campus hate speech constitutes fighting words. Thus
3. Campus hate speech codes punishing and preventing fighting words do not violate the First Amendment.

Though they share a basic argumentative approach, those who appeal to the fighting words doctrine differ in how they interpret and apply that doctrine. One group takes a broader interpretation and the other a narrower interpretation. Here I introduce the "narrower" interpretation, since those who take the "broader" position, for example, Lawrence, Delgado, and Matsuda, also tend to invoke other constitutional doctrines to support the breadth of their proposals, and thus will be considered in a later section.

Thomas Grey, author of the Stanford speech code, defends what he calls a "moderate civil libertarian" position, in which the goals of equality and freedom are balanced by adopting a code that punishes a very narrow category of expression, namely, speech (verbal or nonverbal) that is directed to a specific individual, is objectively insulting, and attacks the identity of the hearer in such a way as to stimulate the "fight or flight" reaction.[47] Clearly, this policy addresses a much narrower category of speech than the statute upheld by the Supreme

Court in 1942, and the reason for this is that a series of later Supreme Court decisions have cut back the scope of the original fighting words doctrine. First, the Court has determined that only fighting words likely to cause immediate violence can be regulated, not fighting words that inflict mere emotional injury, because regulations banning words that cause emotional injury raise too many problems of vagueness and overbreadth. Second, the Court has determined that only fighting words that are targeted at a specific individual or individuals and intended to incite violence can be regulated, not fighting words addressed to the general public, because even fighting words have some expressive value. Finally, the Court has determined that policies regulating fighting words must be content-neutral, that is, they must regulate only the way in which the message is delivered, not the content of the message itself, because content restriction would amount to government censorship of opinions it disagrees with. Thus, it is to ensure the constitutionality of the policy that Grey proposes such a carefully drawn hate speech code.

The statement of the policy makes clear how it satisfies the "targeted" and "incitement to violence" conditions imposed by the Supreme Court. To avoid banning ideas on the basis of their content (which would violate the constitutional requirement that government restrictions on speech be content-neutral), Grey proposes to prohibit only actual epithets such as "nigger," "kike," "faggot," and "cunt" (his examples). Grey writes:

> Racial and other discriminatory hatred and contempt can be effectively expressed without using these words, of course, but (partly in the interests of avoiding vagueness and its chilling effect) such cases are not included under the regulation. A white student can tell a black student, face-to-face, "you people are inferior and should not be here," but not be guilty of harassment. In addition, even gutter epithets are immunized when uttered to the campus or public at large, in order to give the widest possible leeway for speech in the public forum.[48]

He adds that since there are no gutter epithets commonly understood to convey hatred and contempt for whites, males, or heterosexuals as such, the code will be neutral on its face but asymmetrical in practice. This should not trouble us, Grey believes, because the code will then protect those most in need of it, those who are members of groups subjected to "longstanding and deep-rooted prejudices."

Grey's Stanford speech policy is quite narrow and was widely thought, even by many critics of speech codes, to be constitutionally sound. (Moreover, many of the critics who attacked the policy clearly did not understand it.)[49] Its reliance on the fighting words doctrine and careful attention to later court decisions narrowing that doctrine made it one of the most widely discussed and most promising policies in the country.

*The Group Libel/Defamation Model.* This model appeals to the so-called group libel doctrine announced in *Beauharnais v. Illinois*, 343 U.S. 250 (1952), which upheld an Illinois statute making it unlawful to "publish any lithograph, moving picture, play, drama or sketch, which publication or exhibition portrays depravity, criminality, unchastity, or lack of virtue of a class of citizens of any race, color, creed, or religion which said publication or exhibition exposes the citizens of any race, color, creed, or religion to contempt, derision, or obloquy." The Illinois law was passed on June 29, 1917, a time when large numbers of non-Anglo immigrants were moving into the state, primarily the Chicago area. Designed to cool the heated rhetoric of white nationalist supremacists, the law was rarely enforced. But in January 1950, Joseph Beauharnais, the president of the White Circle League, was arrested and charged with violating the statute because he distributed a leaflet petitioning the mayor and city council of Chicago "to halt the further encroachment, harassment and invasion of white people, their property, neighborhoods and persons, by the Negro" and calling for "one million self respecting white people in Chicago to unite." It added, "If persuasion and the need to prevent the white race from becoming mongrelized by the negro will not unite us, then the aggressions . . . rapes, robberies, knives, guns and marijuana of the negro, surely will" (at 252).

The statute was eventually repealed by the Illinois legislature (as all the state laws banning group libel eventually were) and its leading scholarly advocate (David Riesman) abandoned it;[50] but since the group libel doctrine announced in *Beauharnais* has never been directly overturned by the Supreme Court, some legal scholars, including Donald Alexander Downs,[51] Kenneth Lasson,[52] Richard Delgado,[53] and Rhonda Hartman[54] advocate speech regulations punishing those who libel or defame protected groups through hate speech. The logic is straightforward:

1. The First Amendment does not protect group libel.
2. Some hate speech constitutes group libel. Thus
3. Campus hate speech codes punishing and preventing group libel do not violate the First Amendment.

In his 1985 book analyzing the Nazis-in-Skokie case of 1977, Downs maintains that freedom of speech is abused when the law fails to consider properly the content and inherent purpose of speech.[55] Hate groups can willfully inflict harm and defend their unjust actions under the guise of free speech. However,

Downs does not propose a resurrection of *Beauharnais*-type regulations (as they are "not a good idea"); rather, he proposes that "when an expression pertaining to matters of race or ethnic origin is accompanied by the advocacy of death or violence against members of that race or ethnic group, and is targeted at such members, it is constitutionally subject to abridgement."[56] He identifies three necessary conditions: the speech must (1) have an assaultive, intimidating content (explicitly or implicitly), (2) be targeted, and (3) be done with the intention to harm. To those who would object that such a regulation would have a chilling effect, Downs replies that all laws have some chilling effect beyond their intended application and that the speech chilled by such a regulation would be low-value speech. To those who would object that we cannot determine intent, Downs replies that we judge intent in the law all the time (in, e.g., commercial speech, libel of public officials). To those who worry that the regulation will be applied solely for the benefit of minorities and not penalize vilification of majority groups, Downs replies that all vilification is subject to the regulation under his proposal.

Kenneth Lasson, like Downs, addresses group libel in society at large and believes that *Beauharnais* is still good law. On his analysis, it has been used in landmark obscenity cases such as *Roth v. United States*, 354 U.S. 476 (1957), and *New York v. Ferber*, 458 U.S. 747 (1982), to show that libel is not constitutionally protected; and it was only narrowed (not overruled) in *New York Times v. Sullivan*, 376 U.S. 254 (1964), to the extent that it ensured that "a state could not remove speech from judicial scrutiny merely by putting a label on it."[57] He argues that racial defamation "is a form of verbal utterance that is either constitutionally non-speech (akin to hard-core pornography) or, like child pornography, so near the bottom of the hierarchy of protection as to justify either state proscription or civil liability."[58] It "short-circuits democratic principle of self-governance"[59] and "offers no ideas, opinions, or proposals of substance or merit."[60] He adds that traditional arguments against group libel law relying on informed public debate are unpersuasive in light of history, social science, and common sense. After all, "the citizens of Germany had ample opportunity to respond intelligently to Nazi racism; their failure to do so resulted in one of the greatest tragedies of all time."[61] He concludes that

> the proper measure by which any personal liberty must be gauged, particularly freedom of speech, is the degree to which it allows an individual to impose his speech on someone else, and the deleterious effect his actions might have on others. If either is excessive, the liberty must be restricted. The effect of racial defamation is demonstrably deleterious to all persons within the scope of its contempt. It lacks constitutional value;

its imposition is the verbal counterpart of a body blow to all persons swept within the scope of its contempt, as well as to the social fabric of American democracy. The ultimate liberty, after all, is not freedom of speech, but the right to live in peace, secure from harassment.[62]

It is simply false, in Lasson's view, to say that punishing defamation will jeopardize liberty. Democracy in America will not suffer if bigots are prohibited from promoting hatred on public streets.

Delgado and Hartman, in defending campus speech codes, both point out how the Supreme Court has narrowed but never overruled *Beauharnais* and has upheld numerous restrictions on speech (including criminal conspiracy, ordinary contracts, revealing official secrets, libel, obscenity, hostile environment harassment, trademark violations, plagiarism, incitement, "patently offensive" remarks addressed to captive audiences or broadcast on the airwaves, fighting words, disrespect to authority figures, fraud, price-fixing, criminal threats, and perjury).[63] They acknowledge that racist speech is speech and as such entitled to protection unless there is very good reason for not doing so. But they believe there is good reason for doing so. According to Delgado, social science findings demonstrate that antiracism rules will deter speech promoting racial hatred because "the main inhibiter of prejudice is the certainty that it will be remarked and punished." The rule deters racist acts (out of fear both of legal punishment and of social disapproval) and helps eliminate the attitude (it withers away if not acted upon). He further maintains that racist remarks are not harmless, as some critics have suggested, and that the absence of antiracism rules sets the stage for more serious transgressions. The kicker for both Delgado and Hartman is that racist slurs do not serve any First Amendment purposes: they contribute little to self-realization, to dialogue on important matters of public policy, or to the discovery of truth. Rather, they impair the growth of those who use them by encouraging rigid thinking and impeding moral development, they close off dialogue by insulting others, and they amount to a slap in the face rather than the statement or criticism of a proposition. According to Hartman, the First Amendment only protects speech that promotes dialogue; and since hate speech does not promote dialogue, it inhibits both the free marketplace of ideas and democratic self-government.[64]

*Summary.* Although advocates of campus codes debate the relative constitutional pedigrees and legal merits of the different models, they all agree that the deterrence argument can be combined with some version of the First Amendment argument to justify a campus hate speech regulation. (Indeed, there are two further models that have been appealed to: the intentional infliction of emotional distress model, which is discussed in Chapter 3; and the Title

VII hostile environment model, which is discussed in Chapters 5, 6, and 8.) Many scholars (including Charles Lawrence and Richard Delgado) appeal to more than one model in framing their argument, and some university policy statements refer to more than one of these doctrines in order to marshal the most support possible.

Still, another argument was needed, an argument showing how speech codes were especially required on college campuses, how universities were a special sort of community that could legitimately ban hate speech even if such speech were tolerable on the proverbial "Hyde Park street corner." This was needed because these scholars were aware of (1) the long line of Supreme Court decisions permitting various forms of highly offensive speech in public forums and on the university campus and (2) critics who would be quick to maintain that "students will now have less freedom than nonstudents. If there's any place where ignorance ought to be utterable, it ought to be on the university campus"[65] and that "of all institutions that should tolerate varied, even offensive speech, universities are foremost."[66]

## THE UNIVERSITY MISSION ARGUMENT

The general idea shared by all particular versions of the university mission argument is that hate speech is inconsistent with important aims of a university. Stated in its most concise form, its structure is:

1. Universities are empowered to make rules promoting their legitimate aims.
2. A hate speech code will help universities achieve legitimate aims. Thus
3. Campus hate speech codes are justified.

Some version of this argument is included in virtually every defense of campus hate speech codes, for regulations must be consistent with the purposes of the institutions they are designed to serve. Speech code advocates consistently include the goal of promoting racial and sexual equality. Richard Delgado, for example, notes that three constitutional provisions (Amendments XIII–XV) and a myriad of federal and state statutes aim to ensure equal opportunity and protect individuals against discrimination and that universities have the power to protect minority interests.[67] Universities have a special obligation to maintain environments hospitable to minorities and women, who have been shut out for so long and who continue to face obstacles that most white males do not. White students often don't even notice hate speech on their campuses; minority students do.[68] They notice because they know the threats that hate speech conveys are too often acted on. They notice because they are the predominant targets of hate speech and hate crimes.

Charles Lawrence, concerned with showing that campus restrictions on speech are consistent with the "marketplace of ideas" metaphor so widely accepted in First Amendment analysis, points out that hate speech distorts the marketplace in subtle (and not so subtle) ways by "muting or devaluing" the speech of racial and ethnic minorities. For example, a black student may be largely ignored by a professor while a white student with the same ideas may get a lot of attention. A powerful article on racism written by a Native American may be largely ignored by the mainstream media while a simplistic article on racism by a white man may be widely praised. Permitting hate speech also reduces the total amount of speech that reaches the market, because the threats implicit in hate speech silence many minorities.[69]

In addition, advocates point out that the speech marketplace, even the university marketplace, has never been a laissez-faire one. Cass Sunstein, another highly respected scholar of free speech, attempts to outline a theory of the First Amendment in his book *Democracy and the Problem of Free Speech* (1993). In it, he addresses campus hate speech codes and argues that campuses are not like cities. Universities regularly control the speech of faculty and students by limiting topics discussed in the classroom, requiring civility in class discussion and open forums, using viewpoint-biases in grading and assessing in the classroom, hiring and tenure decisions, and more.[70] Sunstein maintains that narrowly designed "fighting words" policies will not jeopardize the free trade of ideas on our nation's campuses any more than other accepted speech regulations do.

Advocates could go even further and attack the marketplace metaphor itself—and not merely its interpretation—along lines laid out by the conservative academic Willmore Kendall over thirty years ago.[71] The marketplace metaphor creates the picture of society as a kind of debating club devoted solely to the pursuit of truth, where ideas are bought and sold in accordance with their perceived market value (truth value). But society is not devoted solely to the pursuit of truth; it also must pursue justice and equality and the common defense and other values. Nor is society a debating club. A debating club, unlike society at large, is like an academic discipline in which all participants are credentialed; have obligations of professional courtesy and respect; and have knowledge of prior arguments and precedents, common frames of reference, and established norms that inhibit criticism of tradition and relegate unsuccessful debaters. In a sense, a debating club is just talk, talk among a well-defined group of peers. However, real life is more than just talk, and it is certainly not conducted among a well-defined group of peers. According to Kendall, if no views are given official status, then people will lose faith in the truth and become intolerant because in the absence of truth, everything is purely a matter of will, and of will power.

Other conservatives, such as Walter Berns,[72] have offered similar critiques, and in an odd union of political persuasions, liberal hate speech code advocates often portray the university as a special community in which free speech concerns diminish in light of other values just as conservatives have long portrayed society at large (or some favored portion thereof) as a special community in which free speech concerns diminish in light of other values.[73] Mari Matsuda, who is surely no conservative, calls for speech codes to protect the values of "inclusion, education, development of knowledge, and ethics that universities exist and stand for."[74] She argues that given the special vulnerabilities of students, universities have an obligation to teach students the values of tolerance and sensitivity to differences. In our pluralistic modern society, we do students a serious disservice if we fail to teach them to respect differences. A university can live up to this promise by enacting a hate speech code, for even if a code is rarely enforced, its symbolic message is that minorities are welcome and their interests will be protected.

Advocates understand that speech codes will not create a campus utopia. However, they insist that a speech code can protect students against the worst abuses and thereby improve the campus climate. John Wilson argues that egregious cases of hate speech can be punished because "the university is not a soapbox; its purpose is to educate students, not to promote absolutely free speech or ensure that every point of view has equal representation."[75] These "academic" reasons (the university mission argument), combined with "moral" reasons (the deterrence argument) and "legal" reasons (the First Amendment argument), led advocates to champion speech codes, and all three arguments are evidenced in the Michigan and Wisconsin cases. Both policies were directed at speech that was thought likely to cause harm (stigmatizing, threatening, hostile speech that interfered with academic activities), had little or no First Amendment value (Michigan's three-tiered approach, Wisconsin's focus on fighting words), and was inconsistent with legitimate university aims (protecting students' academic efforts, employment, extracurricular activities, or personal safety).


CONCLUSION

Reacting largely to student pressure (with faculty assistance) in the face of highly publicized incidents on campuses across the country, university authorities began adopting hate speech codes in the belief that such speech was harmful, unprotected by the First Amendment, and inconsistent with basic university goals. Based on a 1990 survey of 355 colleges and universities, the Carnegie Fund for the Advancement of Teaching estimated that 60 percent of all colleges and universities had a policy on racial harassment and that another 11 percent were considering such a policy.[76] Though the codes were hastily drafted and adopted in some cases (and in others just cloned from some other campus), legal experts were usually consulted in the development of the policies; and many students, faculty, and administrators felt confident they were doing the right thing. The policies were supported by weighty moral, legal, and academic arguments and principles that go far beyond mere arbitrary enforcement of "political correctness." Indeed, we might sum up this chapter with words offered by Charles Lawrence: "To engage in a debate about the first amendment and racist speech without a full understanding of the harm of racist speech risks making the first amendment an instrument of domination rather than a vehicle of liberation."[77] In recognition of the harms of hate speech, universities have actively taken up its regulation. Arati Korwar's 1994 survey of 384 universities showed that 60 percent ban verbal abuse/harassment, 14 percent ban speech causing emotional distress, 23 percent ban libel, 28 percent ban advocacy of offensive or outrageous viewpoint, and so on.[78] Not everyone was convinced by these arguments. As we shall see in the next chapter, critics of campus hate speech codes offered up their own arguments in an attempt to stave off the wave of regulation sweeping U.S. campuses.

# 3

# Wayne Dick's Plea:
# The Critics Fight Back

*If my sentence is not overturned, please advise me as to other views I also am not allowed to criticize, so that I won't unknowingly violate my probation and the standards of Yale University.*

WAYNE DICK, appealing his conviction for verbal harassment,
quoted in Nat Hentoff, *Free Speech for Me—But Not for Thee*

## AN INCIDENT AT YALE

In April 1986, the Yale Gay and Lesbian Co-op held its fifth annual Gay and Lesbian Awareness Days (GLAD, for short) to educate the campus about its members. The usual posters were distributed around campus to inform people about various GLAD events, including lectures, art shows, discussions, and a rally and dance. GLAD went off as planned, but on the following Monday, an anonymous poster parodying GLAD appeared around campus. Headlined "Bestiality Awareness Days," the poster listed a fictitious schedule of events. Some examples of "events" were:

- "PAN: the Goat, the God, the Lover," a lecture by Prof. Baaswell
- Bishop Bleatmore (grad. Dartmouth '69) speaking on THE IMPACT OF HOMO ERECTUS ON THE ORIGIN OF NEW SPECIES, Blight Hall
- Lambda Lambda Lambda—Yale's own Animal House!! announces their first BARNYARD RUSH—Y'all come!!! all night at the Rockinghorse Club

Many people around campus were offended by the crude poster, believing it not merely tasteless but a genuine attack on members of the Yale community. Those most indignant began a search to uncover the identity of the culprit; by

*48*

questioning employees at local copying shops, they discovered that the author of the poster was Wayne Dick, a sophomore from Florida.

At that point, Caroline Jackson, director of the Afro-American Cultural Center and a member of the Yale College Dean's Office Racial and Ethnic Harassment Board, and Yale senior Patrick Santana filed a complaint with Patricia Pierce, associate dean of Yale College and secretary of the Yale College Executive Committee, charging Mr. Dick with illegal harassment under a Yale Undergraduate Regulation banning "any act of harassment, intimidation, coercion or assault, or any other act of violence against any member of the community, including sexual, racial or ethnic harassment." Dick was informed of the complaint in a May 2 letter that also told him that the executive committee coordinating group had found the complaint to have merit and sent it on to the full executive committee for a hearing on May 12, for which he should prepare a written statement.

The ground rules for the hearing (which are, or at least were, typical at campuses around the country) were the following: A decision is reached in closed session. A verdict is announced without any written explanation or justification. No vote is recorded. The accused is permitted a faculty adviser, but the adviser is barred from direct participation in the proceedings (and thus from presenting any arguments or questioning any witnesses). The committee's decision is final, except in the extraordinary situation in which the committee is persuaded in an appeal that relevant new facts have been uncovered. Moreover, the committee conducting the hearing and casting the votes was made up of people ideologically committed to stamping out attitudes they find offensive and harmful.

Aware of these ground rules and the composition of the committee, Wayne Dick took his written defense seriously. In it, he expressed his apologies to anyone offended by the poster and claimed that he did not intend to violate norms of civility through his satire of GLAD. However, he also argued that he could not be charged with harassment since the Yale Report on Free Expression (also known as the Woodward Report), which was a part of the Yale Undergraduate Regulations, states, "Even when some members of the university community fail to meet their social and ethical responsibilities, the paramount obligation of the university is to protect that right to free expression."[1] The Woodward Report also stipulates that expression should not be punished because of its contents or motives; thus, Dick urged that even if his poster caused "shock," "hurt," or "outrage," it was still protected speech. He suggested that a conviction by the committee would amount to Yale allowing only the "politically correct" to speak and silencing the "unenlightened." To say the committee did not agree with Dick is a bit of an understatement. The committee found his speech "worthless" and "offensive"; Dick was of the opinion that some members of the committee thought a summary hanging would be the appropriate way to end the hearing. The next day, May 13, Patricia Pierce announced the committee's decision that Dick was in violation of undergraduate harassment regulations and was sentenced to two years' probation. This would be included in his permanent records and meant that any further offense by Dick would result in suspension or expulsion.

In many cases like this, the accused simply acquiesce, taking whatever punishment or "reeducation" is meted out. But not Wayne Dick. On May 16, Dick appealed his conviction in a letter to Yale president A. Bartlett Giamatti, arguing:

> I have been told that my poster is not protected . . . because it is worthless and offensive. I have seen many posters that I thought were worthless and offensive, but I respect others' right to express their views. . . . I was born and raised in a small town in Florida where the old southern political philosophy and prejudices were commonly accepted. By and large, I accepted these views without really considering them. When I came to Yale as a freshman, I found that my views were held by a small minority and I soon had to justify them for the first time. . . . In defending my beliefs through conversation with various people, I realized that some of my views were ill-considered. For those I have kept, I now, at least, have a philosophical basis for them. Of course, I can hardly claim to be all-wise after having just completed my sophomore year but because of the free interchange of ideas, I have grown. . . . To avoid heated arguments and to avoid hard feelings, I have often kept silent, even when I had strong moral objections to a point of view that was being stated. Recently, though, I decided to criticize an event which was, until recently, considered morally repugnant. My main reason for deciding to state my opinion more publicly was that only one opinion on this issue was being heard. . . . I ask that my sentence be overturned if the free expression regulation is in force or that my sentence be reduced because of my ignorance of the special status of the debate on homosexuality. . . . If my sentence is not overturned, please advise me as to other views that I am also not allowed to criticize, so that I won't unknowingly violate my probation and the standards of Yale University.[2]

Wayne Dick's plea, in effect, was for clarification: Is controversial speech going to be protected at Yale or not? Is the belief that homosexuality is morally acceptable beyond criticism? What speech is protected at the university and what speech is not protected? These were not merely rhetorical questions. His future at Yale, and the future of others who use speech that may be deemed offensive by the powers that be, hung on the answers.

Two weeks later, on May 30, Wayne Dick received a response from President Giamatti (who was leaving Yale to become president of baseball's National League). In the letter, Giamatti assured Dick that he had a right to freedom of expression "on any issue" and that the university would protect that right "in the future as it has in the past." However, he also informed Wayne Dick that the committee's decision stood.

The news that his appeal was rejected was doubly bad because Giamatti also offered no clarification of the university's position on what was protected and not protected speech. Wayne Dick (along with everyone else on campus) was still in the dark as to what views could be criticized and what views couldn't (except he now apparently knew that his view about homosexuality was not protected, although the views of his opponents were protected). Since the committee did not explain or justify its decision, it may be that the committee did not punish his view per se, but rather the way he expressed his view. But that would still leave Dick (and everyone else) in the dark as to the ways they could criticize views and the ways they could not (except for the vague injunction that it not be "harassing"). Since Dick's was an unpopular view seldom expressed, at least on the Yale campus, this likely would have been the end of the story, had not someone intervened.

Nat Hentoff, the free speech journalist, got wind of Wayne Dick's case and began investigating. Hentoff thought that even if Wayne Dick's poster was tasteless and weak satire, it was still protected speech, but he was discouraged in his initial contacts with Yale officials. He wrote Giamatti's incoming replacement, Benno Schmidt, who wrote a noncommittal response saying only that he would look into the matter when he could. Hentoff called Sidney Altman, then dean of Yale College, who expressed private reservations about the committee's decision but stood behind the committee as a matter of public record.

Hentoff persisted in his inquiries, however, and things began to change. He talked with Guido Calabresi, then dean of the Yale Law School, who in no uncertain terms condemned the committee's decision as a violation of student academic freedom. Hentoff discovered that this opinion was shared by Professor C. Vann Woodward, who had chaired the committee that had drafted the Yale Report on Free Expression (the Woodward Report), which was adopted as part of the undergraduate regulations. Woodward thought the committee's decision was a blatant misreading of the Yale Report and thereafter served as Dick's adviser and advocate, taking the case to the *Yale Daily News* and the *New York Times* in an attempt to win public support for Wayne Dick's free speech rights. At the same time, Hentoff published diatribes on Dick's behalf in the *Village Voice* and *Washington Post*. But the signal events must have been when the new Yale president, Benno Schmidt, publicly announced in his inaugural address the next fall that "there is no speech so horrendous in content that it does not in principle serve our purpose" and privately advised Dick to ask for a new hearing. Dick reluctantly agreed (reluctantly because there were no new "facts" on which the committee could base a reversal); to his surprise, the committee announced a reversal of decision in an October 2 press release (again without written explanation or justification or recorded vote).

Now, one might think that this brought a satisfying conclusion to the case from Wayne Dick's point of view. That would be a mistake. For even though he had won a reprieve from his punishment, his plea was not answered. The reasons why his speech became protected were not revealed by the committee. He—like everyone else on campus—was still in the dark as to which views were criticizable and which were not, or, perhaps, how views could and could not be properly criticized. It was still anyone's guess when expression crossed the line from protected speech to unprotected "harassment." Suppose the committee's reversal had emboldened Dick to organize a student group opposing homosexuality that publicly criticized known homosexuals and their heterosexual sympathizers in posters, letters to the editor, and so on. Would that cross the line? Suppose the group started leaving threatening posters of the kind found in Michigan. Would that cross the line? What if the decisions had caused GLAD advocates to direct a campaign of fierce verbal criticism at Wayne Dick, with the intention of driving him from campus. Would that constitute harassment? The failure of the university, and specifically the committee, to state a line dividing protected and unprotected speech leaves everyone—faculty, students, administrators, staff—with no way of knowing when their critical speech is punishable or not. No one can be happy with this situation. Defenders of free speech still did not have any assurance that offensive speech would be protected in future cases; and defenders of equality still didn't have any assurance that their goals were being taken seriously either.

Though the committee was silent about why it reversed its decisions, except to deny it was the negative national publicity that caused it, I think we can reasonably speculate about the causes. All we need to do is point out how the Yale situation differed from the Wisconsin and Michigan cases. First, Yale had the Woodward Report, a formal statement protecting offensive speech that it had developed as a result of earlier hate speech events and that represented an explicit announcement to the Yale community that free speech outweighed civility, solidarity, and the like. Michigan and Wisconsin had no such formal policy, nor did they have Yale's prior experiences of the collision of free expression and equality, which served as the impetus for drafting the Woodward Report.[3] But the Woodward Report and its history are not, in and of themselves, sufficient to explain the events at Yale. Yale also had staunch First Amendment advocates in pivotal positions. Without such people coming forward, the committee would simply have interpreted the Woodward Report out of meaningful existence. Without Nat Hentoff's intervention, without his taking the case public and marshaling opposition to Dick's conviction, it seems unlikely that Dick's speech would have been protected. Without Professor Woodward, Dean Calabresi, and President Schmidt taking public stands, in local and national forums, in support of free speech in the Ivy halls, it seems unlikely that the committee would have reversed its decision. Indeed, this incident launched Benno Schmidt into the forefront of the national debate on hate speech on American campuses.

We must remind ourselves, however, that what happened at Yale (and Michigan and Wisconsin, for that matter) was hardly inevitable. Sam Walker's observation about free speech court precedents holds equally well for these, and many other, campus outcomes: namely, things could have turned out differently, and they turned out as they did largely because of political forces. At Michigan and Wisconsin no organized opposition to hate speech regulation with political clout emerged, although it could have. For example, instead of backing down in the face of student pressure, UW–Madison Chancellor Donna Shalala could have remained resolute in her conviction that the Madison speech incidents were protected by the First Amendment. But she didn't. She became an advocate of regulation, maintaining that "We're talking about harassment here, not impinging free speech."[4] The critics at Yale who stood up for the protection of offensive speech might well have remained silent or changed their tune as Shalala did rather than risk their jobs and reputations by defending the expression of an unpopular point of view.

But they didn't. Perhaps that is the key: the people and how they understand and apply the rules, rather than the rules themselves. Yale had, in effect, a hate speech code (the harassment regulation), but ultimately the university decided to interpret it in a way that protected and encouraged more speech rather than punished and stifled critical expressions. Although policies get lost in a morass of committee work, and today's policy is often viewed as mere fodder for tomorrow's paper shredder, people can, through their own dedicated efforts, bring continuity and sense to this process.

Now, you will have noticed that I have told Wayne Dick's story in a sympathetic manner. Am I correct to do so? Remember, our ultimate goal is not merely to understand what took place and why, but to determine whether the policies and events can be justified. Did Yale make the right choice when it protected Wayne Dick's poster? Or, as we saw argued in the previous chapter, did Michigan and Wisconsin make the right choice in deciding not to protect expressions like Dick's? Is his speech so harmful that it constitutes a violation of constitutional equality and deserves punishment? So egregious it is outside the protective umbrella of the First Amendment because it amounts to fighting words or group libel? So worthless it is inconsistent with the mission of a university? This is no idle inquiry, for speech like Wayne Dick's, speech some hope to censure merely for its perceived offensiveness, still occurs on American campuses daily.

## THE CONSTITUTIONALITY ARGUMENT

As indicated earlier, many critics of campus hate speech codes believe that these regulations are unconstitutional violations of individual free speech rights. It is no accident that the people who stood up for Wayne Dick at Yale (in particular, Benno Schmidt, Guido Calabresi, C. Vann Woodward, and Nat Hentoff) were highly committed to the protection of speech and thoroughly versed in the history and legal interpretation of the free speech clause. They believe, and can cite plenty of legal precedent to support their belief, that however ugly, offensive, or otherwise immoral speech may be, government ought not to censor it except in very narrowly defined areas. Of course, the constitutional status of speech is different at a private institution like Yale than at public institutions like Michigan and Wisconsin, since the First Amendment only restricts the actions of government and its agencies (including school boards and public universities). But Yale, like most leading private institutions, has a historical commitment to follow First Amendment guidelines. (Hence the concern at Stanford by Thomas Grey, for example, to draft a narrow, constitutional policy.) But in any case, the widespread adoption of speech policies on American campuses provoked a chorus of critics to object on constitutional grounds. Put concisely, their argument was as follows:

1. The legal justifications offered for campus hate speech codes rest on invalid or inapplicable First Amendment precedents.
2. Hate speech codes violate accepted standards of First Amendment jurisprudence (i.e., are overbroad, unduly vague, and content-biased). Thus
3. Hate speech codes are unconstitutional.

The argument is widely made, but its classic presentation was made by Nadine

Strossen, then-president of the ACLU and professor at the New York School of Law, in her response to Charles Lawrence III in the *Duke Law Journal*.[5] Acknowledging that some restrictions on speech are constitutional (an extremely narrow range that would probably be satisfied "only in rare factual circumstances"), Strossen attacks three versions of the First Amendment argument for hate speech codes, namely, the fighting words approach, the intentional infliction of emotional distress approach, and the group defamation/group libel approach. On her analysis, each provides an insufficient basis for campus speech codes and has been developed by speech code advocates in ways that go far beyond the kernel of truth contained in each. (That is, the actual codes put into practice restrict much more speech than their own theoretical justifications provide.)

In response to the fighting words model, Strossen argues that it fails because it has (rightly) been dramatically narrowed in scope from its *Chaplinsky* origins. The *Chaplinsky* Court permitted government bans on words that (1) directly inflict injury or (2) tend to incite breach of the peace; however, a long series of later decisions have, in effect, gutted the fighting words model. In *Gooding v. Wilson*, 405 U.S. 518, 523 (1972) (upheld in numerous later decisions), the Court limited the doctrine only to words that tend to incite a breach of the peace. That is, the U.S. Supreme Court no longer considers words that cause injury as fighting words (although in some factual circumstances, words that cause injury may be punished under some other doctrine, e.g., intentional infliction of emotional distress, perjury, bribery, conspiracy, etc.). Moreover, in *Eaton v. City of Tulsa*, 415 U.S. 697, 699 (1974) (*per curiam*), and *Hess v. Indiana*, 414 U.S. 105, 109 (1973) (*per curiam*), the Supreme Court determined that the tendency of the words to incite breach of the peace must be such that the "average person" almost certainly would respond with immediate violence. That is, if a reasonable person could ignore or walk away from the speech or would be moved to violence only later, the expression does not constitute fighting words. Further, even where the words may cause the average person to respond with immediate violence, the state must not allow expected hostile audience reactions to prevent speakers from having their say, for to allow hostile audiences to silence speakers would be to give them a "heckler's veto" and thereby prevent potentially valuable speech from being heard. This is especially true in situations in which the audience is not "captive," that is, in situations where those offended by the speech are free to leave or otherwise avoid the speech. A long line of cases, including *Terminiello v. Chicago*, 337 U.S. 1 (1949), and *Brandenburg v. Ohio*, 395 U.S. 444 (1969), have made it clear that in a public forum even the most highly offensive speech one can imagine regarding race is entitled to constitutional protection.[6] Finally, in *Cohen v. California*, 403

U.S. 15 (1971) (and a long line of other cases[7]), the Supreme Court held that the words must be directed at a specific individual (not an amorphous group) in a face-to-face encounter, and thus invalidated regulations that ban specific words on the grounds that each case must be contextually evaluated. Strossen points out that all of these standards were announced in cases that struck down government restrictions on speech and that "the Court has overturned every single fighting words conviction that it has reviewed since *Chaplinsky*."[8] The upshot? A campus hate speech code based on the fighting words model would apply only to speech that (1) does not bear on issues of social policy, (2) is almost certain to cause a reasonable person to react violently, and (3) is directed at specific individual(s) in a face-to-face encounter that the listener could not avoid. According to Strossen, campus hate speech codes are not tailored narrowly enough to meet these judicial requirements and thus are unconstitutional. The concern about the definition of fighting words is no mere "hypothetical" debate. Every day on campuses all around the country, students, faculty, staff, and administrators engage in heated debate. Sometimes this debate goes beyond, even far beyond, the norms of civil discourse or merely rhetorical ploys. It happens in the classroom, on the quad, in the dorms, in speakers' forums, and other places. A loosely written fighting words policy would enable administrators to punish protected speech and chill the free exchange of controversial ideas.

In response to the intentional infliction of emotional distress model, Strossen argues that it too provides an insufficient basis for a campus hate speech code. As pointed out in the fighting words cases, the Court has repeatedly narrowed the doctrine in order to protect outrageous, highly offensive speech. This means that the emotional distress model must address speech of a different kind or intensity or duration than the fighting words model. And it does: it is based on the "outrageousness" of the speech when intended to inflict psychological injury. Strossen points out, however, that the Supreme Court is reticent to allow judges and juries to make judgments about the kind, intensity, and duration of emotional distress when the First Amendment is at stake. Given the weight the First Amendment carries, its being at stake is a key reason why speech, even offensive speech, must be protected. Strossen quotes *Hustler v. Falwell*, 485 U.S. 46, 55 (1988), to clarify the Court's concern about how the outrageousness standard allows judges and juries to (wrongly) act in highly subjective and arbitrary ways:

> "Outrageousness" in the area of political and social discourse has an inherent subjectiveness about it which would allow a jury to impose liability on the basis of the juror's tastes or views, or perhaps on the basis of their

dislike of a particular expression. An "outrageousness" standard thus runs afoul of our longstanding refusal to allow damages to be awarded because the speech in question may have an adverse emotional impact on the audience.

It is not at all difficult to imagine clever prosecutors winning convictions or lawyers winning awards of damages even in cases of clearly protected speech by playing on the sentiments and prejudices of a jury hostile to the person or point of view of the defendant. Yet it is standard constitutional doctrine that it is the freedom of an unpopular, even hated, point of view or expression that gives the First Amendment bite, that prevents a "tyranny of the majority" from imposing restrictions on their opponents.

Once again, Strossen's point is no idle concern in academia. If all speech that intentionally inflicted emotional distress were punishable, academia would be in serious trouble, for one of its central missions is to challenge vigorously student complacency and social norms; to force students to rethink deeply held assumptions and prejudices; to question and contest student conceptions of the meaning of life, liberty, and the pursuit of happiness; to require them to confront the diversity of opinions, tastes, customs, and attitudes that our world contains. What would prevent a sympathetic jury from awarding damages to a student who sued a professor for emotional damages suffered during a class in which the professor vigorously challenged his or her view of religion or capitalism or patriotism or sexual identity? What would prevent a student from suing another student who vehemently disagreed with him or her in a hallway debate about a social policy of intense personal concern? These are not merely hypothetical fears.

Murry Dolfman, a legal studies senior lecturer at the Wharton Business School of the University of Pennsylvania, was forced to make a public apology and attend a sensitivity training session and was suspended for a year for vigorously challenging students during a classroom discussion of the Thirteenth Amendment.[9] A University of Michigan student was called onto the carpet for maintaining the unpopular view that homosexuals should be counseled to go "straight." A UW–River Falls instructor was forced out when he offended some students (and the chancellor) by burning a flag in a classroom demonstration of First Amendment rights.[10] Moreover, what would count as emotional distress in such cases? Inability to sleep? Mood swings? Anger and resentment? Depression? Loss of concentration? Anguish? Profound educational lessons can be quite unwelcome and emotionally troubling.

It is in view of such concerns that the Supreme Court has imposed a very strict burden of proof in emotional distress cases, a burden that, at least according to Strossen, will rarely be met in campus hate speech incidents. In the *Hustler* case, the standard was that the speech had to be both demonstrably false and made with actual malice. Do we want juries to decide that it is demonstrably false that God does not exist or did not create the world *ex nihilo* when someone attacks a student's religious beliefs as Freudian "illusions" or ridicules creation science as "preliterate"? Will fundamentalist juries take seriously the defendant's assertion that it was his or her intention to benefit, not harm, the student through the critique?

In response to the group defamation/libel model, Strossen argues that the Supreme Court's *Beauharnais* precedent, like the others, has been gutted. In *Milkovitch v. Loraine Journal,* 110 S. Ct. 2695 (1990), the Court held that statements defaming groups convey opinions on matters of public concern and ought to be protected, even if the statements also injure personal reputations. Strossen points out that

> the concept of defamation encompasses only false statements of fact that are made without a good faith belief in their truth. Therefore, any disparaging or insulting statement would be immune from this doctrine, unless it were factual in nature, demonstrably false in content, and made in bad faith. Members of minority groups that are disparaged by an allegedly libelous statement would hardly have their reputations or psyches enhanced by a process in which the maker of the statement sought to prove his good faith belief in its truth, and they were required to demonstrate the absence thereof.[11]

Her point is this: opponents of hate speech will find little satisfaction in trying to prove that Nazis don't really believe blacks and Catholics and Jews are subhuman. The problem, of course, is that they really do believe these things. To make matters even worse for the libel model, the Supreme Court has adopted a very narrow view of what constitutes a false statement in First Amendment contexts, even asserting boldy in *Gertz v. Robert Welch, Inc.*, 418 U.S. 323, 339 (1974), that "there is no such thing as a false idea." The upshot of Strossen's analysis, once again, is that campus hate speech codes are not drawn narrowly enough to conform to these court requirements.

Strossen could also point out how group libel/defamation is a double-edged sword. If government is given the authority to punish racist speech that "defames" minority groups, then it also is given the authority to punish nonracist speech that "defames" racists and other bigots. That is, critics can emphasize that in the years following the *Beauharnais* decision, the Supreme Court has moved away from the majority opinion and toward the dissent of Justice

Hugo Black: "No rationalization on a purely legal level can conceal the fact that state laws like this one present a constant overhanging threat to freedom of speech, press, and religion. . . . The same kind of state law that makes Beauharnais a criminal for advocating segregation in Illinois can be utilized to send people to jail in other states for advocating equality and nonsegregation."[12] The double-edged quality of speech regulation could well have a calamitous effect on universities, opening up wide avenues for censorship of speech and ideas. Law professor Edmond Cahn points out that if universities had a duty to protect students from all statements of group libel, then,

> the officials could begin by prosecuting anyone who distributes the Christian Gospels, because they contain many defamatory statements not only about Jews but also about Christians. . . . Then the officials could ban Greek literature for calling the rest of the world "barbarians." Roman authors would be suppressed because when they were not defaming the Gallic and Teutonic tribes, they were disparaging the Italians. . . . Then there is Shakespeare, who openly affronts the French, the Welsh, the Danes. . . . Dozens of British writers from Sheridan and Dickens to Shaw and Joyce insulted the Irish. . . . Literally applied, a group libel law would leave our bookshelves empty.[13]

To be sure, advocates of campus hate speech codes might complain that Cahn's fear is ridiculous, that universities would never empty the shelves in this way. But is his fear really so far-fetched? Individuals and school boards around the country already try to prevent high school students from reading Mark Twain's *Huckleberry Finn* and Studs Terkel's *Working*, so what would prevent some university presidents or faculty senates or boards of regents from doing the same?

To top off her argument against all three models, Strossen introduces the constitutional requirement of content-neutrality. In *Police Department of Chicago v. Mosley*, 408 U.S. 92 (1972), the Supreme Court made it clear that government is not free to restrict speech on the basis of its content, asserting that "above all else, the First Amendment means that government has no power to restrict expression because of its message, its ideas, its subject matter, or its contents." This principle has been affirmed in a long line of cases, perhaps most famously (to some minds, infamously) in the flag-burning case, *Texas v. Johnson*, 491 U.S. 397 (1989). The trouble, according to critics, is that campus speech codes are not content-neutral. In fact, they maintain that campus hate speech policies are entirely defined by the content of the messages that they seek to suppress (racist ones, sexist ones, homophobic ones, etc.). Of course, the

Supreme Court does recognize limits on speech, but only very narrowly defined ones that are content-neutral. Obscene speech, for example, is not constitutionally protected, but the Court has a very narrow conception of what counts as obscene, and it would not uphold a regulation outlawing obscene expression directed at Republicans but permitting such expression when directed at Democrats.

Once again, this fear is not merely "hypothetical." As we saw earlier, the Stanford code, which was widely considered one of the best in the country, did not consider any epithets used against whites, males, heterosexuals, and the like as sanctionable. Apparently, anti-whites, anti-males, anti-heterosexuals, and so on are free to verbally harass their opponents at will. Alan Charles Kors, a historian at the University of Pennsylvania and vocal critic of campus speech codes, claims that in practice this is what has actually happened at many campuses around the country. He writes:

> You may say anything you wish at most American universities about whites, males, heterosexuals, Catholics, Jews as Israelis, or Jews as white Americans, members of the Unification church, evangelical Protestants, and, offend them as you will, Episcopalians, the least protected sensitivity in the land. You may not offend militant blacks, politicized Hispanics, radical feminists, or activist gays. From the left, you may call moderate blacks "Oreos" or "Uncle Toms" with impunity—that is social criticism, not harassment! You may equally abuse antifeminist women as "Barbie dolls," "mall chicks," and "psychological captives" with impunity (that is analysis, not stigmatization that "creates an offensive environment"!). You may tell white students whose parents died fighting for freedom that their mothers and fathers were, depending on the contexts, oppressors, racists, sexists, or baby-killers (in Vietnam, though not in abortion clinics). You may exhibit a cross in urine. If the issue is the sensitivity of white, male, heterosexuals, however vulnerable their egos, universities will talk about the perils of freedom, and indeed, correctly so! If the issue is the sensibilities of politically correct minorities (evangelicals and "Moonies" need not apply), universities will talk about the vulnerability of egos and the absurdity of an ahistorical definition of freedom.[14]

The problem here, of course, is that this one-sidedness and partiality violates our moral sense of a "level playing field"; and too often, campus hate speech policies and those responsible for their enforcement are not interested in free speech or a level playing field, they are interested in retribution and a competitive advantage in winning the minds of incoming students by silencing and punishing their opponents. Too often, advocates of hate speech codes see the university as the enforcement arm of their social agenda rather than a marketplace of ideas.

Strossen notes that there is a limited class of cases in which the courts will uphold content-based speech regulation, namely, those in which the regulation is both necessary to a compelling state interest and narrowly drawn to achieve that end. However, she also points out that these codes, even assuming their aim is a compelling one, are not narrowly drawn or necessary to attain their desired end. Universities can pursue their egalitarian agenda through educational measures, not punitive ones.

In sum, Strossen's comprehensive and precedent-filled argument is very powerful. If her analyses are correct, campus hate speech codes would be illegal and universities could be held liable for damages for violating student and faculty First Amendment rights under the auspices of these codes. Yet her arguments (like those of the other critics who made the constitutionality argument) seemed to have little effect on the adoption and enforcement of speech codes by universities bent on punishing bigots. Many campus leaders and legal scholars continued to press for hate speech codes where they did not already exist and to defend those codes where they had already been adopted. Apparently, in the opinion of the speech code advocates, either they already had a narrow enough code or else the law needed to expand the range of punishable speech.

It is important to note that critics of campus hate speech codes such as Strossen did not advocate an "anything goes" atmosphere on college campuses. Strossen specifically acknowledges that "the ACLU never has argued that harassing, intimidating, or assaultive conduct should be immunized simply because it is in part based on words."[15] It should almost go without saying that outspoken conservative critics of campus hate speech codes accept some limits on campus expression. Dinesh D'Souza, for example, says that as a matter of policy, "students should not yell epithets at each other."[16] George Will believes that a university requires "a particular atmosphere of civility that can be incompatible with unrestricted expression."[17] Thus, in spite of their rhetoric, the critics' position is not that there should be no speech regulations on campuses at all, but rather that the codes that have been adopted are seriously flawed. That is, the campus hate speech debate should not be understood as a discussion over whether or not campus speech should be restricted, but rather, over what speech should be restricted and why it should be restricted.

Both critics and advocates of campus hate speech codes knew that the constitutional argument could go either way if a case went to the courts. Indeed, a University of Texas committee charged with developing a policy on hate speech concluded, "There can be no guarantee as to the constitutionality of any university rule bearing on racial harassment and sensitive matters of freedom of expression."[18] Thus, to strengthen their position, critics added arguments attempting to establish that campus hate speech codes were unwise or otherwise flawed even if they were constitutional.

## THE CONSEQUENCES ARGUMENT

The arguments of critics, when going beyond constitutional concerns, focus on the harms of speech regulation. Put concisely, their argument is the following:

1. Any public policy that has seriously negative consequences ought not to be adopted, even if it is constitutionally permitted.
2. Hate speech codes have seriously negative consequences. Thus
3. Hate speech codes ought not to be adopted, even if constitutionally permitted.

When it is put in this abstract form, one is left to wonder what harms critics have in mind. In Chapter 2 we saw campus hate speech code advocates identify various benefits to be gained and harms to be avoided by adopting a campus hate speech code. What are the benefits to be gained and harms to be avoided by not adopting a hate speech code of the sort advocates press for? Why do the consequences of the critic's greater freedom outweigh the consequences of the advocate's lesser freedom?

One important "cost" arising from campus hate speech regulations, according to the critics, is the chilling of some legitimate speech. This happens, even if the code does not restrict constitutionally protected speech, because students and faculty are afraid of being accused of hate speech and limit their comments to politically safe truisms or simply don't comment at all on important social issues. Some speech code advocates, John Wilson, for example, have alleged that this fear is purely hypothetical: but is it? Students have been prosecuted for criticizing homosexuals and their sympathizers (Wayne Dick at Yale), for maintaining in a classroom that homosexuality is a biological disease (the Michigan social work student), for questioning the fairness of a minority professor's grading (the Michigan dentistry student), for making jokes in class (the Michigan limerick student), for challenging a professor's belief that lesbians make the best parents (a University of Washington case),[19] for writing a paper deemed to be "racist" by a professor (whose judgment was unanimously overturned by an appeals committee),[20] and for raising a banner advocating restoration of a college's Indian mascot (Dartmouth).[21] Faculty have been prosecuted for using the term "nigger" in a positive way accepted by the students involved (a Central Michigan University case we will examine in the next chapter), for using the term "nigger" as a hypothetical example of protected speech in a law class studying the free speech clause,[22] for using a sexually related metaphor to explain literary concepts,[23] for joining the conservative National Association of Scholars,[24] for maintaining the supremacy of the "sun people" over the "ice people,"[25] for researching the correlation between cranial size and standardized test performance, and for including in a course reading pack an article that used the term "wetback."[26] This is, of course, the short list. The point is this: how is anyone to know what anyone else really thinks in the repressive atmosphere a hate speech code can create? Kaydee Culbertson, who was co-chair of the Stanford Native American Student Association, complained that students were so careful about what they said, out of fear they would say the wrong thing about Native Americans, that she had no idea what they were really thinking. She said, "When it reaches the point that sensitivity stifles communication, it has gone too far."[27] Fears of chilling effects are not merely hypothetical.

Advocates may respond: So what? Why is this such a big deal? So what if some people remain silent who might otherwise have expressed their ideas? Were any of those ideas really worth expressing? Isn't the speech that gets challenged pretty worthless stuff? The hate speech defined by the policies discussed in Chapter 2 isn't really intended to persuade people of anything in a marketplace of ideas, it is intended to hurt victims. Hate speech isn't part of a dialogue, its aim is to silence opponents, to make them want to crawl away. This isn't just a liberal thought police notion: Robert Bork, the conservative judge and social commentator, has said that hate speech may be restricted since it is permissible to censor speech that carries no ideas.[28] To answer this, critics usually argue that the primary mission of universities is to promote knowledge and seek truth, which requires free thought and expression, even offensive thought and expression. Wayne Dick at Yale admitted in his letter of appeal that he had learned the error of some of his earlier prejudices. How? By airing his ideas and having opponents point out their flaws. Without subjecting his views to public scrutiny, Wayne Dick (and countless others) may well never abandon their prejudices. Benno Schmidt, Yale's president, asserts that "the university has a fundamental mission, which is to search for the truth. And a university is a place where people have the right to speak the unspeakable and think the unthinkable and challenge the unchallengeable. . . . Vague and unpredictable possibilities of punishment for expression on campus . . . are antithetical to the idea of the university."[29] If the ideas of racists and anti-racists, the "nature vs. nurture" crowd, homophobes and anti-homophobes, egalitarians and anti-egalitarians,

Communists and capitalists, fascists, Nazis, aristocrats, New Deal Democrats and laissez-faire libertarians are not debated on campuses, where will they be? Gerald Gunther, himself a survivor of Nazi anti-Semitism, writes in response to Charles Lawrence III in a *Stanford Lawyer* debate:

> I am deeply troubled by current efforts—however well intentioned—to place new limits on freedom of expression at this and on other campuses. Such limits are not only incompatible with the mission and meaning of a university; they also send exactly the wrong message from academia to society as a whole. University campuses should exhibit greater, not less, freedom of expression than prevails in society at large.[30]

Critics view the issue in terms of academic freedom and believe that even if the courts weaken their stance on this principle of modern education, the university should not. The campus is a special marketplace of ideas in our society. Dessayer and Burke appeal to *Keyishian v. Board of Regents of the University of New York*, 385 U.S. 589, 603 (1967) (which itself quotes from *United States v. Associate Press*, 52 F. Supp. 362, 372 [S.D.N.Y. 1943]), to illustrate this point: "The classroom is peculiarly the marketplace of ideas. The nation's future depends on leaders formed through wide exposure to that robust exchange of ideas which discovers truth 'out of a multitude of tongues, [rather] than through any kind of authoritative selection.'" Critics usually add that strong academic freedoms were necessary to the advancement of many minority causes. If one group's "knowledge" is permitted to suppress another group's "worthless speech," then the speech of hate speech code advocates might be suppressible by a majority that is offended by their dissident views. The feminist professor who attacks male patriarchy, the minority professor who defends affirmative action or urges black juries to free black defendants even when they are guilty in order to undermine the corrupt white legal system, the homosexual professor who seeks equal employment rights could well be among the first victims of an offended majority given authority to punish content-based speech.

Critics also argue that students are not so vulnerable and in need of a university's protective hand as advocates (such as Matsuda) would like us to believe. In their "libertarian" critique of campus speech codes, David McGowan and Ragesh Tangri maintain (1) that many students are not the thin-skinned, impressionable empty-heads Matsuda assumes them to be; (2) that even if they were, the rationale for regulating speech would then apply to vulnerable audiences outside the university, but that would fly in the face of "heckler's veto" doctrine; and (3) that students are mature enough to realize that a university needs to be neutral between opposing points of view in the debate of social values. McGowan and Tangri defend the marketplace of ideas approach (as opposed to a "command economy" of ideas approach) on the grounds that even if there is no guarantee on the market model that we will not end up as Nazi Germany, there is no guarantee that we will avoid this fate on a "command" model either, and more importantly, "individuals are better judges of what is best for them than is the government."[31] The better bet is to allow individuals to err, for if an individual errs, much less harm is done than if the state errs, and an individual's error is easier to correct than a state's error. This adherence to freedom may come across as an uncaring attitude; indeed, McGowan and Tangri quote Justice Holmes: "If my fellow citizen wants to go to Hell I will help him. It's my job." However, at least from their point of view, it is not so much a matter of caring as a matter of long-term costs and benefits. Their belief is that in the long run, good ideas are more likely to emerge in a free marketplace of ideas than in a constrained marketplace of ideas.

Patrick Garry, author of several books on free speech, defends the marketplace metaphor as the "traditional" understanding of speech on the campus and laments the "ideological" understanding of speech that advocates hate speech codes. He writes:

> The justifications for these codes are the same justifications that have always been used by censors. . . . Speech codes not only reveal an increasingly restrictive attitude toward free expression on college campuses, but also reflect a changing view of truth. As educators traditionally have adhered to the idea that truth emerges from a robust marketplace of ideas, free expression has been seen as vital to the pursuit of truth. In recent years, however, the academic community has taken a more ideological or political view of truth . . . and this ideological approach diminishes the importance of free speech. Because truth is predetermined according to one's ideological beliefs, the need for an uninhibited marketplace of ideas no longer exists. . . . This ideological approach, which tries to attain truth through rules about what can and cannot be discussed, undermines the traditional cornerstone of American education—free and open debate. And by becoming more ideological and less tolerant, the university encourages a less civil form of discourse.[32]

The root of this attempt to change speech paradigms, in Garry's view, is the self-esteem movement, which puts feel-good philosophy ahead of hard truths. This "sacred cow" of the New Left encourages people to fall into victim mentality and invent new histories in an attempt to discern a truth they can feel good about while censoring those that make them feel bad.

After all this talk of the marketplace of ideas, you may wonder where it comes from. In the legal literature, it comes from Justice Oliver Wendell Holmes II, a hero of free speechers, in *Abrams v. United States*, 250 U.S. 616, 630 (1919):

> When men have realized that time has upset many fighting faiths, they may come to believe even more than they believe the very foundation of their own conduct that the ultimate good desired is better reached by free trade in ideas—that the best test of truth is the power of thought to get itself accepted in the competition of the market, and this truth is the very ground on which their wishes safely can be carried out. That at any rate is the theory of our Constitution.

In that case, Jacob Abrams, along with four other Russian-born immigrants, had been convicted under the Espionage Act of unlawfully inciting and encouraging resistance to American war policies. They had thrown out an open factory window thousands of leaflets criticizing President Woodrow Wilson and had been sentenced to twenty years in prison. Abrams and his brethren were self-confessed rebels, revolutionaries, and anarchists, and Holmes believed the government was wrong to jail them for their creed. It is fascinating that Holmes's opinion, written in dissent, a sole dissent which very nearly was not written at all,[33] should come to dominate First Amendment analysis.

Critics also argue that campus hate speech codes will not achieve their aims. Many critics maintain that rather than deter hate speech, these codes will simply cause bigots to get more subtle or go underground, since the policies only touch the outward signs of bias. Margaret Blanchard, a professor of journalism and mass communications, writes, "Part of the problem that these speech codes raise, of course, is beyond the reach of university administrators because the difficulties rest deep within the hearts and souls of many Americans."[34] The codes may even increase bigotry by making martyrs out of hate mongers or by causing a backlash. Nonminorities may believe that minorities are getting special treatment because many codes, for example, Stanford's, ban epithets used against minorities but not epithets used against nonminorities. Second, critics argue that the codes will not advance the interests of equality because debates over them shift the focus away from the plight of minorities and onto legalistic technicalities. Roger Howard, associate dean of students at UW-Madison, admits that UW-17 ultimately was abandoned because defending it would have been counterproductive to the aims of improving the educational environment for minorities and women.[35] Theodore Simon takes the argument further, writing

Enacting and implementing hate speech codes has its price. Considerable time and energy are expended; new foes come to the forefront, and legal and constitutional entanglements abound. Under one scenario, hate speech codes may make it easier to propose more sweeping antiracism policies. However, another scenario seems more likely. The divisiveness caused by the debate over hate speech codes will make universities more reluctant to implement necessary structural changes. Hate speech proponents will have won a Pyrrhic victory, resulting in some exercising more care in their talk but leaving the structural features of racism largely intact.[36]

Others, including academic critic Dinesh D'Souza, law professor Stephen Carter, chair of the Harvard African-American Studies Program Henry Louis Gates Jr., and dean of the Florida Coastal School of Law Donald Lively, make related points, maintaining that these codes benefit only a small number of blacks and other minorities and obscure the real obstacles that impede racial progress and equality, namely, bad laws and too little money.[37] In light of such considerations, critics typically propose other means of dealing with hate speech than institutional speech codes. (For specific proposals, see below.)

Critics also maintain that hate speech regulations encourage attitudes of victimization and reliance on the state rather than promote empowerment and individual initiative for minorities and women. According to Nat Hentoff, "antiracism rules teach black people to depend on whites for protection, while talking back clears the air, emphasizes self-reliance, and strengthens one's self-image as an active agent in charge of one's own destiny." Many minorities agree with Hentoff and view such codes as condescending in their portrayal of minorities as helpless victims of words. Roy Innis, head of the Congress of Racial Equality at the time Yale went through its free speech growing pains prior to the Yale Report and Wayne Dick incident, is appalled at whites who want to silence racists. To his mind, blacks do not need whites who suffer from "the Schweitzer syndrome" to protect them from hateful ideas.[38] University of Wisconsin student regent (and Jew) David Hirsch opposed UW-17, saying, "I've had swastikas painted on my sidewalk on Yom Kippur. But this rule is wrong."[39] Alan Keyes, a black who served in the Reagan administration and was a 1996 GOP presidential primary candidate, denounced campus speech codes as "paternalistic forms of well-intentioned racism that cripple blacks," and added that he would "feel cheated by an education that insulated him from contact with white racist views."[40] And Gerald Gunther, the law professor who debated Charles Lawrence, tells how he was tormented by others for being Jewish while growing up in a small town in Nazi Germany. Yet the lesson he learned was not to seek protection from the state, but rather to seek the freedom to criticize bigots and avoid state orthodoxy.[41] Critics like Hentoff also argue that the codes seem mostly to protect administrators rather than minorities,[42] since the codes are rarely enforced and have been used against minorities in cases in which their speech is constitutionally protected. Marcia Pally points out that the Michigan code was used to prosecute black students twenty times, and the only two cases that led to punishment both involved speech by or on behalf of minorities.[43] Gwen Thomas, a black college administrator from Colorado, says:

> 'I have always felt as a minority person that we have to protect the rights of all because if we infringe on the right of any person, we'll be the next. As for providing a nonintimidating educational environment, our young people have to learn to grow up on college campuses. We have to teach them how to deal with adversarial situations. They have to learn how to survive offensive speech they find wounding and hurtful.[44]

Her point is that minorities have the strongest interest in freedom of speech, for when the majority is given the power to silence, it will use that power to silence those who dissent. Edward Cleary, the lawyer who argued against the St. Paul hate crimes ordinance (a case we'll examine in the next chapter), echoes her concern in his defense of free speech: "Our nation has a history of protecting the individual against the majority, in recognition of the fact that the consensus changes, often as a result of being challenged by an unpopular minority."[45] For all of these reasons, critics maintain that punitive codes will be a less effective way to combat bigotry than counterspeech, education, and other structural changes. Whatever gains on behalf of equality we can hope for when we adopt campus hate speech codes are outweighed by the heavy losses in free expression and the fight for equality that we know will occur. Some critics go so far as to argue that speech codes are self-defeating. Patrick Garry writes:

> Censorship of speech in the name of political action . . . is ultimately self-defeating because it inhibits any real action on the underlying problems. If problems cannot be freely discussed or revealed through speech, they cannot be solved. Consider the analogy of a weed in the lawn. It is easier and temporarily gratifying to cut it down, but unless its roots are pulled out, the weed still lives and grows. So too with social problems: though it may be easier to censor offensive speech, such censorship will not pull out the roots of the underlying problem. Free expression is needed to reveal the social problems, just as the leaves of the weed are needed to

show the location of its roots. Without free speech, for instance, the civil rights movement or feminist movement could never have gotten off the ground.[46]

To those advocates of speech codes who feel the call for education and counterspeech is an empty gesture, critics have offered many responses. Charles Calleros, for example, a law professor at Arizona State University, offers the Campus Environment Team (CET) developed at his school as a method for effectively dealing with offensive speech without curtailing speech rights.[47] The CET is a nine-member campus committee formed of faculty, staff, and students who monitor harassment incidents (without regard to discriminatory content), offer referral services, and sponsor educational forums to promote respect for free speech and tolerance. Calleros agrees that universities should regulate threatening speech and conduct and impermissibly invasive speech, but maintains that they should leave the rest to informal measures. He points out that effective counterspeech does not require face-to-face retorts (as Richard Delgado assumes), since counterspeech may be accomplished through letters, discussions, and demonstrations aimed at a wide audience and designed to show the moral bankruptcy of hateful ideas. Theodore Simon goes further in arguing for anti-racist structural changes, for example, having universities change employment and investment practices, faculty reward systems, and community service projects in ways that promote equality.[48]

## CONCLUSION

In contrast to the benefits of hate speech regulation that advocates focus on, critics of campus speech codes call attention to their costs. As they see the calculation, the small potential gains in equality that speech codes may create are more than offset by the losses to speech and equality that are sure to follow. Rodney Smolla, a First Amendment scholar from the University of William and Mary College of Law, nicely captures the critic's point of view:

> The conflict felt by most decent Americans is that we hate hate speech as much as we love free speech. The conflict, however, is not irreconcilable. It is most constructively resolved by a staunch commitment to free expression principles, supplemented with an equally vigorous attack on hate speech in all its forms, emphasizing energetic leadership and education on the values of tolerance, civility, and respect for human dignity, rather than punitive and coercive measures.[49]

Although critics responded to every argument—constitutional or otherwise—proposed by advocates, it should come as no surprise that many universities did not change their codes to conform to the critics' demands. ("Censorship is the strongest drive in human nature," the journalist Phil Kerby once told Nat Hentoff, "sex is a weak second."[50]) The inevitable result was that the debate moved out of the classroom and into the courtroom. Hate speech was put on trial quite literally.

# 4

# See You in Court:
# The Campus Hate Speech Cases

*If there is any principle of the Constitution that more imperatively calls for attachment than any other, it is the principle of free thought—not free thought for those who agree with us but freedom for the thought that we hate.*

JUSTICE O. W. HOLMES JR., dissenting in
*United States v. Schwimmer*, 279 U.S. 644 (1929)

## JUDGES AND HATE SPEECH

Justice Holmes's words are strong, very strong. He is maintaining that the principle of free thought (by which he means to refer to the First Amendment guarantee of free speech and press) is the most important constitutional principle, more important than any other principle stated in the body of or amendments to the Constitution. He is asserting that this principle requires us to tolerate thought that we hate—thought that might destroy our country, our families, our economic system, our churches. Very strong stuff indeed. Still, Holmes wrote long before the movement for racial and sexual equality gained explicit public acceptance in the Civil Rights Act of 1964, an act that does not allow discrimination on the basis of race or sex, an act routinely upheld and even expanded in court rulings through the years. Thus, we might do well to wonder, even if Holmes meant to allow such speech, what later courts have said on this matter, courts bound by the Civil Rights Act and its guarantees of equal rights. In this chapter we look at how courts dealt with the campus hate speech issue from the initial 1989 University of Michigan case through the 1995 Stanford University case.

As we have seen, the widespread perception that hate speech was reaching epidemic proportions on college campuses and that university hate speech regulations rested on legitimate constitutional precedents ensured that many universities and colleges would continue their ban on hate speech in spite of the objections of critics. This meant that critics could get satisfaction only by litigating. We shall look at six major cases in historical order. Each case brings new particulars to our attention, but the shared features may well be most important, for in every case the federal court refused to enforce the ban on hate speech. In every case, the court ruled that the regulation abridged the plaintiff's right to freedom of speech. This would be surprising, except for the fact that the judiciary has come to be the branch of government most committed to freedom of speech. Judges are the ones who take most seriously Justice Holmes's view about the nature and importance of free speech; there is a standard list of free speech cases, beginning in the aftermath of World War I, in which early denials of dissident and other offensive speech gradually become affirmations of the constitutionality of such speech. It is no accident that Judge Cohn began his holding for Doe by quoting Lee Bollinger, whose 1986 book, *The Tolerant Society*, critically defined and illuminated predominant attitudes of the legal profession toward free speech:

> Taking stock of the legal system's own limitations, we must realize that judges, being human, will not only make mistakes but will sometimes succumb to the pressures exerted by the government to allow restraints [on speech] that ought not to be allowed. To guard against these possibilities we must give judges as little room to maneuver as possible and, again, extend the boundary of the realm of protected speech into the hinterlands of speech in order to minimize the potential harm from judicial miscalculation and misdeeds.[1]

To be sure, this judicial process has been halting, and steps backward have been taken, but the general direction since World War I has been to expand the area of protected speech. The general public as well as the executive and legislative branches of government do not share the same commitment, as their continual calls for censorship and speech regulation indicate (e.g., the flag-burning amendment, the Internet bill). They do not hear the First Amendment call as Holmes and Brandeis and so many other judges did and still do, and the call of this principle is the legal crux of the hate speech issue, as we shall see in our study of six key cases affecting the legal status of campus hate speech codes.

## THE SIX MAJOR DECISIONS

*The University of Michigan.* About one year after the University of Michigan adopted its hate speech code, "John Doe," assisted by legal counsel provided by the ACLU, filed suit in the U.S. District Court, Eastern District, of Michigan, Southern Division, challenging the constitutionality of the university's policy on the ground that it violated his right to free speech. Doe had not been prosecuted under the policy; rather, he sought to have the policy struck down before he would be prosecuted under it. As a psychology graduate student specializing in biopsychology, Doe feared that his open discussion of controversial theories of biologically based racial and sexual difference might be sanctionable under the policy. On September 22, 1989, in the matter of *Doe v. University of Michigan*, 721 F. Supp. 852 (E.D. Mich. 1989), the court ruled in favor of the plaintiff on its finding that the university policy was both overbroad (subjected protected speech to sanctions) and unduly vague (so ambiguous as to allow officials to arbitrarily enforce the policy and violate due process rights).

Judge Cohn found a series of free speech precedents that allow a university to restrict discriminatory behavior, assault and battery, vandalism and property damage, conspiracies to deprive others of their constitutional rights, sexually abusive and harassing conduct, fighting words, intentional infliction of emotional harms, credible threats of violence or property damage, obscenity, and libel and slander and to regulate speech according to time, place, and manner; however, he also found precedent that the university cannot "establish an anti-discrimination policy which had the effect of prohibiting certain speech because it disagrees with the ideas or messages sought to be conveyed. . . . Nor could the University proscribe speech because it was found to be offensive, even gravely so, by large numbers of people."[2] In effect, although he found it "unfortunate," "difficult," and even "painful," Judge Cohn ruled in favor of Doe because he is obligated to uphold a well-articulated set of free speech rights announced by the U.S. Supreme Court.

This well-articulated right to freedom of speech prohibits speech regulations that are overbroad. (Cohn cites *Broadrick v. Oklahoma*, 413 U.S. 601, 611 [1973]; *NAACP v. Button*, 371 U.S. 415, 433 [1963]; *Houston v. Hill*, 482 U.S. 451, 458–60 [1985]; *Kolender v. Lawson*, 461 U.S. 352, 359 n.8 [1983]; *Gooding v. Wilson*, 405 U.S. 518, 521–22 [1972]; *Lewis v. New Orleans*, 415 U.S. 130 [1974]; *Papish v. University of Missouri*, 410 U.S. 667 [1973]; and *Texas v. Johnson*, 491 U.S. 397 [1989].) A speech regulation is overbroad if it prohibits broad classes of speech, some of which may be regulable, if in doing so a substantial amount of constitutionally protected expression is also prohibited. For example, any regulation punishing speech solely on the ground that it is unseemly, offensive, or indecent is overbroad. Such a regulation would in principle apply, for example, to many criticisms of political officials that appear in the popular media. But political speech, even those criticisms of political officials that are widely thought to be offensive, is considered to be at the core of

First Amendment protection. To withstand judicial scrutiny, the regulation must be narrowly drawn to address only the specific evil at hand.

So in what way(s) was the Michigan policy overbroad?

It was overbroad on its face (as it was written), according to Judge Cohn, because the examples provided in the university's interpretive guide, which was purported to be an authoritative interpretation of the policy, described as punishable some conduct that is protected by the First Amendment, including class discussions, jokes, decisions to exclude individuals from a dorm party or study group, and so on. It was overbroad in its application (as it was enforced) because the university informally sanctioned protected speech on at least three occasions. First, the university forced the graduate student in social work to a hearing to answer for his allegedly harassing statements made in the course of academic discussion and research, namely, his belief that homosexuality is a disease and that he ought to develop a counseling plan for changing gay clients into straight ones. Second, the university forced a student in an entrepreneurship course in the School of Business Administration to attend an educational "gay rap" session and write letters of apology to the class and the student newspaper for reading an allegedly homophobic limerick during a scheduled class public-speaking exercise. And third, a dentistry student who aired concerns about a professor being unfair to minorities during informal class discussion of problems anticipated in the course was required to write a letter of apology. Cohn writes:

> The manner in which these three complaints were handled demonstrated that the University considered serious comments made in the context of classroom discussion to be sanctionable under the Policy. The innocent intent of the speaker was apparently immaterial to whether a complaint would be pursued. Moreover, the Administrator generally failed to consider whether a comment was protected by the First Amendment before informing the accused student that a complaint had been filed. The Administrator instead attempted to persuade the accused student to accept "voluntary" sanctions.[3]

This well-articulated right to freedom of speech also prohibits speech regulations that fail to give adequate warning as to which conduct is prohibited and which conduct remains protected, a so-called bright line guiding people's behavior. (Judge Cohn cites *Broadrick*, at 607; *Lanzetta v. New Jersey*, 306 U.S. 451, 453 [1939]; *Smith v. Goguen*, 415 U.S. 566, 573 [1974]; *Young v. American Mini-Theatres*, 427 U.S. 50, 96 [1976]; and *Screws v. United States*, 325 U.S. 91, 98 [1945].) A speech regulation is unconstitutionally vague when "men of common intelligence must necessarily guess at its meaning"; however, the potential chilling effect of the regulation must be real and substantial and a narrowing construction unavailable to the court. For example, a speech regulation that banned obscenity but failed to specify what characteristics a magazine or book or movie must have in order to count as being obscene would be unduly vague. Is Michelangelo's statute of David obscene? Erica Jong's novel *Fear of Flying*? Catharine MacKinnon's attack on pornography in *Only Words* (since it includes many graphic descriptions of sexual violence)? Magazines or movies revealing women's breasts or pubic areas? Even when part of a sex education class or *National Geographic* special? The vagueness of such a law would allow officials to enforce it arbitrarily, that is, to prosecute whomever they wanted. But that would realistically and substantially chill, for example, the creation of works of art and scholarly investigations of human sexuality. To withstand judicial scrutiny, a speech regulation must define the prohibited speech clearly enough to avoid such difficulties.

So in what way(s) was the Michigan policy unduly vague?

Many key terms in the policy lacked clear definitions. For example, it is not clear what would constitute a "threat" under the policy. This might mean a threat to one's life, limbs, or property, or it might be a threat to defeat one's opponent in some competitive endeavor or to begin a campaign to damage an opponent's credibility that might undermine one's academic "success." Again, what would constitute "interference" with academic work? Judge Cohn writes:

> Looking at the plain language of the Policy, it was simply impossible to discern any limitation on its scope or any conceptual distinction between protected and unprotected conduct. The structure of the Policy was in two parts: one relates to the cause and the other to the effect. Both cause and effect must be present to state a prima facie violation of the Policy. The operative words in the cause section require that the language must "stigmatize" or "victimize" an individual. However, both of these terms are general and elude precise definition. Moreover, it is clear that the fact a statement may victimize or stigmatize an individual does not, in and of itself, strip it of protection under the accepted First Amendment tests.[4]

Not only did the policy fail to state any bright line, the interpretive guide the university published to clarify the policy's requirements had to be withdrawn as "inaccurate" and was not replaced, indicating that the university itself and those charged with enforcing the policy were unsure of its precise meaning and scope. This was verified during the hearing. Judge Cohn writes:

During oral argument, the Court asked the University's counsel how he would distinguish between speech which was merely offensive, which he conceded was protected, and speech which "stigmatizes or victimizes" on the basis of an invidious factor. Counsel replied, "Very carefully." The response, while refreshingly candid, illustrated the plain fact that the University never articulated any principled way to distinguish sanctionable from protected speech. Students of common understanding were necessarily forced to guess at whether a comment would be later found to be sanctionable under the policy. The terms of the Policy were so vague that its enforcement would violate the due process clause.[5]

If the university officials charged with enforcing the policy cannot even state its parameters, then how is a student or faculty member to know what is permitted and what is prohibited? When the officers charged with enforcing the policy do not know First Amendment requirements well enough to answer such a question, can there be any doubt that the policy will be arbitrarily enforced according to their own personal feelings and beliefs?

Thus, Judge Cohn, bound to uphold the law, found that the University of Michigan campus hate speech regulation was unconstitutional because it both restricted protected speech and would be arbitrarily enforced—just as critics had argued. The court's view, in the end, was simply that the First Amendment has little meaning if the government or its agents are allowed to punish people under these conditions.

*The University of Wisconsin.* In several ways, the University of Wisconsin hate speech code was superior to the University of Michigan code. This was intentional, of course, since officials there were aware of the Michigan case. (It is worth noting, on the other hand, that at least one school dropped its hate speech policy as a result of the *Doe* decision.)[6] First, it was both clearer and narrower in scope because it specifically excluded comments made in classrooms to the group and required the behavior to create a hostile environment. Second, the justification for the hostile environment requirement was grounded in the belief that speech that created a hostile environment constituted fighting words and that it therefore constituted a narrow category of speech consistent with a court-defined category as well as common law interpretations of Title VII of the 1964 Civil Rights Act. Third, the interpretive guide issued to explain its scope was much more sophisticated, taking into account both the kind of speech involved and its context. Yet less than one year after its adoption, the policy was in the courtroom. On March 29, 1990, the UW-Milwaukee student newspaper, UWM Post, Inc., and an anonymous student prosecuted under UW-17 filed suit against the board of regents, challenging the policy on the grounds that it was both overbroad and unduly vague, thereby violating their First Amendment rights to freedom of expression. The university argued that the policy should be upheld since (1) UW-17 falls within the category of unprotected speech called fighting words; (2) even if it is not technically within the fighting words doctrine, UW-17 is justified under the balancing test approach the *Chaplinsky* court used in ruling fighting words unprotected speech; (3) UW-17 parallels court-developed Title VII law; and (4) even if UW-17 is overbroad, the Court may apply a narrowing construction to limit the rule's reach to unprotected speech. The court rejected every university argument.

On October 11, 1991, in *UWM-Post v. Board of Regents of the University of Wisconsin*, 774 F. Supp. 1163 (E.D. Wis. 1991), the court held in favor of the plaintiffs since the rule was overbroad and unduly vague, did not meet the requirements of the fighting words doctrine, and could not be saved by the limiting construction urged by the university. District Judge Warren, writing for the court, began by pointing out how the fighting words doctrine has been narrowed through the years, identifying three salient features (the same ones that Strossen identified to criticize campus hate speech codes) identified by the U.S. Supreme Court: (1) the words must be likely to result in a breach of the peace ; (2) to constitute a "breach of the peace," the words must be highly likely to result in imminent violence (not merely be capable of doing so or merely result in a breach of decorum); and (3) the words must be addressed to "the person of the hearer" (that is, be directed at a specific individual in a face-to-face encounter). Turning to UW-17, the District Court found that although the policy conformed to then-current fighting words requirements in identifying speech that might cause a breach of the peace and speech directed to the person of the hearer, it violated the requirement that the speech tend to incite violent reaction. Judge Warren writes:

> An intimidating, hostile, or demeaning environment certainly "disturb[s] the public peace or tranquility enjoyed by citizens of [a university] community." However, it does not necessarily tend to incite violence. The creation of a hostile environment may tend to incite an immediate breach of the peace under some circumstances. Nevertheless, the term "hostile" covers non-violent as well as violent situations. Moreover, an intimidating or demeaning environment is unlikely to incite violent reaction.[7]

Thus, the District Court could not uphold the policy under the fighting words doctrine.

Turning to the balancing test argument, Judge Warren conceded that the *Chaplinsky* court used a balancing approach in ruling that New Hampshire's ban on fighting words regulated speech that had minimal social value and had harmful effects; however, he went on to maintain that this provided no support for the university in this case because (1) the Supreme Court has not given the power to use balancing tests to lower courts and (2) the Seventh Circuit (the relevant appellate court) has determined that a balancing test approach is appropriate only for content-neutral speech regulation, and UW-17 was not content-neutral because it restricted expression based purely on the message conveyed. That is, it regulated only fighting words with racist, sexist, and similar messages, and not fighting words with other messages.[8] Moreover, Judge Warren asserted that discriminatory speech does have some First Amendment value (and must therefore be counted on the "benefits" side of a balancing test) since it can both inform or convince the listener of at least the fact that the speaker is a racist, sexist, or the like and serve as an expressive vehicle for the speaker's emotions. For all of these reasons, the court ruled that it could not uphold the policy under a balancing test approach.

The parallel to Title VII law argument was quickly dismissed by the court for three reasons. First, Title VII addresses employment, not educational, settings. Second, Title VII law is based in agency principles, and students are not normally agents of the university. Third, Title VII is only a federal statute and cannot supersede the requirements of the First Amendment.

Finally, the court declined the university's request that it apply a limiting construction (add a fifth requirement, namely, that the speech lack any intellectual value) to avoid regulating protected speech. According to Judge Warren, even the limiting construction is overbroad and without basis in any balancing test or Title VII common law.

To make matters worse, Judge Warren stated that UW-17 was unduly vague insofar as it failed to specify whether the speaker must actually create a hostile environment or must merely intend to do so. While this ambiguity could be corrected in a limiting construction, that would be of no help because the rule would still be overbroad. Thus, Judge Warren concludes,

> The problems of bigotry and discrimination sought to be addressed here are real and truly corrosive of the educational environment. But freedom of speech is almost absolute in our land and the only restriction the fighting words doctrine can abide is that based on the fear of violent reaction. Content-based prohibitions such as that in the UW Rule, however well intended, simply cannot survive the screening which our Constitution demands.[9]

Now, you don't have to be a constitutional scholar to realize that the *Doe* and *UWM-Post* decisions had strong negative implications for hate speech regulations on all campuses, but to cement the point, let us briefly consider a case from the same time period in which a university sought to punish students for a hate speech incident even though the university did not have a campus hate speech code per se.

*George Mason University.* During the week of March 11, 1991, "Derby Days" at GMU, the Iota Xi Chapter of the Sigma Chi Fraternity staged a "Dress a SiG" contest (dress members like ugly women)." In the event, one student dressed in blackface, used pillows to represent breasts and buttocks, and wore a black wig with curlers. One week later, several GMU student leaders signed a letter to a dean requesting sanctions be imposed on the fraternity because it offended them by perpetuating racial and sexual stereotypes. The dean ruled that the fraternity would be barred from holding social and sports activities for a two-year probationary period and, during that same period, must get advance university approval for other planned activities. The fraternity sued on the grounds that the discipline abridged their right to free speech. The university argued that the speech was not protected under the First Amendment and that even if it was, there were compelling educational interests at stake that justified the discipline.

On August 27, 1991, in the matter of *Iota Xi Chapter of Sigma Chi Fraternity v. George Mason University*, 773 F. Supp. 792 (E.D. Va. 1991), the court ruled in favor of the plaintiffs. Citing essentially the same litany of legal precedents as Judges Cohn and Warren, District Judge Hilton held that government agents cannot ban performances in blackface nor expressive messages that offend merely because the administration or some other students disapprove of the message. Citing *Gay Alliance of Students v. Matthews*, 544 F.2d 162, 166 (4th Cir. 1976); *Healy v. James*, 408 U.S. 169, 187–88, 92 (1972); *Barnes v. Glen Theatre, Inc.*, 111 S. Ct. 2456 (1991); *Schad v. Borough of Mt. Ephraim*, 452 U.S. 61, 101 (1981); *Berger v. Battaglia*, 779 F.2d 992 (4th Cir. 1985), *cert. denied*, 476 U.S. 1159 (1986); and *Piarowski v. Illinois Community College*, 759 F.2d 625, 630 (7th. Cir. 1985), *cert. denied*, 474 U.S. 1007 (1985), Judge Hilton writes, "In this instance, GMU sought to discipline the students based precisely on the 'heckler's veto.' That is not permissible."[10] Moreover, the court rejected the university's appeal to that part of its educational mission flowing from the Fourteenth Amendment (to educate minorities and women, to promote learning through a culturally diverse student body, to eliminate racist and sexist behavior on campus, and to accomplish maximal desegregation of the student body) because the "Dress a SiG" event did not substantially or materially disrupt these aspects of GMU's educational mission.

These three cases served notice to the nation's campuses that any speech restrictions (whether in the form of an official speech code or not) that they intended to enforce had better be very carefully drafted and very carefully justified. That the rationale and legal precedents cited by the judges in each case were virtually identical shows just how entrenched and well recognized the free speech precedents are, and many commentators thought that the constitutional threshold these precedents set was too high for any campus code to meet. The code must (1) not regulate protected speech on its face or punish protected speech in its application, (2) be sufficiently clear to provide a "bright line" for students to guide their conduct by, (3) be content-neutral, and (4) promote a compelling state interest that cannot be adequately furthered by other means. In order for a campus to be confident its code would be upheld in a federal court, the code's advocates would have either to develop a narrower code that would survive judicial reasoning or to convince a higher court (preferably the U.S. Supreme Court) to reverse these decisions. That hope seemed dashed when the Supreme Court announced its ruling on a St. Paul, Minnesota, hate crimes ordinance.

*The St. Paul Case.* In response to public concern and outrage over a growing number of hate speech incidents, the city of St. Paul, Minnesota, adopted an ordinance in 1990 providing that "whoever places on public or private property a symbol, object, appellation, characterization or graffiti including but not limited to, a burning cross or Nazi swastika, which one knows or has reasonable grounds to know arouses anger, alarm, or resentment in others on the basis of race, color, creed, religion, or gender commits disorderly conduct and shall be guilty of a misdemeanor."[11] Shortly after passage of the ordinance, R.A.V. (Robert Viktora, a minor at the time, hence the court's use of initials) was arrested and charged with violating the ordinance for participating in a cross burning inside the fenced yard of an African American family's home. R.A.V. never contested the facts of the case, only the city ordinance under which he was charged. The trial court dismissed the charge prior to trial on grounds that the ordinance censored expressive conduct in violation of the First Amendment, but its ruling was overturned by the Minnesota Supreme Court on appeal. The Minnesota Supreme Court ruled the city ordinance was not overbroad because it was limited to fighting words within the proper meaning of *Chaplinsky* and was not impermissibly content-based because it was narrowly tailored to serve a compelling state interest in protecting the community against bias-motivated threats to public safety and order within the meaning of *Schaumburg v. Citizens for a Better Environment*, 444 U.S. 620, 637 (1980). The court wrote, "Resort to epithets or personal abuse is not in any proper sense communication of information or opinion safeguarded by the Constitution, and its punishment as a criminal act [raises] no question under that instrument."[12] On appeal, however, the U.S. Supreme Court unanimously ruled that the ordinance was unconstitutional in virtue of its overbreadth, and a majority also ruled it was impermissibly content-based. Since the case adds nothing new to our discussion of overbreadth or vagueness, we can pass over a discussion of those points and look solely at the content-neutrality argument.

Justice Antonin Scalia, joined by Chief Justice William Rehnquist and Justices Anthony Kennedy, David Souter, and Clarence Thomas, acknowledged that there are narrow categorical exceptions to First Amendment protection (such as "fighting words" since *Chaplinsky v. New Hampshire*, 315 U.S. 568 [1942], "defamation" since *Beauharnais v. Illinois*, 343 U.S. 250 [1952], and "obscenity" since *Roth v. United States*, 354 U.S. 476 [1957]), and that state regulations based on "time, place and manner" are permissible (he cites *Ward v. Rock against Racism*, 491 U.S. 781, 791 [1989]), but the requirement of content-neutrality prohibits government from selectively regulating speech in regard to the message it conveys, as the St. Paul ordinance did.[13] Scalia offered four examples to clarify his point:

1. A state may prohibit obscenity only in certain media and markets (such as telecommunications, as the Court ruled in *Sable Communications of California, Inc. v. FCC*, 492 U.S. 124 [1989]) because it is regulating only the "time, place or manner" and not the message it conveys.
2. A state may choose to prohibit only obscenity that is most patently offensive in its prurience, that is, that which involves only the most lascivious displays of sexual activity; but it may not prohibit only obscenity that includes offensive political messages.
3. A state may criminalize threats of violence against the president, since the reasons why threats are outside the First Amendment have special force as applied to the person of the president (*Watts v. United States*, 394 U.S. 705 [1969]), but it may not criminalize only those threats based on opposition to the president's policy on inner cities. And
4. A state may regulate price advertising in one industry but not in another because of special risks of fraud (*Virginia Pharmacy Board v. Citizens Consumer Council, Inc.*, 425 U.S. 748 [1976]), but it may not prohibit only advertising that depicts men in a demeaning fashion.

Since the St. Paul ordinance banned only those fighting words involving race, color, creed, religion, or gender and only symbols expressing racist and sexist attitudes, it was not content-neutral because it did not ban, for example, fighting words involving "political affiliation, union membership or homosexuality." Even worse, the ordinance was viewpoint-biased because it only banned fighting words used against the "favored" viewpoint of racial and gender equality and did not ban fighting words used by egalitarians against bigots. Scalia writes, "St. Paul has no such authority to license one side of a debate to fight freestyle, while requiring the other to follow Marquis of Queensbury Rules."[14] He continues, "Selectivity of this sort creates the possibility that the city is seeking to handicap the expression of particular ideas. That possibility would alone be enough to render the ordinance presumptively invalid, but St. Paul's comments and concessions in this case elevate the possibility to a certainty."[15] Moreover, Scalia cites *Boos v. Berry*, 485 U.S. 312 (1988), to show that even though speech can be regulated for its "secondary effects" in some special instances, the secondary effects do not ever include the listeners' reactions or the emotive impact of the speech on its audience. Finally, Scalia cites *Burton v. Freeman*, 504 U.S. (1992), to show that even though the state interest in this case is a compelling one, to be upheld the ordinance must be necessary to serve that interest, and the existence of content-neutral alternatives in this case proves the ordinance is not necessary to serve that interest. Scalia writes, "Let there be no mistake about our belief that burning a cross in someone's front yard is reprehensible. But St. Paul has sufficient resources at its disposal to prevent such behavior without adding the First Amendment to the fire."[16] He maintains that the only interest essentially being served by the ordinance is to display the city council's special hostility toward the particular biases being singled out, but government is not allowed to select favored and disfavored biases.

Since campus hate speech codes are essentially the same as the St. Paul ordinance in regard to their content- and viewpoint-bias and their overbreadth and vagueness, the *R.A.V.* decision suggested that critics had at last won the debate. Every code had failed the constitutional tests, from the trial court to the Supreme Court. Although free speech critics might concede to speech code advocates that clearer and narrower codes could be developed, they could still point out that (1) every such code singles out speech on the basis of its racial, sexual, ethnic, and similar content, thereby violating the content-neutrality requirement and that (2) the goals of the codes may be furthered purely through educative measures, thus making their punitive sanctions appear constitutionally suspect.

In a bellwether article, Heiser and Rossow conclude that

> it now appears that most readily available arguments in favor of broad antiracism regulations have now been rejected, if only cursorily and in dicta. . . . As long as courts and commentators frame the debate in terms of a one-sided struggle between a vague principle of equality and a well-articulated principle of free speech rights, it seems unlikely that universities will be able to tailor regulations that specifically address the problems of racist speech on campuses.[17]

Edward Eberle, in his painstaking legal analysis of *R.A.V.*, puts it more bluntly: "The court resolved the debate between hate speech and equality by preferring the right to freedom of speech. . . . R.A.V. dramatically reinforces the precept that freedom of expression is the dominant organizing principle in our society."[18] Such opinions were not limited to the law reviews. In light of the *R.A.V.* decision, Vanderbilt University dropped its policy on discriminatory harassment.[19] The university's community affairs board initially recommended an amendment to the policy to accommodate the content-neutrality requirement of *R.A.V.*, but after discussion of the policy on campus, the university decided not to accept the amendment and dropped the code. It substituted a statement in the student handbook discouraging personal vilification, along with a conduct rule prohibiting threats of violence. Jeff Carr, general counsel and vice-chancellor of university relations, recommended this course of action in a letter to the chancellor, writing (among other things) that

> the difficulty lies entirely in creating a code that reaches certain speech under certain circumstances, but does not limit or have a chilling effect on other speech. The difficulty is enhanced because both the circumstances and intent are relevant to the question of whether particular words should be prohibited. The same words that can be used to express personal contempt, hatred, and vilification can under other circumstances and with different intent give no offense at all. While theoretically it might be possible to draft a rule that reached only hate speech directed at an individual rather than that individual's ideas, as a practical matter that line may be too fine.[20]

But advocates continued to hope for success, either by developing narrower codes or by successfully challenging the judicial precedents. Unfortunately for advocates, yet another hate speech code went to court and was struck down for exactly the same reasons as the others.

*The Central Michigan Case.* Keith Dambrot was head basketball coach at Central Michigan University (CMU) during the 1992–1993 season. As a "motivational tool," he repeatedly used the word "nigger" during closed-door locker-room team sessions. His use of the term was intended to be "positive and reinforcing," connoting a "fearless, mentally strong and tough" player, a use of the term that was accepted and employed by the players themselves, including the black players on the team (several of whom joined the coach in challenging the CMU policy). Dambrot's use of the term eventually became known, and an investigation began in February 1993. At that point, a former player filed a complaint with the university affirmative action (AA) officer, the official charged with enforcing the policy. The AA officer informed Dambrot that in her opinion, the term "nigger" could not be used in a positive manner and that his speech was in violation of the university anti-harassment policy. Dambrot acquiesced and accepted as punishment five days without pay. Soon after, news of the incident spread around campus. Just as in the Ann Arbor and Madison cases, large numbers of vocal students demonstrated to express their contempt for the coach, and local and national media attention followed. In view of all this bad publicity, the athletic director informed Dambrot on April 12, 1993, that his contract would not be renewed. Dambrot then sued the university on the grounds that it violated his First Amendment rights to free speech and academic freedom and constitutional right to due process.[21] The Central Michigan University policy at issue (Plan for Affirmative Action at CMU, Section III[b][1], Racial and Ethnic Harassment) sought to prevent

> any intentional, unintentional, physical, verbal, or nonverbal behavior that subjects an individual to an intimidating, hostile or offensive educational, employment or living environment by (c) demeaning or slurring individuals through . . . written literature because of their racial or ethnic affiliation; or (d) using symbols, epitaphs [*sic*, epithets] or slogans that infer [*sic*, imply] negative connotations about an individual's racial or ethnic affiliation.

And once again, the court found the policy overbroad and void for vagueness. It is directed at all human conduct (intentional, unintentional, physical, verbal, or nonverbal) and does not specify what subjects a person to an offensive environment. Indeed, as in *Doe*, the university officials themselves were unable to describe the prohibited behavior except as that which a person "feels" has affronted either him or some group.[22] This invites arbitrary and overzealous enforcement because the definition of its terms depends entirely on the viewpoint of the enforcement officers,[23] and it creates a realistic and substantial chilling effect:

> It is not much of a stretch to imagine a treatise (or a student's term paper or even a cafeteria bull session) which explores the source of conflict among residents of some middle-eastern region and posits that one tribe involved in the conflict is the more blameworthy due to some ancient ethnic traditions which give rise to barbarian combativeness or a long-standing inability to compromise. When and if it were complained of, would such a treatise (or term paper or conversation) be judged to violate

the CMU policy. . . ? It would be a good fit with the policy language. . . . Any behavior, even unintentional, that offends any individual is to be prohibited under the policy.[24]

When faculty, students, and staff of common sense are unable to discern what is permitted and what is prohibited, the policy will be struck down as unconstitutional. When vague language permits enforcement officers to punish selectively according to their own personal beliefs and feelings, the policy will be struck down as unconstitutional.

We see in *Dambrot* the fears of Vanderbilt confirmed. The coach is punished for using a word that can be intended and heard to express hatred, contempt, and the like or be intended and heard to be free of such vilification. A word has no meaning devoid of context, and its intended meaning need not be its heard meaning; university policies, however, cannot take adequate account of these facts. Indeed, although CMU assured the court it would not interfere with university members' rights to free speech, the court was "not willing to entrust the guardianship of the First Amendment to the tender mercies of this institution's discriminatory harassment/affirmative action officer."[25] We also see in *Dambrot* the emergence of hate speech code legal precedents. Judge Cleland explicitly rules the policy unconstitutional in view of its content- and viewpoint-bias, citing and quoting Justice Scalia's *R.A.V.* analysis at length.[26] The policy is content-biased because it is limited to the content of the speech (words involving race and ethnicity) and viewpoint-biased because it only punishes the racist viewpoint (anti-racists would be free to offend racists *ad libitum*). And, citing and quoting Judge Hilton's *Iota Xi* analysis, he explicitly rules the policy unconstitutional because it is based purely on the offense taken by the audience.[27] If the *Dambrot* decision was not enough to convince universities that courts take a dim view of campus hate speech codes, critics urge that the Stanford case should put the final nail in the coffin.

*The Stanford Case.* In September 1988, a group of students got into an argument in Stanford's Ujaama House, an African American–theme dormitory. A black student claimed that Ludwig van Beethoven was a mulatto, and a white student argued that that was preposterous. The next night a group of white students got drunk, defaced a picture of Beethoven by drawing the composer in black caricature, and posted it near the black student's dormitory room. Shortly thereafter, a poster of a black fraternity was marred with the word "niggers." The student responsible for defacing the poster was identified, but disciplinary proceedings ended with the recommendation of no discipline (other than to move the white student to different housing) in light of the student's First

Amendment rights. In response to the incidents, Thomas C. Grey, a law professor and faculty cochair of the campus judicial council, drafted a disciplinary standard for racial harassment. The relevant portion of the proposal stated:

> Speech or other expression constitutes harassment by personal vilification if it:
> (a)  is intended to insult or stigmatize an individual or small number of individuals on the basis of their sex, race, color, handicap, religion, sexual orientation, or national and ethnic origin; and
> (b)  makes use of insulting or "fighting words" or non-verbal symbols. In the context of discriminatory harassment, insulting or "fighting words" or non-verbal symbols are those "which by their very utterance inflict injury or tend to incite to an immediate breach of the peace," and which are commonly understood to convey direct and visceral hatred or contempt for human beings on the basis of their sex, race, color, handicap, religion, sexual orientation, or national or ethnic origin.[28]

The proposed policy was adopted by the campus legislative body and became effective in June 1990. After four years, nine Stanford students sued the university on the grounds that the policy permanently damaged the quality of education at Stanford by artificially chilling open discussion of important issues (even though the policy was never used to punish anyone).

In *Robert Corry, et al. v. Leland Stanford Junior University*, County of Santa Clara Superior Court, Case no. 740309, February 27, 1995, the court ruled the policy in violation of the First Amendment, following earlier campus speech code precedents. Citing the usual litany of precedents, including the *UWM-Post* decision, Peter G. Stone, judge of the Superior Court, ruled that Stanford's code was overbroad since on its face it prohibited a word that "merely hurts the feelings of those who hear it."[29] And even if it were not overbroad, it would still be unconstitutional because it was content-based speech regulation, of the sort struck down by the *R.A.V.* decision (not a conduct regulation that incidentally sweeps up some speech as in *Wisconsin v. Mitchell*, 113 S. Ct. 2194 [1993]), that was not necessary to serve a compelling state interest.[30] Even worse, Judge Stone cited Judge Cleland in finding that the Stanford policy was viewpoint-biased, just as the Central Michigan University code was ruled to be in *Dambrot*.[31] As pointed out earlier, since Stanford is a private university and not considered a state actor (even though it receives public funds, is publicly regulated, and performs a public function), a demonstration that the code is unconstitutional by itself would have no legal force. However, California in section 94367 of its Education Code (hereafter referred to as the Leonard Law) stipulates:

(a) No private nonsecondary educational institution shall make or enforce any rule subjecting any student to disciplinary sanctions solely on the basis of conduct that is speech or other communication that, when engaged in outside the campus or facility of a private post-secondary institution, is protected from government restriction by the First Amendment to the United States Constitution or Section 2 of Article 1 of the California Constitution.

(b) Any student enrolled in a private postsecondary institution that has made or enforced any rule in violation of subdivision (a) may commence a civil action to obtain appropriate injunctive and declatory relief as determined by the court. Upon motion, a court may award attorney's fees to a prevailing Plaintiff in a civil action pursuant to the section.

Judge Stone, ruling that the Leonard Law applied to Stanford and survived the university's constitutional challenges,[32] found for plaintiffs.

*Conclusion.* Every campus (and municipal) hate speech code that has been challenged on First Amendment grounds in a court has been ruled unconstitutional. The courts have invariably found the codes overbroad, unduly vague, content- and viewpoint-biased, and not essential to the legitimate aims they are intended to further. The codes have been arbitrarily enforced by university officers who have little or no understanding or appreciation of binding First Amendment doctrines. Does it follow, then, that universities should abandon their hate speech codes, that advocates should roll up their tents and go home?

Some advocates of campus speech codes have responded that the courts have erred in these decisions. John K. Wilson, for example, argues in *The Myth of Political Correctness* that although the court correctly struck down the Michigan code, the Wisconsin and Stanford codes should have been upheld. He maintains that those codes are dramatically better than the vague old policies in force at universities across the country and that critics of the new campus speech codes were misguided: "By some curious logic, the colleges that revised their disciplinary policies in the late 1980s were the ones accused of having speech codes, while the colleges that retained older, usually vaguer and more easily abused policies were praised for not censoring students."[33] What "older, usually vaguer and more easily abused" policies is he referring to here? Ones like the policy Stanford had before the new code, which allowed sanctions for students who failed to show "respect for order, morality, personal honor, and the rights of others"?[34] Ones like the policy at the University of Chicago, which prohibits any conduct that "threatens the security of the University community, the rights of its individual members, or its basic norms of academic integrity" and adds that "personal abuse, whether oral or written, exceeds the bounds of appropriate discourse and civil conduct"?[35] Wilson also argues (as several First Amendment scholars have) that to accept Scalia's interpretation of content-neutrality is to rule the Civil Rights Act of 1964 is unconstitutional; he suggests further that the Court backed down from Scalia's interpretation of content-neutrality in *Wisconsin v. Mitchell*, 113 S. Ct. 2194 (1993), in which it upheld a state law affording greater punishments for crimes motivated by racial or gender bias.[36] Wilson agrees with Henry Louis Gates Jr. that speech codes will have little if any effect in combating discriminatory attitudes,[37] but like Gates, he still maintains that the best choice for universities is a narrowly defined code that targets only the most egregious cases, such as threats, harassment, and the mass theft of newspapers.[38] Wilson and other advocates of campus speech codes can, of course, argue whatever they want; the fact remains that every campus hate speech code that has been challenged has been struck down, and so long as courts facing new challenges are required to consider precedent (the Michigan, Wisconsin, GMU, CMU, St. Paul, and Stanford cases now stand as precedent), a university will be very hard pressed to defend successfully a campus hate speech code. Unless, of course, as Heiser and Rossow imply, the courts suddenly begin to frame the issues in non–First Amendment terms. In order to understand how this might be accomplished, we must first examine the "accepted" judicial view of the nature and value of free speech. Why do judges believe "freedom of speech is almost absolute in our land," as Judge Warren wrote in his decision?

## THE NATURE AND VALUE OF FREE SPEECH

I do not for a minute believe that there is a uniform understanding of the nature and value of free speech among the American judiciary. Clearly, judges disagree about its scope and meaning, and this is reflected in dissenting opinions, reversals of lower court rulings, and the pages of our nation's law journals. I invite the reader to compare, for example, the opinions of Justice Brennan for the majority and Chief Justice Rehnquist in dissent in the flag-burning case *Texas v. Johnson*, 491 U.S. 397 (1989).[39] At the same time, however, I think it is clear that these two men are bound by the same litany of precedents and operate within a conceptual framework that can usefully be called the "accepted" view of free speech.

Law professor Thomas Emerson wrote the classic statement of the judiciary's "accepted" view of free speech in his 1966 book *Toward a General Theory of the First Amendment*. In Chapter 1, Emerson weaves together individual strands of argument popularized by the philosopher John Stuart Mill,[40] legal scholars such as Zechariah Chafee[41] and Alexander Meiklejohn,[42] and U.S. Supreme Court justices Oliver Wendell Holmes Jr. and Louis Brandeis into a clear, comprehensive, and coherent account of the value of free speech. He writes, "We as a nation are presently committed to the theory, that alternative principles have no substantial support, and that our system of freedom of expression must be based upon and designed for the realization of the fundamental propositions embodied in the traditional theory."[43] The "traditional" theory he articulates (which I call the "accepted" view) has been clarified and in some measure criticized by later First Amendment scholars, but Emerson sets out the framework within which these people operate. According to Emerson, free speech is valuable (1) as a method of assuring individual self-fulfillment, (2) as a means of attaining the truth, (3) as a method of securing the participation of citizens in social and political decision making, and (4) as a means of maintaining a balance between stability and change in society. According to the traditional, or accepted, view, this value is so overwhelming that the judiciary should uphold a speech restriction only when the speech is inseparably locked with action. Let us consider these claims about the value of free speech a bit more closely.

First, Emerson maintains that free speech is essential to one's self-realization because "thought and communication are the fountainhead of all expression of the individual personality. To cut off the flow at its source is to dry up the whole stream."[44] His point is that to deny individuals the right to explore new ideas, to express and explain one's opinions, to engage in rational or symbolic or vitriolic debate with those who disagree, is in effect to deny individuals the opportunity to grow as individuals. If I am not free to express my ideas, how can I test their validity? Suppose I begin to believe that "life is a bitch and then you die." How can I determine the meaning and significance of this belief except in discourse with others, even though they may find my ideas highly offensive, even evil? How am I to understand who I am and what my place in the world is if I am prevented from articulating my hypotheses, my convictions, my speculations, my hopes, my fears? How am I to learn of alternative perspectives on life and its meaning if I am not allowed to hear opposing viewpoints? Who has the right to decide for me which viewpoints I can grow from and which will only harm me? I can only grow if I am allowed to make those determinations and if I am allowed to learn from my mistakes. Stifling ideas will result in stunted individuals. Thus, free speech has value to individuals in their understanding and pursuit of the good life.

Second, Emerson maintains that free speech is essential to the attainment of truth, since many "acknowledged truths have turned out to be erroneous."[45] How are we to discern the defects and limitations of current opinions if we suppress all others? It seems inordinately self-righteous to believe our present state of knowledge precludes further discoveries. Permitting dissent enables us to test our ideas in open competition. It teaches us to tolerate new and different ideas and to acquire the discipline to rethink assumptions. Even in those cases where we are most convinced of the truth of our ideas, we are well served by freedom of speech because permitting dissent enables us to keep the meaning of and reasons for the "accepted" doctrine alive. Suppressing dissent will result in a stunted society. Thus, free speech has value to the society as a whole in its understanding and pursuit of the truth.

Third, Emerson maintains that free speech is essential to securing the participation of citizens in social and political decision making because suppression of ideas effectively eliminates some of the body politic from playing its role in the democratic process. In this regard, the anti-segregationist's message in the 1960s is no different from the white supremacist's message in the 1990s, and the Christian fundamentalist's argument that women ought to be subservient to men is no different from the feminist's argument that women ought to be viewed as equals. If the government suppresses ideas, adherents of the suppressed ideas will be strongly inclined to quit the political process and resort to other measures, very likely violent ones, to express their opinions and demonstrate their dissatisfaction with the status quo. Of course, this does not mean that extensive political participation is guaranteed by free speech (our relatively strict protection of free speech coexists with a voting rate of less than 50 percent) nor that the absence of free speech guarantees little political participation. (The former Soviet Union had little concern for free speech but apparently did have high voting rates.) What it does mean, according to Emerson, is that a genuine democracy in search of the common good needs citizens of divergent perspectives to participate freely in the deliberative process on pain of stagnation and eventual dissolution. Moreover, suppression makes informed judgment impossible by eliminating different sides of the argument. It is only by permitting dissent by minorities that majority opinion can be fully informed and, in some cases, swayed. Thus, free speech has value to individuals and society by reinforcing democracy and democratic values.

Finally, Emerson claims that free speech is essential as a means of maintaining a balance between stability and change in society. A closed society promotes inflexibility and becomes vulnerable to violent uprisings by asserting its possession of absolute truth. An open society, on the other hand, can adapt to new circumstances and technologies with fewer growing pains and reinforce the legitimacy of its authority through its willingness to tolerate dissent.

Emerson also suggests that free speech may have value in and of itself and not merely as a means to individual or social ends, but he does not elaborate on this intriguing possibility.[46] One can find some support for this view in some Supreme Court decisions. For example, in *Palko v. Connecticut*, 302 U.S. 314, 327 (1937), the Court held that "freedom of thought and speech . . . [are] the matrix, the indispensable condition, of nearly every other form of freedom." And some major philosophers of law, including Ronald Dworkin,[47] have echoed this sentiment. Critics of this view sometimes suggest, as Stanley Fish has, that "the trouble with a nonconsequentialist position is that no one can maintain it because it is always sliding over into consequentialism."[48] But several attempts to clarify the intrinsic value of free speech appear promising. One strategy has been to tie free speech to individual autonomy, as the political philosophers Thomas Scanlon[49] and Joseph Raz[50] have. Raz in particular offers the interesting suggestion that freedom is good in itself by virtue of its being a constitutive good of an autonomous life, that is, freedom of expression is good in itself and not merely as a means because it is an essential component of the intrinsic good of autonomy (self-direction and self-rule based on adherence to rational rules).[51] Another strategy has been to tie free speech to toleration, as former law school dean and University of Michigan president Lee Bollinger[52] and political philosopher David A. J. Richards[53] have. In this view, free speech is understood to be one of the manifestations (along with, e.g., freedom of religion) of our commitment to the right of each individual to make judgments of conscience, to form and express their conscience independently of state control, even when the state may have good grounds for believing the expressed opinions to be false. Richards writes:

> The principle of free speech plays the central role it does among our constitutional principles and structure because it deprives the State of power over speech based on self-entrenching judgments of the worth or value of the range of speech that expresses sincere conviction about matters of fact and value in which a free people reasonably has a higher order interest. That interest is nothing less than the free exercise of the moral powers of their reason through which persons give enduring value to their lives and community. . . . The idea is not that the state is always mistaken in judging certain views to be false or noxious; rather, judgments of that sort cannot, in principle, be made by a State committed to respect for the right of people reasonably to exercise their own judgment in these matters.[54]

Still, whether its value is purely consequentialist or not, the traditional/ accepted view does not permit literally all speech or expression. Even so-called free speech absolutists such as Alexander Meicklejohn and Supreme Court Justices Hugo Black and William O. Douglas acknowledge legitimate limitations on speech.[55] Emerson admits that free speech is not the only social good, but insists that it is "essential" to achieving other social goods (such as public order, justice, equality, and moral progress), and therefore, that these other values must be pursued by regulating action, not expression,[56] except in those cases in which speech is inseparably locked with action (and therefore should be treated as conduct, not speech, e.g., fighting words, threats, solicitation, perjury, obscenity) and in which the restriction is "clear-cut, precise and readily controlled."

The concern that speech be overprotected rather than underprotected is heightened by a skeptical attitude toward the law and its officers. The inherent difficulties of clearly framing and impartially enforcing speech regulations require courts to protect zealously even the speech they personally find horrific. In virtually every case in which a court has struck down a hate speech regulation, the court notes its own strong opposition to the message conveyed or locution employed. The view can be understood as a parallel to the maxim of criminal justice, "Better a few guilty go free than an innocent be convicted." That is, the accepted view's maxim may be expressed as "Better some bad speech be permitted than some good speech be punished."

This is the view judges have been enforcing in their decisions, and the view that will have to be replaced if such restrictions as campus hate speech codes are to be upheld by the courts. In recognition of this fact, many scholars have begun to criticize the accepted view. Cass Sunstein, for example, has argued that the traditional view has lost sight of the main purpose of the free speech clause.[57] Sunstein contrasts the "Holmesian" ideal of free speech (marked by interest-group pluralism, the marketplace metaphor, and skepticism) with the "Brandeisian" ideal of free speech (civic republicanism). Sunstein opts for the latter, arguing that we should regulate speech with an eye toward protecting and enhancing deliberative autonomy in "Madisonian" terms: Do the rules promote greater attention to public issues? Do the rules ensure greater diversity of view?[58] If we take this "Brandeisian" approach, our general strategy is not "categorical" like the traditional view (speech versus conduct), it is "two-tier," putting political speech at the core of protection and offensive means of expressing nonpolitical ideas at the penumbra. Sunstein thus argues that campus speech codes that narrowly target low-value speech (fighting words) in nonpublic contexts (dormitories, workplaces) in order to eliminate second-class citizenship for members of historically disadvantaged groups (the civic republican angle) should be upheld.[59] He compares the kind of hate speech he wants to prohibit to an obscene phone call: both are highly likely to cause harm to the hearer and are not intended or received as a contribution to public deliberation about some issue.[60]

Sunstein's argument is very strong, and his marshaling of cases to support the "Brandeisian" ideal is inspiring; but the plain fact is that the fighting words approach and the attempt to design codes that privilege members of historically disadvantaged groups have been emphatically rejected by the courts, as demonstrated in our review of the Michigan, Wisconsin, George Mason, St. Paul, Central Michigan, and Stanford cases. Clearly, the courts are still viewing campus hate speech in traditional/Holmesian terms. Indeed, taken together, these cases emphatically signal the judiciary's view that free speech is valuable in and of itself and deserves protection even when it may cause tangible personal or social harms.

We are left, then, to wonder: If the traditional view stands more or less firm against outside attack, is there anything within the accepted/Holmesian view (other than the failed fighting words, group libel/defamation, and emotional distress categories) to which an advocate may appeal to defend a campus hate speech code? When a black student hurls anti-Semitic insults at a white Jewish student, calling him a "dirty Jew," "stupid Jew," and "fucking Jew,"[61] are universities able to respond only with official proclamations of their disapproval? When two white men taunt a black student, pouring urine on her out their window as she walks past,[62] can we punish their "conduct" but not their "speech"? Should students be allowed to express their beliefs about homosexuality by writing slogans like "Step Here, Kill a Queer" and "Stay in the Closet Fag" on university sidewalks[63] and promote the arrival of an anti–gay and lesbian speaker on campus just as other students are permitted to promote campus events by writing on sidewalks or hanging banners? Must the university and the judiciary, should the university and the judiciary, leave students to these fates, to the whims of the marketplace of ideas, because of the nature and value of free speech? Or is there some way not previously recognized to combat effectively the near absolutism of the traditional view?

## FREEDOM OF EXPRESSION AND HOSTILE ENVIRONMENTS

Beginning in the early 1990s a number of scholars began arguing that the well-articulated free speech rights critics rely on can be defeated by the well-articulated equality rights developed in Title VII hostile environment harassment cases. Their argument is more promising than the ones defeated in the courtrooms (fighting words, group libel, intentional infliction of emotional suffering) for three main reasons. First, Title VII hostile environment doctrine has the force of law. It is grounded in current judicial opinions routinely upheld, not in isolated precedents from forty or fifty years ago that have been whittled away to nothing. Second, Title VII hostile environment doctrine has widespread, though not unanimous, public support and its scope had been broadening, not eroding. Unlike the fighting words, intentional infliction of emotional distress, and group libel approaches, it is familiar to many Americans rather than to a mere handful of lawyers and free speech scholars. Finally, even most critics of campus speech codes acknowledge the importance of avoiding Title VII–like hostile environments and punishing those who harass innocent victims. Nadine Strossen and the ACLU, whose arguments are near paradigms for critics of speech codes, accept hostile environment harassment restrictions on campus speech.[64] Justice Antonin Scalia, who wrote the majority opinion in *R.A.V.*, carves out an exception for hostile environment harassment.[65] Even Nat Hentoff, who frequently rails against hostile environment regulations, admits that "any systematic, repeated verbal harassment that substantially interferes with the target's functioning is not protected speech."[66] This confluence of favorable factors put the hostile environment harassment model in the front seat, so to speak, of the arguments supporting campus regulations of student and faculty conduct and speech codes.

But can this model make good on its promise? After all, Judge Warren, firmly in the grip of the traditional view, explicitly rejected the University of Wisconsin's appeal to Title VII law to defend its speech code. What exactly does a hostile environment speech code say? Where does hostile environment law come from? How can we determine its scope and meaning? Why should it apply to a campus environment? On what terms can it overcome the near-absolutism of the "accepted" view? In the next chapter, we investigate the origins and nature of hostile environment law and its application to the campus hate speech debate.

# 5

# Hostile Environment
# Takes a Front Seat

*When equality is constitutionally adopted, the idea that some people are inferior to others on the basis of group membership is rejected as the basis for public policy. This does not mean that ideas to the contrary cannot be debated or expressed. It should mean, however, that social inferiority cannot be imposed through any means, including expressive ones.*

CATHARINE MACKINNON, *Only Words*

## CIVIL RIGHTS AND HATE SPEECH

A public figure as vocal and policy-driven as Professor Catharine MacKinnon of the University of Michigan Law School is bound to be lauded as a savior by some and reviled as a demagogue by others, but her appeal to our ideal of equality and her attempt to distinguish legitimate differences of opinion and permissible offensive expressions (debating or expressing anti-egalitarian ideas) from illegal discrimination (imposing anti-egalitarian ideas) are important for us to consider. As discussed in Chapter 4, although courts struck down all the college hate speech codes they were called upon to scrutinize, those very same courts routinely uphold Title VII hostile environment regulations. We should note, however, that even though MacKinnon literally wrote the book on sexual harassment,[1] her 1993 book *Only Words* was not the first to look at campus speech codes through a Title VII lens. Ellen Lange,[2] John Shapiro,[3] and Mary Ellen Gale[4] began independently to outline a Title VII approach as early as 1990 to 1991. Aware of the limitations of the fighting words, group defamation, and intentional infliction of emotional distress models, they urged universities to look at the hostile environment regulations developed over a twenty-year period by federal courts and the Equal Employment Opportunity Commission (EEOC) to protect civil rights guaranteed to employees and stu-

95

dents by Title VII (employment) and Title IX (education) of both the 1964 and 1990 Civil Rights Acts. This approach, explicitly accepted by even some of the most vocal critics of hate speech regulations (e.g., Nadine Strossen, past president of the ACLU, and Antonin Scalia of the U.S. Supreme Court), boils down to a basic argument:

1. Titles VII and IX of both the Civil Rights Acts are embodiments of the Fourteenth Amendment's guarantee of equality under the law and are interpreted by federal courts to prohibit discriminatory speech and conduct that materially alter the conditions of an individual's employment or education by creating a hostile or abusive environment.
2. Some campus hate speech incidents meet the legal threshold for hostile environment infringements of equal opportunity in education and employment. Thus
3. Hostile environment campus hate speech codes are justified.

The difference between the Title VII codes these scholars advocate and other codes appealing in some way to hostile environment regulations—for example, the Wisconsin and Stanford codes defining hostile environments in terms of the use of fighting words—is that these codes are defended and developed through extensive current case law and EEOC guidelines rather than the isolated, old, and narrowed precedent of *Chaplinsky*. As noted earlier, the main political and legal advantage of this approach is its stronger legal pedigree and broader base of public support. But serious questions have arisen for this approach too: What exactly is a "hostile" environment? Why should this be sanctionable by employers and educators? Even if this law applies to the workplace, isn't a public university importantly different from a mere job site in its free speech interests? How would hostile environment regulations be implemented in a campus speech code? What exactly would such a code permit and prohibit? In this chapter we examine the development of hostile environment law and its application to campus hate speech.

## THE DEVELOPMENT OF HOSTILE
## ENVIRONMENT REGULATIONS

Prior to the Equal Pay Act of 1963 and the Civil Rights Act of 1964, no federal laws prohibited discrimination in employment. Employers were free to hire or not hire employees because they liked or disliked the color of one's skin or one's national origin. Employers were free to pay women less than men for doing the same work and free to fire women if they refused their employers' sexual advances. However, those federal laws banned discrimination in employment (and education through the Civil Rights Act's Title IX Educational Amendment of 1972) on the basis of race, religion, color, sex, or national origin. Section 703(a) of Title VII of the Civil Rights Act of 1964 states, "It shall be an unlawful employment practice for an employer to fail or refuse to hire or to discharge any individual or otherwise to discriminate against any individual with respect to his compensation, terms, conditions, or privileges of employment, because of such individual's race, color, religion, sex, or national origin." Other revisions to the law brought protection to workers over the age of forty (1967), the handicapped (1973), and the pregnant (1975). All of these laws were deemed necessary to protect equal opportunity in our society, and the EEOC—the government agency responsible for enforcing these laws—was involved in the very first case in the development of hostile environment law.

In *Rogers v. EEOC*, 454 F.2d 234 (5th Cir. 1971), *cert. denied*, 406 U.S. 957 (1972), a Hispanic worker in an optical company filed a complaint with the EEOC against her employer for racial discrimination because he segregated patients on the basis of national origin. In a landmark decision, the appellate court upheld the EEOC's claim that Title VII protected an employee's psychological and pecuniary interests in its pronouncement that a workplace that was "so polluted with discrimination as to completely destroy the emotional and psychological stability of minority group workers" is illegal. The *Rogers* decision on racial harassment did not use the term "hostile environment," but its implicit acknowledgement of environmental discrimination would be followed and then broadened in sexual harassment cases in the upcoming years.[5]

In *Tomkins v. Public Service Electric and Gas Co.*, 568 F.2d 1044 (3d Cir. 1977), a secretary had been propositioned by a supervisor during a lunch to discuss her job evaluation. The supervisor indicated that her acceptance of his proposition was necessary in order to receive a satisfactory evaluation. Her refusal led to a transfer to a lesser position in a different department, inferior evaluations, and ultimately a disciplinary discharge. The original court (like other courts before it)[6] did not uphold Tomkins's suit, stating that

> an invitation to dinner could become an invitation to a federal lawsuit if a once harmonious relationship turned sour at some later time. And if an inebriated approach by a supervisor at the office Christmas party could form the basis of a federal lawsuit for sex discrimination if a promotion or raise is later denied to the subordinate, we would need 4,000 federal trial judges instead of 400.

However, on appeal, following *Williams v. Saxbe*, 11 EPD Par. 39,106 (D.C. Dist. of Col. 1976), the appellate court reversed, ruling that a claim of sexual discrimination could be maintained if (1) sexual advances were imposed as a condition of employment and (2) these sexual advances were imposed by the employer in a sexually discriminatory manner, and that Tomkins's suit met these two conditions.[7]

Once sexual harassment cases were made actionable under Title VII, the EEOC could pursue a case on behalf of a plaintiff, protect plaintiffs from retaliatory action, and reduce the amount of time to bring action. To assist employers and employees in determining whether their employment practices were legal or not, the EEOC issued "Final Guidelines on Sexual Harassment in the Workplace" on November 10, 1980, which defined sexual harassment as:

> Unwelcome sexual advances, requests for sexual favors and other verbal or physical conduct of a sexual nature constitute sexual harassment when, (1) submission to such conduct is made either explicitly or implicitly a term or condition of an individual's employment, or (2) submission or rejection of such conduct by an individual is used as a basis for employment decisions affecting such individual, or (3) such conduct has the purpose or effect of unreasonably interfering with an individual's work performance or creating an intimidating, hostile offensive work environment.

Although these EEOC guidelines do not have the force of law in and of themselves, the hostile environment doctrine expressed in them soon gained the force of law in the District of Columbia when the D.C. Circuit Court of Appeals ruled in *Bundy v. Jackson*, 641 F.2d 934 (1981), that purely verbal sexually discriminatory remarks constitute a violation of Title VII even when they do not involve "tangible" job benefits:

> We recognize that this holding requires differing treatment of respondeat superior claims in the two types of sexual harassment cases. In the classic quid pro quo case an employer is strictly liable for the conduct of its supervisors, while in the work environment case the plaintiff must prove that higher management knew or should have known of the sexual harassment before the employer may be held liable.

*Bundy* was the first case in the country in which a court upheld a sexual harassment suit on any terms other than job harm. The court supported its decision, at 945, on the ground that "unless the *Barnes* holding is extended, an employer could sexually harass a female employee with impunity by carefully stopping short of firing the employee or by not taking any other tangible actions against her in response to her resistance. [T]he employer could thus implicitly and effectively make the employee's endurance of sexual intimidation a condition of her employment." The *Bundy* decision evidenced a changing attitude on the part of courts, and a survey of 23,000 civilian government employees conducted by the United States Protection Board Office brought additional judicial and public attention to sexual harassment claims when it revealed that 42 percent of female and 15 percent of male employees had suffered some form of sexual harassment between the years 1978 and 1980.[8]

This interpretation of Title VII became the law of the nation when the U.S. Supreme Court ruled in *Meritor Savings Bank, FSB v. Vinson*, 477 U.S. 57 (1986) that sexual harassment is a form of illegal gender discrimination and that a complaint may be based on the alleged creation of a hostile or abusive working environment. As further evidence of the judiciary's changing attitude, Vinson's claim was upheld even though Vinson did not file any complaints under the bank's policy and grievance procedure for dealing with harassment and did not resist the supervisor's sexual overtures. According to the *Meritor* court the sexual activity need not be involuntary; it need only be "unwelcome." But what was going on in this case that was so bad? What exactly was this abusive, hostile environment employees were subjected to? Was this just an overly sensitive woman griping about innocent jokes or were there some serious wrongs being done?

Mechele Vinson was hired as a teller trainee by Sidney Taylor, a branch manager of the bank, and worked at the bank for four years before she was fired for excessive use of sick leave. She then sued Taylor and the bank, alleging sexual harassment by Taylor. The court found the following to have occurred: In her first year of employment, Taylor had invited her to dinner and suggested they have sex. She refused the proposition at first, but eventually relented because she feared losing her job if she continued to refuse his advances. After that, Taylor increased his sexual demands, forcing Vinson to engage in sex from forty to fifty times during and after business hours, even to the point of raping her on some occasions. In addition, Taylor fondled Vinson in front of other employees and followed her into the rest room when she was alone there to expose himself to her. Vinson said that she did not report any of this activity out of fear of Taylor.

The *Meritor* court held for Vinson on the grounds that illegal sexual harassment occurs when (1) it is sufficiently severe or pervasive enough to create an abusive working environment and (2) it is unwelcome in the sense that the plaintiff did not desire the sexual activity to take place. It seems clear that being forced to engage in sex or lose your job changes the terms of your employment based on your sex. But that is quid pro quo harassment ("quid pro quo" is a Latin expression meaning "this for that"; in this context it refers to harassment stemming from requests for sexual favors in return for job benefits), not hostile environment harassment (harassment arising from offensive or abusive conduct and/or speech that unreasonably interferes with job performance without conditioning job benefits on the performance of sexual favors). The hostile environment part is constituted by the remarks, the fondling, the exposing, and the like. Was that sufficiently pervasive to alter the conditions of Vinson's employment? The court thought so, but stated no standard or guidelines for lower courts to follow when addressing future cases.

Thus, although the *Meritor* decision explicitly endorsed the EEOC interpretation of sexual harassment as including hostile work environments, the Supreme Court left a number of important issues unresolved. How hostile does an environment have to be to be illegal? If Taylor had kept his hands to himself and his pants on and had limited himself to sexually charged verbal banter, would he have created an illegal hostile environment? If Vinson had not been fired or suffered loss of any other tangible job benefit, could she have sued purely on the grounds that his activities seriously affected her psychological well-being? What if most people would say the environment is abusive but the individual is not seriously harmed by it? What about a case where the conduct is abusive from a "woman's" point of view but acceptable from a "man's" point of view?

Some of these questions were answered in *Harris v. Forklift Systems, Inc.*, 510 U.S. 17 (1993). The situation was this: Teresa Harris was a manager at an equipment rental company for about a year and a half. She alleged that the company's president, Charles Hardy, frequently insulted her because of her gender and made her the target of unwanted sexual innuendos. On several occasions he told her "you're a woman, what do you know," "we need a man as the rental manager," and "you're a dumb ass woman" in the presence of other employees. He also made unwanted sexual advances, inviting her to go to the Holiday Inn to negotiate her raise, asking her to retrieve coins from his front pants pocket and to pick up coins from the floor he purposely dropped. Harris complained to Hardy, and he stopped for a brief period. Then, when Harris was arranging a deal with a customer and Hardy commented, "What did you do, promise the guy some [sex] Saturday night?" she quit and sued the company. The Supreme Court held that "a reasonable woman manager under like circumstances would have been offended by Hardy; but his conduct would not have risen to the level of interfering with that person's work performance" or caused her injury. However, Sandra Day O'Connor, writing for the majority, added that

Title VII comes into play before the harassing conduct leads to a nervous breakdown. A discriminatorily abusive work environment, even one that does not seriously affect employees' psychological well-being, can and often will detract from employees' job performance, discourage employees from remaining on the job, or keep them from advancing their careers. Moreover, even without regard to these tangible effects, the very fact that the discriminatory conduct was so severe or pervasive that it created a work environment abusive to employees because of their race, gender, religion, or national origin offends Title VII's broad rule of workplace equity. . . . So long as the environment would reasonably be perceived, and is perceived, as hostile or abusive . . . there is no need for it also to be psychologically injurious.

The decision expanded hostile environment doctrine beyond the *Meritor* decision in at least two important ways. First, although it reaffirmed the "objective" or "reasonable person" standard and did not adopt a "subjective" or "reasonable woman" standard, it eliminated any conduct requirement in a finding of hostile environment. That is, the Court held that even purely verbal behavior, offensive words—not threatening or extortive words—can be found to create a hostile environment. Second, it eliminated the psychological harm requirement. That is, not only does a plaintiff not have to show any tangible loss in job benefits, he or she also need not show that the defendant's behavior caused any psychological or emotional injury.

How then is a reasonable person to decide if the words used in a workplace are illegal or not? What test are employers to use to determine what actions to prohibit? O'Connor answers:

This is not, and by its nature cannot be, a mathematically precise test. We need not answer today all the potential questions it raises, nor specifically address the EEOC's new regulations on this subject. . . . But we can say that whether an environment is "hostile" or "abusive" can be determined only by looking at all the circumstances.

These may include the frequency of the discriminatory conduct; its severity; whether it is physically threatening or humiliating, or a mere offensive utterance; and whether it unreasonably interferes with an employee's work performance.

The Court's decision still leaves us in the dark as to what constitutes illegal harassment in a wide variety of circumstances, as Justice Scalia notes in a separate concurring opinion:

Today's opinion does list a number of factors that contribute to abusiveness . . . but since it neither says how much of each is necessary (an impossible task) nor identifies any single factor as determinative, today's holding lets virtually unguided juries decide whether sex-related conduct engaged in (or permitted by) an employer is egregious enough to warrant an award of damages.

(Incidentally, while still a circuit judge, Scalia had joined Judge Starr in Judge Robert Bork's dissent in *Vinson v. Taylor*, 753 F.2d 141 (1985), holding that the majority was "plainly wrong" in holding for Vinson.)

To fill in the gaps and provide more specific guidelines than the Supreme Court has been willing to state, hostile environment advocates have looked to lower court holdings and various philosophical distinctions (which we will examine in Chapters 6 and 7), but before advocates of Title VII–like campus speech codes can legitimately begin that process, they must first establish that the hostile environment doctrines of Title VII, which were developed in the context of employment, are applicable to the campus. This is not so easy as it may seem at first blush. Why should laws governing private workplaces be extended to public education settings? Perhaps these laws can be used to regulate faculty conduct in their capacity as employees, but what about as teachers entitled to academic freedom? What about students, who typically are not employees of the university?

## WHY TITLE VII REGULATIONS SHOULD
## APPLY TO EVERYONE ON CAMPUS

One way to try to justify application of the hostile environment model to everyone on campus is to find legal precedent. John Shapiro, in his *Minnesota Law Review* Note, cites *Lipsett v. University of Puerto Rico*, 864 F.2d 881 (1st Cir. 1988), to support the use of workplace guidelines in a campus environment. In that case the plaintiff, who was both an employee and a student at the university in the medical residency program, was subjected to constant assertions that women in general—and the plaintiff in particular—should not be surgeons; threats that she would be driven out of the program; unwanted sexual advances; hostile reactions when she did not give in to sexual demands; and degrading pinups (including *Playboy* centerfolds, a sexually explicit drawing of the plaintiff's body, and a list of sexually charged nicknames of the female residents, including her own, "Selestraga," meaning "she swallows them"). The appellate court found that the conditions constituted an illegal hostile environment and that the university was liable for damages since the program directors condoned, acquiesced in, or even encouraged the illegal behavior.

The circumstances of the case suggest that a student who was not an employee but faced similar harassment would be just as much a victim and just as much entitled to protection. Where did her employment stop and her studies begin? Where did the employment responsibilities of her professors and supervisors end and their teaching duties begin? The implication is that their conduct is deplorable and subject to sanctions in either capacity. After all, Title IX language mirrors Title VII language, so if Title VII is interpreted to prohibit abusive environments, so should Title IX be.

This argument can be supported by pointing out how the workplace and campus are similar. Shapiro, for example, acknowledges that there are two common differences between universities and workplaces—namely, (1) an employee is a more "captive audience," unable to avoid the harassing behavior, than a student in a university, and (2) a workplace, unlike a university, is primarily a place of productivity, not ideas or the sharing of ideas. He acknowledges that the First Amendment has greater importance at a university than at a place of employment, but suggests that there are campus contexts that in effect place students in "captive audience" roles and that a university also has an interest in creating an environment conducive to intellectual growth. He concludes that colleges and universities can accommodate free speech rights by simply limiting a campus policy to only the most egregious cases.

Mary Ellen Gale adds to Shapiro's comments by emphasizing the importance of a college education and how discriminatory environments can destroy equal liberty. According to Gale,

> the principle of equal liberty is especially relevant when speakers in a university setting use prejudiced speech as a weapon to destroy the right to educational equality of blacks, women, and other devalued minorities, and to deny them equal access to university dialogue and dispute. Education, like the vote, is a right preservative of other rights. It is fundamental not only to individual self-realization but to democratic self-governance as well. If we can ever construct rules that successfully balance the rights and liberties of dominant and subordinate groups in hopes of creating a more just and equal society, the university, increasingly the site of racist and sexist incidents, seems like an appropriate and necessary place to begin.[9]

She claims that most areas of a campus function essentially like a workplace, in which prejudiced speech may be regulated, rather than a public forum, in which nearly anything can be uttered.[10] The classroom, the lab, the dorm, the dining hall, and the like are all places in which students must live and work and perform successfully if they are not to be denied tangible future benefits, in just the same way that the workplace is a place in which employees must live and work and perform successfully if they are not to be denied tangible future benefits. Indeed, Gale sees the university as a "company town."

But Ellen Lange offers the most detailed discussion of the similarities of the workplace and the campus, arguing that "from an organizational standpoint, the workplace and the campus differ, if they really differ, in degree more than in kind."[11] She notes six important common features: (1) both employees and students routinely encounter the same people; (2) both employee and student body compositions change (due to promotions, transfers, termination, graduation, transfer, dropout); (3) just as an employee does different tasks within a job description, a student engages in discrete school activities (does class or lab work, lives in a dorm, joins an extracurricular activity, etc.) that can be viewed as "mini-jobs"; (4) both employees and students share common experiences and may share a common goal; (5) employees and students face similar problems with respect to the availability of alternative schools or jobs; and (6) both the workplace and the campus are discrete, definable "experiences." By virtue of these similarities, she concludes that

> what Title VII has achieved in the workplace should logically be done for the academic environment. The value and necessity of a college education warrant giving the campus the same protected status as the workplace. The protective rights accorded individuals in the workplace—protection from harassment and discrimination—ought to be accorded to students as they pursue their education.[12]

If we accept the premise that the campus environment is sufficiently like the workplace environment that Title VII–like guidelines are appropriate for the campus environment, it would seem to follow that the constitutional goal of equality can, at least in some cases, outweigh the constitutional goal of free speech. That is, courts firmly in the grip of the traditional view of free speech have not worried about a supervisor's right to verbally harass employees, so why should they worry about a campus member's right to verbally harass another campus member? Given the parallels, by what rationale could a judge (say, Scalia) strike down a hostile environment campus speech code as unconstitutional, but uphold a hostile environment workplace speech code?

Catharine MacKinnon, who extensively discusses pornography as well as discriminatory harassment, maintains that the central premise of the accepted view of free speech is flawed, for "discrimination does not divide into acts on one side and speech on the other. Speech acts. It makes no sense from the action side either. Acts speak."[13] Recall that the accepted view sharply distinguishes speech from conduct, and strictly protects speech. MacKinnon's point is that this distinction is untenable. She offers several examples to show that much "speech" is considered "conduct" and thus regulable: saying "kill" to an attack dog, bribery, price-fixing, a storefront sign saying "Whites Only," a job advertisement reading "help wanted—male."[14] A professor saying "sleep with me and I'll give you an A" or a dean saying to a work-study student "fuck me or you're fired" are no different. She maintains the courts fashion exceptions to the First Amendment in view of the value and harm of the speech in question, and maintains that the low First Amendment value of permitting abusive speech is outweighed by the high Fourteenth Amendment value of punishing abusive speech.

To bolster her point about the value of the constitutional ideal of equality, MacKinnon points out that it is not only in the sexual harassment area that the law has recognized equality as a "compelling state interest" that outweighs First Amendment rights. Illegal discrimination was also found in *Roberts v. U.S. Jaycees*, 468 U.S. 609 (1984),[15] a case in which the expressive interests of the Jaycees to exclude women were outweighed by the equality interests of women. Rather than focus on whether or not government itself is suppressing speech, MacKinnon wants us to focus on how private groups can use the government's free speech rules to suppress speech. That is, "these days, censorship occurs less through explicit state policy than through official and unofficial privileging of powerful groups and viewpoints."[16] In her view, the state needs to correct this imbalance by regulating pornography and hate speech. In the absence of state regulation, the anti-egalitarians are effectively able to impose their viewpoint, and this is not merely the debating or expressing of ideas. After all, "it is not ideas they are ejaculating over."[17]

Linda Greene, a law professor at UW-Madison, echoes MacKinnon's attack on the "accepted" theory of free speech, which views all speech-related cases as ones in which the right to free speech is infringed acceptably or unacceptably. Like MacKinnon's, her concern is that the anti-egalitarians are able not merely to express their ideas, but also to impose their ideas on others because of flaws in the "marketplace of ideas." She writes:

Questions of autonomy, conscience, and free will have implications for the person addressed as well as the speaker, and we cannot dismiss the autonomy and conscience-formation concerns of the hearer of derogatory words that are chosen to destroy confidence and effectiveness. In addition, the general importance of facilitating the search for truth in a free marketplace of ideas both assumes that racial hate is just another idea rather than an original and enduring flaw in our historical experience and also assumes that the epithets contribute to that search.[18]

Advocates of Title VII–like campus speech codes thus argue that courts have outlawed speech, pure speech, that creates a hostile environment in the workplace and should extend this protection to members of the campus community, since this equality-oriented regulation outweighs the limited First Amendment concerns involved in the speech affected by the rules. Universities, no less than employers, should be liable for hostile environment harassment and thus should adopt and enforce speech regulations to protect student, faculty, and staff rights.

But what about the four legal requirements that emerged from our discussion of the campus hate speech trials in Chapter 4? What about overbreadth and arbitrary enforcement? What about content-neutrality? What about other, less coercive means to attaining the legitimate university goals involved in these cases?

In response to charges of overbreadth and arbitrary enforcement, Title VII advocates maintain that universities should take guidance from Title VII case law and EEOC guidelines, since courts have not found these regulations overbroad or arbitrarily enforced. Gale, for example, cites *U.S. v. City of Milwaukee,* 395 F. Supp. 725 (E.D. Wis. 1975), in which the court rejected a First Amendment overbreadth challenge on the ground that the guidelines provided sufficient notice to employers and employees even if they were cumbersome technically. Moreover, the U.S. Supreme Court has twice upheld hostile environment awards based on EEOC Title VII guidelines and felt it unnecessary to provide more detailed definitions. Given general court deference to university policy making, this objection should be no more of a concern to universities than it is to private employers.[19] The speech that universities seek to punish has little or no First Amendment worth (which the courts have recognized in their holdings), just as libel, slander, obscenity, and the like are beyond the pale; and the restrictions Title VII regulations impose are no less vague than those imposed by libel, slander, obscenity, and the like.

In response to charges of content-bias, Title VII advocates maintain that if these regulations are in fact impermissibly content-based, then the 1964 Civil Rights Act would have to be struck down as content-based, since the categories and justifications of Title VII campus codes are drawn straight from civil rights law. If universities must prohibit all verbal harassment that creates a hostile environment (not merely words directed at race, color, creed, gender, ethnicity, and so on) on pain of unconstitutionality, then the Civil Rights Act must do so too. So, rather than accept *R.A.V.* at its face value in condemning content-based speech regulations, Title VII advocates look at Scalia's acceptance of hostile environment harassment as an opening. Linda Greene claims that "a close reading of [the separate judicial opinions in *R.A.V.*] reveals that there may be ample room for debate about the constitutionality of hate speech codes and laws, and the *R.A.V.* case did not categorically foreclose them. Rather, the case suggests that in certain circumstances all members of the court would sanction suppression of racial hate speech."[20] John Wilson goes one step further, arguing that "Scalia's simplistic dismissal [of bans on racially motivated fighting words] was ignored by the Court in *Wisconsin v. Mitchell* [113 S.Ct. 2194 (1993)], which upheld enhanced penalties for racially motivated crimes" and that "while *R.A.V.* still outlaws vague and overbroad hate speech laws (as the concurring liberals ruled), Scalia's extreme attack on speech codes has been effectively overruled. There is no constitutional barrier to narrowly written university speech codes, even if not all fighting words are punished equally."[21] Cass Sunstein agrees, maintaining that if *R.A.V.* is correct, then civil rights laws penalizing racists for firing blacks are unconstitutional, since civil rights laws are content-based.[22]

In response to charges of unnecessary sanctions, Title VII advocates play up the educative aspects of their policies and emphasize their limited punitive nature. Few complaints are filed, and in only a small percentage of the complaints is any punitive action taken. Besides, if in fact the workplace and university are similar in the ways advocates maintain, the charge that these policies are unnecessary at a university would apply equally well to the workplace! But no court is prepared to abandon Title VII sanctions in the workplace. The sanctions, softened as they are due to the free speech concerns present in a campus environment, are needed to promote legitimate state interests and protect legitimate individual rights, interests that will not be attained and rights that will not be protected through purely educative measures. Whether or not statutes against murder and rape do much to deter those crimes does not change the fact that they are violations of individual rights and ought to be illegal.

Title VII advocates conclude that their approach, although not perfect, represents the best balance between the competing ideals of equality and free speech. It is constitutionally sound as judged by the courts and morally and strategically imperative as judged by campus administrators. This is borne out in Arati Korwar's 1994 survey, in which she reports that 78 percent of the universities surveyed (three hundred of them) had a sexual harassment rule regulating the conduct of university members.[23] But what exactly does such a regulation say and how would it actually apply? In the abstract it may sound fine, but the proof is in the pudding, as they say.

## A HOSTILE ENVIRONMENT SPEECH CODE

To determine the nature and scope of Title VII–like campus hate speech codes, let us consider proposals from Title VII advocates Mary Ellen Gale, Ellen Lange, and John Shapiro. According to Gale,

> universities may prohibit and punish direct verbal assaults on specific individuals—severe or pervasive harassment based on membership in a group whose identifying characteristic is practically or historically linked to serious and persistent prejudice—if the speaker intends to do harm and if a reasonable person would recognize the potential for serious interference with the victim's educational rights. I would add further limiting principles as well: that sanctions, proportionate to the harm intended and done, may be imposed only when they are the least restrictive means available to discourage prejudiced harassment; that harassment must be clearly evident to an objective observer; that the incident or incidents must be highly likely to produce serious psychological harm and a hostile or intimidating educational environment; and that the university regulations must be accompanied by specific illustrations of punishable harassment that warn students in advance of the types of expressive acts that fall within the prohibited zone. In doubtful cases, a presumption in favor of free speech should prevail.[24]

Lange's proposal mirrors Title VII language exactly (harassment occurs when the verbal or physical conduct (1) has the purpose or effect of creating an intimidating, hostile, or offensive educational environment; (2) has the purpose or effect of unreasonably interfering with an individual's academic performance; or (3) otherwise adversely affects an individual's educational opportunities),[25] with the following two modifications. First, given the vulnerability of students and the university's role in promoting their growth, fewer occurrences of harassment should suffice to violate a campus policy than a strict Title VII policy.[26] Second, the scope of the rule should be limited to dormitory common areas, libraries, dining commons, research labs, school-sponsored organizations, and "the quad."[27] She adds that a fairly brief code should be supplemented by interpretive guides and educational seminars. Shapiro suggests a lengthier "model policy" (with a preamble and call for more detailed supplements), the relevant portion of which is as follows:

> III.   Protected free expression ends and prohibited discriminatory harassment begins when vilification of, or threats of violence against

members of the University community on the basis of race, religion, disability, sexual orientation, national origin, ancestry, ethnic origin creates a hostile environment. Speech or other expression constitutes hostile environment harassment if it

A. [Intends] to insult or stigmatize an individual or a small, identifiable group of individuals on the basis of their [membership in a protected category];

B. [Addresses] directly . . . the individual or individuals whom it insults or stigmatizes; and

C. Amounts to fighting words or is so pervasive that it creates a hostile academic environment. These expressions, in addition to their insulting or stigmatizing content, must be commonly understood to convey, in a direct and visceral way, hatred or contempt for an individual or identifiable small groups based [on membership in a protected category].

IV. Whether certain behavior constitutes harassment must be examined in light of the particular incident. A single harassing act may be so severe or pervasive as to constitute a hostile environment in violation of this Policy.

V. Intent to discriminate on the basis [of membership in a protected category] is necessary to sanction a person under this Policy. Intent will be determined by consideration of all the relevant circumstances.

A. If a member of the University community asks another member of the community to stop a harassment action or expression, and that person continues the action, intent will be presumed.

B. Expression of an opinion, no matter how abhorrent to the community, which does not contain epithets, is not directed to a particular individual or identifiable group, and does not demonstrate intent to harass when all the circumstances are considered, is not a violation of this Policy.

VI. An objective legal standard will be used to help define and evaluate harassment claims.

VII. This Policy applies to every member of the University community, including students, faculty, and staff. This Policy will be in effect in every University-owned or operated facility, including classroom and administrative buildings, research facilities, libraries, and athletic and recreation centers. This Policy does not apply to university sponsored publications or open spaces on campus grounds, but the University reserves the right to make reasonable time, place, and manner restrictions in keeping with legal precedent.[28]

There are some clear and important differences in the policies suggested by Gale, Lange, and Shapiro. For example, Gale and Shapiro require intent, whereas Lange does not (she requires purpose or effect). Again, Gale and Shapiro indicate greater protection for campus speech than EEOC workplace guidelines, whereas Lange indicates even less protection for campus speech than EEOC workplace guidelines. They also differ on what campus areas are subject to the policy. And I have not even introduced some more aggressive versions of Title VII campus regulations.[29] These disagreements in policy will, of course, produce differences in how individual incidents are addressed.

Given these differences, how should we proceed?

Mindful of the law's dim view of speech restrictions evidenced in Chapter 4, and in particular, Judge Warren's dismissal of Wisconsin's appeal to Title VII law, let us proceed on the assumption that a policy will need to be quite narrow to be expected to survive judicial review. To this end, I suggest that a Title VII–like code meet three basic conditions (which are essentially in line with Gale's and Shapiro's proposals). In order to be sanctioned, the speech must

1. Be directed at a captive audience;
2. Be intended to harm or otherwise interfere with the education or employment of the targeted individual or identifiable small group; and
3. Be judged by a reasonable person in light of all the relevant particulars to be severe or pervasive enough to constitute a hostile or abusive environment.

To clarify these requirements, we can survey Gale's analysis of eight situations adapted from reported cases.[30]

Case 1: Students form a White Supremacy Council and hold meetings on the campus lawn at which they display a swastika, protest affirmative action admissions and the presence of nonwhite students on a campus that is one-fifth nonwhite, and use racial epithets to express their feelings and opinions. According to Gale, this is protected speech, not illegal harassment. Although it is intended to insult and stigmatize on the basis of a protected category, it is not targeted at any specific individual and does not have the effect of creating a hostile environment in its particular circumstances: anyone offended by the activities can simply walk away or use counterspeech. This is, Gale writes, simply the famous Nazis-in-Skokie case translated onto the campus.

Case 2: White students draw a blackface cartoon of the composer Beethoven and post it on the bulletin board of a predominantly black dormitory. Gale would protect this speech too, since it still constitutes more of a contribution to public debate of race and racism than a targeted attack of harassment at an individual. She points out that her judgment would be different were the poster hung on an individual's dormitory door. That would cross the line and make it a "targeted" act. She also notes that the size of the dorm, the racial makeup of the students in the dorm, the proportion of black students on campus, and the frequency of the speech would play a role in an intelligent decision and could tip the balance the other way.

Case 3: Black students tear the poster down. Gale would permit this too. She says this example simply acknowledges that provocative statements can be answered and that rules against a "heckler's veto" should not be extended to preclude effective responses by the victims of racism.

Case 4: In a classroom discussion of biological differences between the sexes, a male student contends that women's brains are insufficiently compartmentalized to permit first-rate analytical thought. This is permitted speech, according to Gale, since the classroom is a place where students, in pursuit of knowledge, must be allowed to make erroneous claims so they can be corrected. It is, she says, an opportunity for more speech, not less, for the classroom can be organized in such a way to level the playing field by including the perspective of the victims of racism and sexism.

Case 5: Someone enters the room of two black college students and scrawls a note on the mirror inside, "African monkeys, why don't you go back to the jungle?" Gale finds this to violate a hostile environment code. It is targeted at specific individuals and intended to inflict harm on them, and in the circumstances alters the conditions of their education. Gale adds that the speech seems to have no redeeming value: it is not part of any public dialogue on educational, social, or political issues. Rather, people invade a home, destroying the victim's sense of physical and psychological security. Such an invasion cannot be avoided by the victims; it isn't like Nazis yelling on the quad.

Case 6: A group of white male students follow a black female student across campus, shouting racist and sexist epithets and suggesting the possibility of imminent sexual assault. This too is unprotected speech in Gale's analysis, since it is targeted at a specific individual with the intent to cause harm. The speakers in this case use words as weapons, words that amount to nothing more than threats and that in the context could well be acted on, causing great harm to the victim.

Case 7: A fraternity selects a particular woman as "Jewish American Princess" and ridicules her over the loudspeaker at a football game. This too is sanctionable speech since it targets an individual and is intended to inflict harm. Her home is not invaded (as in case 5), nor is she threatened with physical assault (as in case 6), but she has been singled out for harm and is unable to respond with counterspeech. Such a case of public humiliation cannot be defended as free speech when its intention is to create a hostile environment for a specific individual.

Case 8: A student (of either sex) corners a male student in a library hallway and harangues him, employing no epithets but using hostile words that demean his sexual orientation, for organizing a gay rights group on campus. According to Gale, this is the closest call of the lot, since he is not confronted in his home, threatened physically, or subject to public humiliation. It is, however, a case in which he is an unwilling listener subjected to face-to-face verbal assault. He is, at least at the moment, an unwilling captive audience.

A Title VII–like code such as Gale's clearly avoids many of the difficulties of rival approaches. Unlike the fighting words approach, it is not misguided by some attempt to list banned words, nor is it bogged down in a vain attempt to show violence is imminent. Sexual harassment case law adequately demonstrates that words do not have to be "fighting words" to be actionable under the hostile environment rubric. The concern is not so much to prevent fights from breaking out between students because someone has hit a hot button with a naughty word; rather, the concern is to make sure individuals of all races, creeds, colors, religions, and nationalities have a fair chance to succeed in college. It also avoids the difficulties of the intentional infliction of emotional distress. Instead of getting caught up in a disingenuous attempt to prove bigots falsely believe their racist and sexist creeds, it allows them to believe whatever they want and express whatever they want so long as they are not interfering with the rights of other individuals by altering the conditions of their employment or education. Instead of getting caught up in showing the "libel" of bigoted beliefs and the alleged harms of words on groups, it focuses on the real and demonstrable harms suffered by specific individuals.

A Title VII–like campus hate speech code like Gale's also is superior to the codes courts struck down in the cases examined in Chapter 4. John Doe at the University of Michigan need not fear prosecution under Gale's code, since his classroom discussion of a controversial theory is not intended to cause harm to a specific, targeted individual in a captive-audience context.

Nor would any of the students confronted under the policy be subject to discipline, at least under the factual conditions reported in court documents. The student newspaper that successfully sued in the *UWM-Post* case need not fear prosecution, because Gale exempts such publications from the code. To be sure, some of the students prosecuted under UW-17 might violate such a code—for example, the student who stole a credit card out of racial bias—not because the conduct or speech might provoke a fight, but because it unreasonably interfered with the victim's right to equal educational opportunities. So, too, the fraternity that successfully sued in the *Iota Xi* case need not fear prosecution because its speech was not directed at specific individuals in a captive-audience context. The coach and players at CMU would be immune, since in their view no hostile environment was created and the coach's accepted intent was positive.

To be sure, this code offers no precise definition of what constitutes a "hostile" or "abusive" environment, and to that extent the code is vague and arguably overbroad. But advocates maintain that this is consistent with court holdings. Advocates like Gale can maintain that a carefully drawn Title VII code would address only egregious cases of discriminatory speech and conduct and leave individuals free to state and defend their beliefs in a variety of contexts and in a variety of ways and in a variety of forums. Racists and sexists would not be prevented from airing their views even in ways that offend lots of people, but they would be prevented from imposing their views on others in ways that infringe on an individual's right to equal educational opportunities.

Interestingly enough, many people object to a carefully tailored Title VII code like Gale's on the grounds that it is too narrow, that it doesn't do enough. They wonder why a right-wing student newspaper should be allowed to harangue a critical race theorist or feminist professor for weeks with demeaning cartoons and derogatory articles. They wonder why a student group should be allowed to bring onto campus a hate-spewing speaker who is likely to increase racial tensions and hostilities on campus. They wonder why people should be allowed to leave racist and sexist fliers on car windshields or hallway bulletin boards.

Title VII advocates like Gale must respond that the ideal of equality does not trump the ideal of free speech as in a game of Rook or pinochle; rather, it works with the free speech ideal, not as in some game, but as in real life, where both ideals are essential means to common goals. As discussed in Chapter 4, freedom of expression is needed to attain self-realization. But so is equal opportunity.

How can a person attain his or her full potential if he or she must face personal persecutors every day on the job or in the dorm? We also saw how freedom of expression is needed to preserve other rights. But so is equality under the law. For without equality under the law, how are members of disfavored groups to be sure they will get their day in court to protect their free speech (or any other) rights? Without an equal opportunity in the law to get an education, how are people to have a fair chance to learn what the true nature and value of free speech (or any other constitutional ideal) is? Freedom of expression is needed to ensure democratic self-governance. But so is equality under the law and equal opportunity. Without these guarantees, democracy is a sham and self-governance is an illusion. John Wilson suggests that there is no conspiracy to deprive students of their rights to express ideas on American campuses, only a concerted attempt to formulate carefully crafted rules to protect individual rights.[31]

Title VII advocates like Gale can also respond that the arm of the law should be kept short when fundamental constitutional values are at stake. We cannot expect or trust government officials to solve all our social ills. Government officials are as likely to use their authority to pursue their own personal agendas as they are to promote social interests or protect constitutional values. Let us not forget that the very same men who vigorously advocated freedom of speech in criticizing the British and other political opponents also enacted the Sedition and Libel Act when they gained political power after the Revolution.[32] Giving free rein to campus officials to enforce equality would likely lead to a campaign to silence their critics. We must recover our sense of civic pride and individual responsibility and stand up against bigotry whether it is expressed legally or illegally; however, we don't have to file a complaint or initiate a lawsuit every time we encounter offensive speech or ideas or discrimination. We can try to deal with it through private discussion or negotiation, through informal channels or secondary groups, or through public forums. We can learn to fight back against bigots rather than remain their victims. We can learn to grow from difficult experiences rather than dwell on them. It is possible to learn to tolerate differences in our pluralistic society and create a more inclusive national identity based on shared ideals rather than on similar skin color or national origins.

## CONCLUSION

Title VII hostile environment harassment law is not settled. There are important areas of disagreement in its definition and application. In spite of this, courts have upheld the demands of equality that Title VII law represents even in some cases involving pure speech. In recognition of this exception to or expansion of the "accepted" judicial view of free speech, many advocates of campus speech codes want to extend Title VII–like regulations to the campus to attack the problem of campus hate speech and ensure equal educational conditions and opportunities for all students, faculty, and staff regardless of their race, sex, religion, and so on. Given the unsettled nature of this area of law, these advocates do not agree on the wording or application of campus policies, but they uniformly agree that such a policy is both lawful and necessary.

It is worth noting that advocates of other approaches earlier in the debate later moved more toward the hostile environment justification. Kent Greenawalt, for example, devotes a chapter in his book *Fighting Words* to the approach and offers a qualified endorsement of hostile environment restrictions.[33] Even Richard Delgado, who long campaigned for the group libel approach, came to accept the workplace harassment approach. Changing argumentative tactics, Delgado eventually argued that campus hate speech codes are purely a matter of "policy" rather than "legal status" (i.e., justifiable on multiple legal grounds, viz., fighting words and workplace harassment, and debated only as a matter of strategy) and that it is only a matter of time until we accept hate speech regulation as other Western nations do. Delgado has proposed that we prohibit in a race-neutral way "severe, face-to-face invective calculated to seriously disrupt the victim's ability to function in a campus setting,"[34] thereby bringing his definition into alignment with the key requirements I postulated for the hostile environment standard, namely, being targeted, being intentional, and seriously disrupting the learning environment.

Perhaps more importantly, Delgado has gone after the critics, replying to their arguments one-by-one in a series of articles.[35] In his "Pressure Valves and Bloodied Chickens" article in a 1994 issue of the *California Law Review*, Delgado addresses four arguments. First, where critics maintain that allowing bigots to express their prejudice through speech may serve as a "pressure valve" release and prevent them from acting out their hate, Delgado cites the Allport studies (once again), indicating that permitting hate speech increases the likelihood of violence. Second, where critics maintain that these regulations will be used against, rather than for, minorities through a kind of "reverse-enforcement" strategy, Delgado cites police agency statistics indicating that hate crimes are predominantly white-on-black and that the distribution of enforcement seems consistent with that data. Third, where critics maintain that the First Amendment is a minority's "best friend" by allowing them to dissent from the majority, Delgado argues that the gains of minorities during the civil rights era have been greatest when done in defiance of the First Amendment (at least as it was then understood). Finally, where the critic maintains that it is best to "talk back" to opponents rather than silence them, Delgado argues that (1) the result of a minority replying face-to-face to a bigot is likely to be a beating and (2) there is no talking back to most hate speech, for example, racist graffiti or posters.

In his "Neoconservative" article in a 1994 issue of the *Vanderbilt Law Review*, Delgado replies to six more arguments. First, where critics maintain that hate speech regulation is a waste of time because it deflects attention from the real causes and problems of racism on campuses, Delgado argues that such codes may deflect some underlying racism by removing racial stereotypes from public discourse. And, given the connection between thought and language and behavior, this linguistic "purification" may also clean up student behavior. Second, where critics maintain that the battle for hate speech regulation is "quixotic" or unwinnable, Delgado argues that success is possible given the international view of hate speech regulation, campus activism, and the success of other groups determined to carve out exceptions to free speech (e.g., libel, defamation, false advertising, copyright, plagiarism, threats, words of monopoly). He writes, "The history of free speech doctrine, especially in the landscape of 'exceptions,' shows that need and policy have a way of being translated into law. The same will continue to happen with the hate speech movement."[36] Third, where critics maintain that it is better to allow bigots in the open where they can be confronted rather than drive them underground, Delgado argues that the rules may cure some bigots and do not prevent universities from institutional self-examination or town-hall meetings discussing racism and similar topics. Fourth, where critics maintain that codes will encourage a "victim mentality," Delgado argues that "hate-speech rules simply provide an additional avenue of recourse to those who wish to take advantage of them. Indeed, one could argue that filing a complaint constitutes one way of taking charge of one's destiny."[37] Fifth, where critics find a subtle kind of "classism" or "elitism" at work in campus speech codes by punishing blue-collar hate speech but permitting more refined, more indirect, but potentially more devastating expressions of contempt devised by more educated persons, Delgado argues that his code applies with equal force to all classes and that more subtle expressions are more open to response than gutter expressions. Finally, where critics maintain that adopting a hate speech code to combat hate speech amounts to "two wrongs to make a right," Delgado argues that the university isn't censoring speech critical of the university; rather, he states, it is restricting private speech aimed at individuals, and this protection ought to enhance rather than restrict overall public debate by giving minorities and women confidence in their campus status.

What all this suggests is that even though campus speech code advocates are often highly critical of the "accepted" view of free speech and its philosophical and political assumptions, they recognize the need to work within the parameters which that view sets for the judiciary and legal profession. Thus, where early advocates of Title VII–like codes often viewed the issue as a stark contest between free speech and equality (just as critics did), later advocates suggested that a careful rethinking of the "accepted" view can show us how free speech and equality must work together to bring about a just society. For example, Laura Lederer, director of the Center on Speech, Equality and Harm at the University of Minnesota and editor of *The Price We Pay* with Richard Delgado, suggests that hate speech must be regulated because when we examine the problem of hate speech from the perspective of what best contributes to building real democracy, we may find that genuine free speech is dependent upon equality, and genuine equality upon free speech. The future of both may lie in our understanding that they are not contradictory forces, but rather interdependent and in need of one another for full expression of both.[38]

Yet it also is worth recalling that this was the position taken by Nadine Strossen, then-president of the ACLU, in her critique of Charles Lawrence's argument for a campus hate speech code.[39] Indeed, the continuing support of Strossen and the ACLU for Title VII regulations was a major reason why campus Title VII regulations did not face direct First Amendment challenges in the way that campus hate speech codes based on other grounds did.

There are, however, those who believe Title VII regulations should not be sustained, that hostile environment regulations are more costly than the speech they aim to suppress. In the next chapter we examine their arguments.

# 6

# The Attack on Hostile Environment

*Certainty about the correctness of one's views should not lead to certainty about the correctness of silencing one's opponents. . . . We feared communists in the 1950s, hippies in the 1960s, and Nazi marchers in the 1970s. Today's bogey men are the racists and the sexists. Of one thing we may be certain: any precedents established "just this once" to permit regulation of racist and sexist speech will be later called upon to support regulation of other speech.*

KINGSLEY BROWNE, "Title VII as Censorship"

## TITLE VII AND FREE SPEECH

The push for and adoption of Title VII–like hostile environment harassment campus speech codes provoked a number of critical responses. The quote from Kingsley Browne illustrates a common concern of these critics: when it comes to hostile environments, there is no way to draw good lines to guide conduct, and the doctrines we invoke to censor speech we oppose may serve in the future as doctrines our opponents use to silence us. But Browne doesn't limit his criticism of hostile environment speech regulations to just this objection; he also argues that they fail to fit any of the accepted categorical restrictions on free speech and fail to recognize the value of offensive speech. Another critic of hostile environment campus speech codes is Nat Hentoff, the free speech journalist involved in the Wayne Dick case at Yale, who acknowledges that physical harassment and quid pro quo harassment should be prohibited in the workplace and on campus, but insists that hostile environment harassment ought not to be because it will chill legitimate speech, fail to deal with the underlying attitudes that cause bigotry, and increase reliance on government rather than self-initiative.[1] Jonathan Rauch, a writer for the *Economist* in London, goes even further, maintaining that "by all indications, Homo sapiens is a tribal species for whom 'us versus them' comes naturally and must be continually pushed back" and that we must simply "make the best of prejudice rather than try to eliminate it."[2] And the attack is not limited to legal commentators, for Judge Warren in the *UWM-Post* decision threw out the university's appeal to Title VII law on the grounds that (1) Title VII law addresses employment contexts, not educational ones, (2) Title VII law is based on agency principles that do not apply to campuses (students are not normally agents of the university), and (3) Title VII is merely statute and cannot supersede the requirements of the First Amendment.[3] More recently, in a case we shall look at later in this chapter, the U.S. Court of Appeals for the Ninth Circuit ruled the San Bernardino Valley College sexual harassment policy unconstitutionally vague.[4] Although these critics do not always have the same specific target (Hentoff, for example, attacks Title VII campus speech codes regulating students, Browne attacks Title VII workplace speech regulations, and Rauch attacks hostile environment speech regulations in any context), we can usefully sort their arguments into two basic groups (as we did in our Chapter 3 study of critics' arguments): those attacking the legality of a Title VII–like campus speech code and those attacking the morality or desirability of such a speech code.

## TITLE VII–LIKE CODES ARE UNLAWFUL

Critics of Title VII hostile environment harassment–based campus speech codes offer three basic legal reasons why such codes should not be enforced by courts: (1) Title VII–like codes should not be extended to educational settings, (2) Title VII–like requirements should not supersede First Amendment guarantees of free speech, and (3) Title VII–like codes fail to meet legal administrative requirements. Any one of these reasons, if sustainable, could be sufficient for a court to strike down a Title VII–like campus speech code.

*Title VII and Educational Settings.* We saw in Chapter 5 how advocates of hostile environment harassment speech codes try to extend Title VII–like codes to the campus environment by pointing out how employment and education contexts are alike. The trouble with this argument, according to critics, is that courts have not accepted, and should not accept, this extension. Judge Warren was quite specific in the *UWM-Post* decision that "Title VII addresses employment, not educational settings"[5] and is based on agency principles, which are not applicable to students. Title VII law makes employers liable for the actions of their employees when acting as agents of the company; however, students per se are not agents of the university:

> Even if Title VII governed educational settings, the *Meritor* Court held
> that courts should look to agency principles when determining whether
> an employer is to be held liable for its employee's actions. . . . Since
> employees may act as their employer's agents, agency law may hold an
> employer liable for its employee's actions. In contrast, agency theory
> would generally not hold a school liable for its students' actions since stu-
> dents normally are not agents of the school.[6]

The critic's point is that even if the workplace and university are alike in some
ways, it is their dissimilarities that count most. Members of the university community are entitled to academic freedom, whereas employees of private com-
panies are not. The freedom to express one's ideas (whether one is an agent of
the university or not) is an essential part of the academic, but not corporate,
enterprise.

This difference has not been lost on the courts, which have developed harassment law differently for Title VII cases than Title IX cases (which is, of course,
why advocates appeal to Title VII law rather than Title IX law to defend their
proposals). That is, although courts have applied the hostile environment standard to academia beginning with *Moire v. Temple School of Medicine*, 800 F.2d
1136 (3d Cir., 1986), that standard has been limited to programs and activities
receiving direct federal funding, *Grove City v. Bell*, 104 S. Ct. 1211 (1984); and
the more recent *UWM-Post* and *Dambrot* decisions both struck down Title VII–
like hostile environment campus hate speech codes. Why is this? Because courts
simply hold universities to different standards than private employers: it is not
an essential part of the mission of a business to discover and disseminate ideas.

Advocates try to rebut the agency argument by finding cases in which students have been held to be agents of the university. For example, in *Levin v.
Harleston*, 770 F. Supp. 895 (S.D.N.Y. 1991), the district court found the university liable when it failed to sanction a group of students who had disrupted
the classes of Michael Levin, a philosophy professor known for his attacks on
affirmative action based on lower intelligence test scores by blacks. But critics
will emphasize that such cases are the exception, extremely rare exceptions. This
is why Judge Warren says students are not "normally" considered agents of the
university. A student would normally be an agent in cases where he or she stood
in some official university capacity, for example, as a resident director of a dormitory, so that he or she could be reasonably understood to be an agent of the
university. More importantly, however, the cases in which students are treated
as agents are analogous to Title VII hostile environment hate speech cases. In
the *Levin* decision, the court simply upheld reasonable time, place, and manner
restrictions to prevent disruption of the classroom; and all of the decisions strik-

ing down campus hate speech codes have acknowledged the legitimacy of reasonable time, place, and manner restrictions on campus speech. What they have not upheld are content- and viewpoint-biased regulations that are overbroad and unduly vague and whose aims are attainable without the sanctions.

Now, even if we agree with critics that the university is not enough like the workplace to warrant Title VII–like harassment regulations, we must be careful not to overstate their point. The agency objection to Title VII extension to campus speech only applies to codes insofar as they restrict nonagent student speech; it does not apply to a code regulating faculty or university staff or students employed at a public university, since they are agents of the employer in an employment context. However, the next objection tries to extend the critique to hostile environment laws as applied even to university employees.

*Title VII and the First Amendment.* As a matter of legal hierarchy, constitutional requirements take precedence over all other laws, whether federal statutes, state constitutions or enactments, or county or municipal ordinances. Title VII is a federal statute, and as such is constrained by constitutional requirements, including the requirement that government not restrict freedom of speech and press. Again, Judge Warren is quite explicit: "Even if the legal duties set forth in *Meritor* applied to this case, they would not make the UW Rule constitutional. Since Title VII is only a statute, it cannot supersede the requirements of the First Amendment."[7] Of course this would be no problem if Title VII–like codes were consonant with constitutional requirements; thus, when critics make this argument, they must also show how Title VII–like codes fail to meet constitutional requirements. To understand this, recall how in Chapter 4 we saw courts lay down four explicit requirements for campus speech regulations and how in Chapter 5 we saw Title VII advocates respond to these concerns by arguing that Title VII–like codes pass the four requirements. Given this background, the critic of hostile environment harassment campus speech codes is arguing here that the Title VII advocates' responses are not adequate. Here we shall examine the critics' arguments that Title VII–like codes fail the vagueness and content neutrality tests.

Are EEOC Title VII guidelines unreasonably vague in spite of the fact that courts have upheld them as reasonably clear? Have courts erred in their judgment? Kingsley Browne thinks so.[8] As we noted earlier, government regulation of speech or expression is unconstitutional unless it provides reasonably clear notice of what speech is permitted and what is not. Browne cites *NAACP v. Button*, 371 U.S. 415, 433 (1963), to show that such a law is unconstitutional because it creates a substantial risk of deterring speech that is constitutionally protected and *Smith v. Georgia*, 415 U.S. 566, 575 (1974), to show that such a law allows judges and juries to impose liability on the basis of their own personal preferences. Browne maintains, then, that both EEOC and court holdings wrongly deter and punish speech that is constitutionally protected and allow judges and juries to impose liability on the basis of their own personal preferences in two ways and, thus, that the guidelines are unconstitutional.

First, Browne argues that EEOC and court definitions provide little notice of what expression is prohibited or permitted because even distinguished federal appellate judges cannot agree in a wide variety of cases. Is a desk plaque stating "even male chauvinist pigs need love" (see *Rabidue v. Osceola Refining Co.*, 805 F.2d 611,624 (6th Cir. 1986), *cert. denied*, 481 U.S. 1041 [1987]) constitutive of a hostile environment? Some judges in that case thought so, while others dissented. Is abusive conduct and speech directed at all employees in violation of Title VII? Some courts have thought so (e.g., *Bailey v. Binyon*, 583 F. Supp. 923 [N.D. Ill. 1984]), while some courts have not (e.g., *Sheehan v. Purolater, Inc.*, 839 F.2d 99 [2d Cir.1988]). Are nude pinups posted throughout a workplace in violation of Title VII? Some courts have thought so (e.g., *Robinson v. Jacksonville Shipyards, Inc.*, 1991 U.S. Dist. LEXIS 794 [M.D. Fla. 1991]), while some courts have not (e.g., *Rabidue v. Osceola*). If our nation's most distinguished legal experts, the people who determine the law, cannot agree about such matters, how is a company/university or employee/member of the academic community to know what is permitted and what is not? Browne adds in a footnote that this concern is especially strong because of subjective elements in the determination of facts. For example, male judges have been instructed not to "substitute their perceptions of the balance of positive and negative messages the plaintiff was receiving" from coworkers (*Robinson v. Jacksonville Shipyards* at 123–24) and told that the "fact finder must walk a mile in the victim's shoes" and employ the standard "of a reasonable black person, as that can be best understood and given meaning by a white judge" (*Harris v. International Paper Co.*, 1991 U.S. Dist. LEXIS 4340, at 21). But how am I to know how a co-worker will react to all my speech, whether something I say will be taken as offensive? It is important to remember that a person does not have to intend to offend someone to be found guilty of creating a hostile environment under EEOC guidelines, since it looks to either the purpose (intent) or the effect (consequences) of the speech.

Interestingly, Browne appears to have some sympathetic judges. Supreme Court Justice Antonin Scalia, for example, in his concurring opinion in *Harris* wrote:

"Abusive" (or "hostile," which in this context I take to mean the same thing) does not seem to me a very clear standard—and I do not think clarity is at all increased by adding the adverb "objectively" or by appealing to a "reasonable person's" notion of what the vague word means. Today's opinion does list a number of factors that contribute to abusiveness . . . but since it neither says how much of each is necessary (an impossible task) nor identifies any single factor as determinative, today's holding lets virtually unguided juries decide whether sex-related conduct engaged in (or permitted by) an employer is egregious enough to warrant an award of damages. One might say that what constitutes "negligence" (a traditional jury question) is not much more clear and certain than what constitutes "abusiveness." Perhaps so. But the class of plaintiffs seeking to recover for negligence is limited to those who have suffered harm, whereas under the statute "abusiveness" is to be the test of whether legal harm has been suffered, opening more vistas of litigation.[9]

Thus, even if courts currently accept EEOC guidelines as reasonably clear, a change in those who occupy the bench (i.e., more Scalia types) could result in a rejection of those guidelines as unreasonably vague.

This is what appears to have happened in the San Bernardino case. In 1992 Dean Cohen, an English professor teaching a remedial course, "discussed subjects such as obscenity, cannibalism, and consensual sex with children in a 'devil's advocate' style"; told students of his writing for *Hustler* and *Playboy* magazines, sometimes reading from them; and required students to write an essay defining pornography. Anita Murillo, a thirty-five-year-old student in the course, asked for a different assignment, and when that request was refused, stopped attending. When she received a failing grade for the course, she filed a complaint. The relevant administrative bodies (a faculty panel, the college president, and its governing board) found Cohen had violated the sexual harassment policy by creating a hostile environment. Cohen was required to warn students in his syllabus of the nature of his courses, attend a sexual-harassment seminar, and modify his teaching strategy. Cohen sued and won. The court found the policy (which is nearly identical to the EEOC statement) void for vagueness, pointing out that since Cohen had taught that way for years and had been given no notice of how the policy would affect him, the policy amounted to "a legalistic ambush," a violation of fair-notice requirements.

Second, Browne argues that EEOC and court guidelines are impermissibly vague and permit arbitrary enforcement because judges and juries are instructed to look at the "totality of circumstances" to determine the existence of a hostile environment, which leads to overregulation because the determination thereby depends not only on the content and context of that particular statement but also everything else the speaker and plaintiff and co-workers have said and done through the years. If so, however, an employer/university cannot possibly for-

mulate basic rules for employees/members of the academic community to follow, since the particular mix of expression (and conduct) that will be judged
to constitute a hostile environment will be unknown until the lawsuit comes
and a verdict is rendered. That is, in some circumstances the desk plaque in
*Rabidue* may constitute a basis for a finding of harassment and in other circumstances not. In some circumstances "pinups" or "girlie magazines" may constitute a basis for a finding of harassment—as in *Robinson v. Jacksonville Shipyards,
Inc.,* 760 F. Supp. 1486 (M.D. Fla. 1991)—and in other cases not—as in
*Rabidue*. Can anyone say in advance what circumstances are determinative of
guilt? No. The most anyone can say is that some forms of "abusive" expression
are generally frowned upon. We are left to make our best guess, a guess which
a judge and jury may well decide is wrong.

Other critics attack EEOC guidelines on these grounds as well. Nat Hentoff,
for example, quotes Eleanor Holmes Norton, former chairwoman of the
EEOC: "It is technically impossible to write an anti-speech code that cannot
be twisted against speech nobody means to bar. It has been tried and tried and
tried."[10] Even a director of the EEOC admits that its guidelines can be used to
punish protected speech and applied by judges and juries in arbitrary ways!
Jonathan Rauch argues that

> distinguishing prejudice reliably and nonpolitically from non-prejudice
> . . . is quite hopeless. . . . At the University of Michigan, a student said in
> a classroom discussion that he considered homosexuality a disease treat-
> able with therapy. He was summoned to a formal disciplinary hearing for
> violating the school's policy against speech that "victimizes" people based
> on their "sexual orientation." Now evidence is abundant that this partic-
> ular hypothesis is wrong, and any American homosexual can attest to the
> harm the student's hypothesis has inflicted on many real people. But was
> it a statement of prejudice or of misguided belief? Hate speech or hypoth-
> esis? Many Americans who do not regard themselves as bigots or haters
> believe homosexuality is a treatable disease. They may be wrong, but are
> they all bigots? I am unwilling to say so, and if you are willing beware.
> The line between a prejudiced belief and a merely controversial one is elu-
> sive, and the harder you look the more elusive it becomes. "God hates
> homosexuals" is a statement of fact, not of bias, to those who believe it;
> "American criminals are disproportionately black" is a statement of bias,
> not of fact, to those who disbelieve it.[11]

These critics are trying to underscore the point that when it comes to sexual
harassment, the plain fact is we all do not "know it when we see it," for whether

a remark or plaque or joke is seen as harassing is a highly subjective matter. Browne reports a case in which a plaintiff contended that her supervisor had told her she should turn her house into a brothel; on deposition, it turned out that her supervisor, who sold real estate in his spare time, had said, "You should make your house work for you."[12] In another case, the plaintiff alleged that she had been subjected to "pornographic radio shows"; on deposition, it turned out that employees had been listening to the "Dr. Ruth" show.[13] In *Carter v. Sedgwick County*, 705 F. Supp. 1474, 1476 (D. Kan. 1988), a harassment claim was based on the presentation of several sexual "novelties," including a "Mr. Peter Party Mold," a "Pecker Pop Top," a "Mouth Organ," a "Sexy Hot Dog," and nude male and female figurines that the alleged harasser and his wife gave as jokes they thought the plaintiff would enjoy. Indeed, in *Ellison v. Brady*, 924 F.2d 872, 880 (9th Cir. 1991), the appellate court found that even a "well-intentioned compliment" can form the basis for a sexual harassment claim. Can judges and juries make such discriminations free from personal bias and subjective attitudes? Is their judgment based on the (dubious) empirical claim that all women object to being viewed in a sexual manner in the workplace or on the normative judgment that all women should object to being viewed in that way? How is a man to know if a woman will welcome the advance or reject it and sue for harassment? In *Howard v. National Cash Register Co.*, 388 F. Supp. 603, 606 (S.D. Ohio 1975), the court held that

> the Archie Bunkers of this world, within limitations, still may assert their biased view. We have not yet reached the point where we have taken from individuals the right to be prejudiced, so long as such prejudice did not evidence itself in discrimination. This court will secure plaintiff against discrimination; no court can secure him against prejudice. The defendant in this case is charged by law with avoiding all discrimination; the defendant is not charged by law with discharging all Archie Bunkers in its employ. Absent a showing of something other than disrespect and prejudice by his fellow workers, plaintiff cannot bring himself within the terms of [Title VII].

Yet in *Davis v. Monsanto Chemical Co.*, 858 F.2d 345, 350 (6th Cir. 1988), *cert. denied*, 109 S.Ct. 3166 (1989), the appellate court held that

> in essence, while Title VII does not require an employer to fire all "Archie Bunkers" in its employ, the law does require an employer to take prompt action to prevent such bigots from expressing their opinions in a way that abuses or offends their coworkers. By informing people that the expres-

sion of racist and sexist attitudes in public is unacceptable, people may eventually learn that such views are undesirable in private, as well. Thus Title VII may advance the goal of eliminating prejudices and biases in our society.

So which is it: Are courts charged with eliminating prejudice or not? If they are charged with eliminating prejudice, to what lengths can they go to eliminate it? If reasonably clear lines to guide our conduct cannot be agreed upon and articulated by legal experts, if federal appellate judges cannot even agree on the proper bases for harassment claims, how is a university or member of the academic community to know when he or she is approaching the line or crossing it? If a black co-worker of mine tells me some ethnic jokes, and I respond by telling one too, and he is offended by it, can he file a claim of racial harassment against me? If a female employee willingly joins in sexual banter, but then takes offense at someone's remarks, can she file a claim of sexual harassment? As we shall see below, it appears so. Given these ambiguities and outright inconsistencies, how can a court hold that the guidelines are reasonably clear and consonant with the First Amendment?

Browne also contends that Title VII codes are impermissibly content-based. Are they? On first glance, it would seem that Title VII advocates are on safe ground, since even Justice Scalia in the *R.A.V.* decision carved out an exception to First Amendment rights to allow courts to enforce hostile environment harassment regulations in spite of their regulation of speech on the basis of content. Browne, however, maintains that this exception is entirely ad hoc and should not be sustained.

The standard justification for a content-based restriction on speech in the workplace is based on captive-audience theory. Browne points out that this doctrine is most strictly applied in the context of one's own home (see, for example, *Frisby v. Schultz*, 487 U.S. 474, 484 [1988], and *Rowan v. United States Post Office Department*, 397 U.S. 728 [1970]), but has been extended to state proprietary areas in the case of *Lehman v. Shaker Heights*, 418 U.S. 298 (1974).[14] In that case, the U.S. Supreme Court ruled that a city could justifiably ban political ads from city buses since a bus is not a public forum and the city's interests in avoiding appearances of endorsing a candidate and in protecting riders from the "blare of political propaganda" were legitimate aims that could be promoted in no less restrictive way. In other words, the Court ruled that the city could legitimately ban the speech based purely on its content (being a political advertisement) because it would, in effect, be forced on an unwilling audience that could not reasonably avoid it. Title VII advocates maintain, then, that hostile environment harassment regulations banning speech based on its bigoted content are justifiable, since a workplace/academic setting (classroom, dormitory room, etc.) is not a public forum and a company's/university's interest in avoiding appearances of endorsing racism and sexism and in protecting employees/members of the academic community from the "blare of bigoted propaganda" are legitimate aims that can be promoted in no less restrictive ways.

This argument by analogy fails, according to Browne, because the *Lehman* decision upheld only content-based regulations, not a viewpoint-based regulation like a Title VII hate speech code. That is, although it may be justifiable (in narrowly defined conditions) for government to regulate speech on the basis of content (ban political ads on city buses, but permit nonpolitical ads on those same buses), it does not follow that a government agency may regulate speech on the basis of its viewpoint (ban Republican political ads on city buses, but permit non-Republican ads on those same buses). The latter would constitute a government privileging of one viewpoint over another, and this assault on speech our republic of free and equal citizens cannot withstand. Thus, although it may be justifiable (in narrowly defined circumstances) for a company/university to regulate speech on the basis of content (ban quid pro quo speech, but permit political speech), it does not follow that a company/university may regulate speech on the basis of its viewpoint (ban racist and sexist speech, but permit anti-racist and anti-sexist speech).

Browne claims that harassment cases are "more analogous to a ban on political advertising by extremist candidates but not by mainstream candidates," a ban that would never be upheld in court, and offers *Erznoznik v. Jacksonville*, 422 U.S. 205 (1975), as the appropriate analogy. In *Erznoznik*, the U.S. Supreme Court struck down a city ordinance prohibiting the exhibition of films containing nudity on drive-in movie screens visible from a public street since the ordinance was underinclusive. That is, the ban on skin-flicks was underinclusive of the rationale (to protect drivers from distractions that might cause traffic hazards). If that really was the rationale, then all movies that might distract motorists would have to be banned. The fact that all such movies were not banned strongly implies the city was trying to ban speech it simply disapproved of, and this the Constitution does not permit. Similarly, hostile environment laws cannot be justified on the basis that they protect workers/members of the academic community from all harassing or offensive speech in the workplace/academic setting, because they single out harassment based only on privileged categories. If Title VII restrictions giving government the power to ban harassing speech with a racist or sexist message but allowing such speech with an anti-racist or anti-sexist message were justifiable, then restrictions giving "the state the power to ban obscene films having an antidemocracy message, while allowing such films with a pro-democracy message" would be justifiable too. But it just ain't so, says Browne, citing *American Booksellers Ass'n v. Hudnut*, 771 F.2d 323, 331 (7th Cir. 1985), *aff'd*, 475 U.S. 1001 (1986), for a "regulation prohibiting scatological descriptions of Republicans but not scatological descriptions of Democrats" would not be sustainable. That is, if scatological descriptions or harassing speech or political ads or fighting words or obscene films (etc.) are to be banned, then the state must ban them no matter what their viewpoint is.[15]

Browne concludes that

> speech that is intended to cause emotional distress is entitled to little First Amendment protection, especially if uttered with the conscious intent to compel an employee to resign. It is difficult to see any first amendment value in such speech and tempting to consider such expression "conduct." If a standard could be devised that would fairly limit restrictions of expression in such contexts, the first amendment would not be imperiled, even if the restriction was not, strictly speaking, viewpoint neutral. The difficulty would be in identifying the proper cases and ensuring that no liability would attach to other cases and that an inordinate amount of expression would not be chilled. Surmounting that difficulty seems impossible.[16]

According to the critics, then, Title VII–like speech codes violate First Amendment guarantees, and since constitutional requirements supersede federal statutes, Title VII–like hostile environment campus hate speech codes should not be upheld.

To be sure, advocates (such as Catharine MacKinnon, Richard Delgado, and Thomas Grey) will argue that Title VII is not merely federal law; it is grounded in the constitutional ideal of equality espoused in the Fourteenth Amendment and has outweighed the ideal of free speech in several cases. But critics can respond to this point in three ways.

First, critics can challenge the claim that there is any clearly recognizable ideal of equality in the Constitution. Is the ideal equal opportunity or equality of outcome? Equality of treatment or equality of access? Equality of material possessions or equality of respect or equality of power? Advocates don't agree in their answers to such questions. The ideal of equal opportunity came long after the Fourteenth Amendment was framed and ratified, and there is substantial disagreement about the nature of equality. Many current provisions thought to promote equality under the Civil Rights Act of 1991 are significant additions to or modifications of the provisions thought to promote equality under the Civil Rights Act of 1964; for example, prior to 1991 sexual harassment cases could be filed only by individuals, not as class action suits. Because of such disagreements about the nature of equality and what is legally necessary to promote it, some critics point out the essential role freedom of speech plays in pursuing a better understanding of and implementation of policies for equality. Martha Minow, a law professor at Harvard, points out in her keynote address to the 1989 National Association of Colleges and Universities Attorneys Meeting:

> The goal of equality . . . will remain elusive so long as we attribute differences to others and then pretend that differences are discovered, not socially created. Equality will remain elusive so long as we neglect perspectives other than our own that should challenge the labels, like lazy, we assign.
>
> Does one have to have a kindred experience of discrimination in order to recognize inequality in the treatment of others? It helps, but so does talking with others, asking when differential treatment is injurious, and when it is necessary, or preferred by those who are treated "differently." . . . You can't know, sitting alone at your typewriter, whether what you or others believe fits the experiences of people unlike yourself. You have to talk with them and learn from them.
>
> In short, can we learn to look at perspectives other than our own, and then still others, continually unsettling our assumptions that we know what others think? This struggle, I think, is critical to the search for equality. It is a process of continual reexaminations of the treatment we allow our institutions to accord people. The lines used to divide people must be scrutinized and rescrutinized to incorporate the perspectives of those who have not in the past been consulted. Hearing a perspective does not require deferring to it. The search is not simply for the fox's perspective, nor the dog's, but for the perspective that can see them both. That is still a perspective—but it is not one implying the normal and the deviant, the average and the marginal, but one looking to the relationships between human beings.[17]

Minow's attempt to see the struggle over the nature and value of equality as one of the contests waged in the free speech arena reinforces the importance of strong free speech guarantees. When advocates style their proposals as anti-caste or anti-subordination rules, the unconverted are left to wonder who exactly are members of what castes in our mobile society and how a campus speech rule eliminates castes (presumably held in place by legal, political, and other institutional means).

Second, critics can argue that even if there is a generally acceptable constitutional ideal of equality, it doesn't follow that it ought to apply to universities in the same way that it does to private employers, given the primacy of ideas and their dissemination on the campus. For example, the *Jaycees* decision Mac-Kinnon appeals to (the only decision she offers in support of her contention that equality outweighs free speech) is not analogous to campus hate speech codes. First, the case does not involve a public university or university members with strong free speech and academic freedom concerns; it involves a private community-service organization. Second, in that case the Supreme Court required the Jaycees to correct their conduct (stop barring women from becoming members), not to change their view of women or its expression (as ill-suited to the work of the Jaycees). The problem was not that the Jaycees were suppressing speech in overbroad and unduly vague ways, the problem was they denied women equal access. In fact, critics can point to a much more relevant case, *Dube v. The State University of New York at Stony Brook*, 1990 U.S. App. LEXIS 6038, No. 88-7980 (2d Cir., April 12, 1990), that suggests free speech outweighs equality in offensive speech cases. Dube, a South African who had been hired in the Africana Studies program in 1977, taught a "Politics of Race" course in 1981 in which he discussed Nazism, South African apartheid, and Israeli Zionism as manifestations of racism. Although Dube was initially cleared of charges in view of his academic freedom, the Anti-Defamation League of B'nai B'rith and some faculty began a campaign to oust Dube, which culminated in him being denied tenure in 1985. In its decision, the appellate court noted that courts should give deference to academic decisions, but "it has been clearly established that the First Amendment tolerates neither laws nor other means of coercion, persuasion or intimidation 'that cast a pall of orthodoxy' over the free exchange of ideas in the classroom."[18]

*Title VII and Administrative Requirements*. Even if a law passes First Amendment tests on its face, it must also pass certain administrative requirements in its application. For example, the Fourteenth Amendment has been interpreted by courts to require the government and its agents to follow "due process of law." This means, for example, that the accused must be presumed innocent until proven guilty and that the state cannot deny a defendant such rights as the right to legal counsel or a timely hearing. Yet many universities deny or otherwise abridge these very rights when investigating, prosecuting, and punishing alleged harassers.

First, universities too frequently presume the accused guilty and attempt to coerce him or her into accepting informal or formal sanctions without any consideration of First Amendment rights (as in the Wayne Dick, Michigan, and George Mason cases). In the Central Michigan case, they apparently didn't even bother with a hearing before sanctioning and then firing the coach. The fact that there are cases in which universities do not pursue allegations of harassment vigorously enough (I suspect that there are even more cases of this sort than the other) does not absolve universities of the obligation to afford the accused due process of law. This difficulty is compounded by the fact that enforcement officers tend to be affirmative action officers or their equivalent, whose institutional role is to advance the cause of members of historically disadvantaged groups, not to protect academic freedom or freedom of expression.

Second, universities can follow Title VII guidelines in allowing plaintiffs to file complaints in conclusory terms such as "racial slurs," "racist jokes," "sexual innuendo," "dirty jokes," "sexist remarks," "pornographic pictures," and so on rather than by listing the specific words used.[19] However, as Kingsley Browne points out, this can subject people to needless and annoying investigation at the minimum, and worse, to gossip, innuendo, or misleading publicity that damages one's career. Due process requires those falsely accused of harassment to be able to extricate themselves as quickly as possible. If specificity were required, meritless complaints could be weeded out in an initial interview process. And if the enforcement officers had training in free speech doctrines, they would know when the complaints were substantial enough to merit further investigation. In the highly politicized academic environment, a charge of harassment (whether it is ultimately upheld or not) can quickly turn one's life upside down.

Third, universities can follow a "double standard" or "continuing veto," which some courts have upheld.[20] Kingsley Browne notes that some courts have maintained that women may engage in the same sexual vulgarities as men, yet be able to charge the men with sexual harassment. In *Lynch v. Des Moines*, 454 N.W. 2d 827 (Iowa 1990), and *Loftin-Boggs v. Meridian*, 633 F. Supp. 1323 (S.D. Miss. 1986), female plaintiffs "gave as much as they got," that is, participated in and even initiated the sexual language, jokes, and the like as much as the co-workers they were charging with sexual harassment, but were still able to say that the speech was "unwelcome" and thus harassment. In *Swentek v. US Air, Inc.*, 830 F.2d 552 (4th Cir. 1987), the plaintiff had (among other things) placed a dildo in her supervisor's mailbox to get her to loosen up, urinated in a cup and given it as a drink to another employee, and grabbed the genitals of a pilot with a frank invitation to a sexual encounter. Yet she complained of a hostile environment. Is it fair for someone to engage in such activities willingly and then declare at some later date that the environment was now hostile? How could anyone be reasonably expected to know the later conduct would be construed as harassing if it had been willingly accepted and joined in by the plaintiff for years? At a minimum, due process requires fair notice, but universities are not doing that.

To be sure, universities typically hold some kind of sexual harassment seminar, but these often are uninformative. On my own campus, faculty leaders of the 1996 new student academic workshops were asked to discuss sexual assault and harassment during their sessions and were given handouts to assist them. Several faculty members at the meeting expressed concerns about this, given their lack of expertise in such subject areas and the extremely limited information contained in the one-page handouts they were given to lead their discussions with. When they appealed to the campus affirmative action officer and other officials present at the meeting for clarification, none was forthcoming. No examples of legal or illegal conduct were mentioned. No relevant guidelines or principles were introduced, just a vague injunction to refer students with questions to the relevant campus offices. After attending an International Sexual Assault and Sexual Harassment conference in November 1996, I learned that such situations existed all over the country, not just at my campus.

Now, one might well wonder whether such problems or even abuses are the exception or the rule, and whether universities can take reasonable steps to reduce or eliminate them. So far as I can tell, critics have offered no concrete evidence of widespread abuse (though they imply it through the examples they emphasize), and they have not shown that universities cannot correct their procedures to ensure due process, with the possible exception of "fair notice." Of course, critics can respond that they don't need to show abuse is widespread; in any case of abuse a university can be sued for failure to provide due process. Moreover, so long as universities fail to clarify the nature of a hostile environment, they run the risk of having their policies ruled void for vagueness, just as the Michigan, Wisconsin, Central Michigan, and San Bernardino Valley policies were.

The failure to provide due process can be costly, as the University of New Hampshire discovered.[21] On February 24, 1992, English instructor Donald J. Silva, a thirty-year teacher, tried to explain writing focus to his technical writing class in this way: "I will put focus in terms of sex, so you can better understand it. Focus is like sex. You seek a target. You zero in on your subject. You move from side to side. You close in on the subject. You bracket the subject and center on it. Focus connects experience and language. You and the subject become one." Two days later Silva gave as an example of metaphor, "Belly dancing is like Jell-O on a plate with a vibrator under the plate." Eight female students, encouraged by a faculty member, filed a complaint. Without even informing Silva of the complaint, the university began searching for a replacement, and after the relevant panels found him guilty, Silva was suspended without pay and ordered to undergo psychological counseling. Silva sued. In a preliminary hearing, Judge Shane Devine found the students' complaints factually inaccurate (apparently as a result of sharing misinformation in "rap sessions") and the professor's comments likely to be protected by the First Amendment, since they "advanced the educational objectives of conveying certain principles related to the subject matter of his course" and "were made in a professionally appropriate manner." It also was pointed out that Silva's examples were not even original: writers like Ernest Hemingway and Ray Bradbury have compared writing focus to sex and the belly dancing example was taken from the belly dancer Little Egypt. Rather than go to trial, the university settled out of court for $230,000 ($60,000 back pay and $170,000 attorneys' fees). Surely the university could do better things with this money than try to censor faculty speech.

## TITLE VII–LIKE CODES ARE WRONGHEADED

Even if the three legal objections to hostile environment harassment campus speech codes can be overcome, critics maintain that such codes are morally wrong or otherwise undesirable as a matter of public policy for many of the same reasons that critics attacked other speech codes: they do not deal with the underlying attitudes, which can be better dealt with through educational measures; they increase individual dependence on government; they can, and will, be used to silence, not strengthen, minority speech; they shift focus away from the welfare of minorities to legalistic debates; they make martyrs of bigots and may cause a backlash; and they make the fight against bigots harder by driving them underground. Nat Hentoff, for example, argues that hostile environment codes won't do a bit of good:

> Let us suppose these codes were in place on every campus in the country. Would racism go away? Racism would go underground, in the dark, where it's most comfortable.
>
> The language on campus could become as pure as country water, but racist attitudes would still fester. The only way to deal with racism is to bring it out into the open—not to pretend it has been scared away.[22]

Jonathan Rauch points out that the war on words waged by hostile environment theorists and the "verbal absolutism" of some schools cannot succeed, since

> as long as they remain bigoted, bigots will simply find other words. If they can't call you a kike then they will say Jewboy, Judas, or hebe, and when all those are banned they will press words like "oven" and "lamp-

shade" into their service. The vocabulary of hate is potentially as rich as your dictionary, and all you do by banning language used by cretins is to let them decide what the rest of us may say.[23]

Rauch adds that such codes do great harm by equating "verbal violence" (words that wound, in Mari Matsuda's expression) with real physical violence:

> The fear engendered by these words is real. The remedy is as clear and as imperfect as ever: protect citizens against violence. This, I grant, is something that American society has never done very well and now does quite poorly. It is no solution to define words as violence or prejudice as oppression, and then by cracking down on words and thoughts pretend that we are doing something about violence and oppression. No doubt it is easier to pass a speech code or hate-crimes law and proclaim the streets safer than to actually make the streets safer, but the one must never be confused with the other. Every cop or prosecutor chasing words is one fewer chasing criminals.[24]

Kingsley Browne adds that "the only effective method of altering a world view that is deemed pernicious is to provide a persuasive response—that is, 'more speech.' 'Shut up!' is not a persuasive response."[25] Rather than rehash these criticisms, which were presented already in Chapter 3 and responded to in Chapter 5 in some measure, let us move on to a final argument urged by critics: offensive speech has significant value that Title VII advocates overlook.

Browne argues that at least some of the speech involved in hostile environment harassment cases has some value.[26] First, it constitutes expression of views on matters of social policy. Since political speech is at the "core" of First Amendment protection and the state must remain neutral on viewpoints concerning social policy ("its paramount obligation," *Young v. American Mini Theatres. Inc.*, 427 U.S. 50, 70 [1976]), it must allow people to attack the idea of racial and sexual equality just as it protects people who defend the idea of racial and sexual equality. That we as a society have enshrined racial and sexual equality in law (in, e.g., the Civil Rights Acts) does not make criticisms, even highly offensive ones, of racial and sexual equality unworthy of protection. Supreme Court Justice Louis Brandeis stated in *Whitney v. California*, 274 U.S. 357, 374 (1927), "A state is, ordinarily, denied the power to prohibit dissemination of social, economic, and political doctrine which a vast majority of its citizens believes to be false and fraught with evil consequence." Justice Brennan echoes this in *Texas v. Johnson*: "The First Amendment does not guarantee that other concepts virtually sacred to our nation as a whole—such as the principle that discrimination on the basis of race is odious and destructive—will go unquestioned in the market-place of ideas." Judge Warren in *UWM-Post* points out that such speech at least has the expressive values of convincing the listener of the speaker's discrimina-tory position and expressing the speaker's emotions.[27] To deny this (i.e., to accept a ban on ideas offensive to the majority) is to accept a "tyranny of the majority" that John Stuart Mill warned us against over a century ago. It is to ignore all four of Mill's reasons why offensive speech must be permitted:

> We have now recognized the necessity to the mental well-being of mankind (on which their other well-being depends) of freedom of opin-ion, and freedom of the expression of opinion, on four distinct grounds, which we now briefly recapitulate:
>
> First, if any opinion is compelled to silence, that opinion may, for aught we can certainly know, be true. To deny this is to assume our own infallibility.
>
> Secondly, though the silenced opinion be an error, it may, and very commonly does, contain a portion of truth; and since the general and prevailing opinion on any subject is rarely or never the whole truth, it is only by the collision of adverse opinions that the remainder of the truth has any chance of being supplied.
>
> Thirdly, even if the received opinion be not only true, but the whole truth; unless it is suffered to be, and actually is, vigorously and earnestly contested, it will, by most of those who receive it, be held in the manner of a prejudice, with little comprehension or feeling of its rational grounds. And not only this, but, fourthly, the meaning of the doctrine itself will be in danger of being lost or enfeebled, and deprived of its vital effect on the character and conduct; the dogma becoming a mere formal profes-sion, ineffectious for good, but cumbering the ground and preventing the growth of any real and heartfelt conviction from reason or personal experience.[28]

Indeed, Jonathan Rauch's defense of prejudice is essentially a 1990s version of Mill's argument. He echoes Mill's belief that we need a competition of ideas to discern the truth by noting that

> we cannot know in advance or for sure which belief is prejudice and which is truth, but to advance knowledge we don't need to know. The genius of intellectual pluralism lies not in doing away with prejudices and dogmas but in channeling them—making them socially productive by pitting prejudice against prejudice and dogma against dogma, exposing

all to withering public criticism. What survives at the end of the day is our base of knowledge.[29]

And he points out how offensive speech can lead to the discovery of new truths: "I know of no modern idea more ugly and stupid than that the holocaust never happened, nor any idea more viciously motivated. Yet the denier's claims that the Auschwitz gas chambers could not have worked led to closer study, and, in 1993, research showing, at last, how they actually did work. Thanks to prejudice and stupidity, another opening for doubt has been shut."[30] Browne gives the example of the character Archie Bunker from *All in the Family*, a character that taught the American public a lot about the ugliness and error of prejudice. Rather than persuade others to take up the banner of racism and sexism, hearing prejudice in its baldest form may well have the effect of demonstrating the poverty of the belief expressed. Rauch and Browne maintain that by letting people make errors, even intentionally harmful ones, we allow challenges to orthodoxy, imaginative thinking, and bold experimentation—all of which are necessary to discover, verify, and teach truths and keep their meaning alive.

Second, Browne argues that racist and sexist speech may serve a valuable function by acting as a "safety value," a function Justice Brandeis also recognized in *Whitney* (at 375):

But [the founders] knew that order cannot be secured merely through fear of punishment for its infraction; that it is hazardous to discourage thought, hope and imagination; that fear breeds repression; that repression breeds hate; that hate menaces stable government; that the path of safety lies in the opportunity to discuss freely supposed grievances and proposed remedies; and that the fitting remedy for evil counsels is good ones.

In many cases, the expression of racist and sexist ideas may serve to "displace aggression, protect self-esteem, define self-image, and reduce uncertainty about the perceived world," *Snell v. Suffolk County*, 611 F. Supp. 521,529–30 (E.D.N.Y. 1985), and thereby have "cathartic value," *Snell* (at 531). And in the extreme case, the expression of racist and sexist ideas in crude jokes and barbs may prevent its repression and eventual expression in physical violence or even a fit of murderous rage.

Rauch and Browne do acknowledge the harm that can stem from words. Rauch tells a story relating the fear and hurt he felt upon hearing some teenagers joke about "faggots" in a Washington, D.C., subway.[31] He wonders:

Who are they? How many are there? How dangerous? Where is the way out? Is it just a joke, or will they recognize me as a homosexual and attack? Yet he also recognizes that freedom of expression ceases to exist when offensive speech is banned. Browne notes that much protected speech is viewed as posing a real risk of concrete harm—speech advocating the violent overthrow of our government, flag burning, criticism of the U.S. government during times of war—and points out that to reject such attempts to regulate speech does not rest on a rejection of the premise that harm may flow from the speech, but rather on the judgment that the value of free speech is sufficiently high that the risk of harm must be tolerated.[32] David A. J. Richards and Lee Bollinger have pointed out that the principles of tolerance are most in need when the speech expresses a dissenting, not conventional, point of view. That is the whole purpose of tolerance: to allow what one does not necessarily approve of.

At bottom, there are two basic problems with regulating offensive (harassing) speech. First, everything can offend somebody—a vegetarian's attack on the morality of eating meat may be thought fraught with evil to a carnivore (and vice versa), an atheist's attack on the truth of belief in God may be thought fraught with evil to a theist (and vice versa), a defense of the morality and legality of abortion may be thought fraught with evil to anti-abortionists (and vice versa), an argument supporting democracy can be thought fraught with evil by a fascist, cynic, or anarchist (and vice versa). The list never ends. If all offensive speech, all speech thought fraught with evil, were banned, we would be left with nothing to say! Cartoonist Garry Trudeau captured this consequence with great comedic effect in a *Doonesbury* strip in which a college commencement speaker is reduced to saying only "thanks and good luck" by the student and faculty committees that enforce the current orthodoxy. Nothing more would pass their standards of political correctness.[33] Of course, what is more likely, given the realities of enforcement, is that the group in power (whether it is a majority or minority) will censor only its opponent's offensive speech. That produces the second problem. Without the freedom to urge ideas and practices offensive to and thought fraught with evil by racists, blacks and their sympathizers would not have been allowed to criticize southern segregation and Jim Crow laws. Without the freedom to speak of ideas and practices thought sinful by many Americans, homosexuals and their sympathizers would not be allowed to defend gay and lesbian lifestyles. Without real guarantees of free speech and court decisions upholding and expanding free speech, wartime dissidents would not have been able to criticize American involvement in Vietnam. It may not be a pretty freedom, but it is a necessary one. The sword of censorship is double-edged: if nonracists have the right to ban racist speech as offensive, then racists have the right to ban nonracist speech as offensive.

In response, some advocates of campus speech regulations, in particular Richard Delgado,[34] have suggested that this is merely a free speech myth and have maintained that free speech has acted more often as an obstacle to egalitarian progress than as a helping hand.

Here one simply has to look at history. When people who have nothing to gain by support of free speech, including prominent veterans of the civil rights movement like Benjamin L. Hooks and leading academic experts on the civil rights movement like Harry Kalven Jr. concur on the centrality of the First Amendment in advancing the cause of black equality, I find it difficult to believe the revisionist. William Rubenstein makes essentially the same point in a convincing article on the gay and lesbian search for equal treatment.[35] He offers powerful evidence that the First Amendment has been gays' and lesbians' best friend, upholding rights to a great many things, while the Fourteenth Amendment has delivered only one confusing and thus insignificant verdict in support of equal treatment for homosexuals.

Browne also skewers the self-righteous rhetoric of many hostile environment advocates.[36] Mari Matsuda, for example, defends hate speech regulation because society knows hate speech is wrong. Browne points out that this obviously is not the case, else there would be no need for the code. Judge Keith, dissenting in *Rabidue*, also had supreme confidence in his judgment that it is his norms, not society's, that ought to guide interpretation of the law. Keith rejected the court's reliance on societal norms as a basis for the decision, holding instead that "the relevant inquiry at hand is what the reasonable woman would find offensive." Browne quips, "Needless to say, it would be a rare judge for whom the views of [the reasonable woman] were in conflict with his own."[37] Robert Post adds that the campus hate speech code advocates' appeal to a "universal condemnation" of hate speech rings hollow given their beliefs about the "epidemic" of hate speech incidents and their rhetoric about racial and gender "castes."[38] If racism, sexism, and homophobia are as pervasive in U.S. society as hate speech code advocates maintain, then their disapproval of hate speech simply cannot be universal. In fact, if bigotry is pervasive (as they maintain), the condemnation of hate speech is not even a majoritarian opinion. It is a minority view.

The critics' argument has reached a point where even a committee of the American Association of University Professors (AAUP) complained about hostile environment regulations on American campuses.[39] Beginning with the observation that "the history of academic freedom is, in fact, the history of protecting speech that was found deeply offensive by members of the community at the time," the committee argues that applying this broad definition of sexual harassment to speech in the context of the academic mission necessarily assumes that the presence of and risk of offending women requires that certain limits be placed on the free exchange of ideas. This invites other groups to make similar claims, depending on their perception, or that of others, as to how "at risk" they are. Thus, the teaching of any of a variety of subjects—sociology, history, political science, literature—might become a minefield of forbidden expression. There is no principled basis for distinguishing, and therefore for supplying less or more stringent protection for, expression that offends one group as opposed to another, on the ground that the message conveyed or the locution employed is offensive to a group more or less "at risk."[40]

The committee suggests that concerns of "hostile environments" be handled by the standards or codes of professional conduct already governing academe, since the ill-defined "hostile environment" standard will inevitably conflict with the central mission of the university, which is the discovery and assessment of ideas. Thus, the AAUP filed an *amicus* (friend of the court) brief on Professor Cohen's behalf in the San Bernardino case.


CONCLUSION

Analysts of Title VII law and social scientists investigating sexual harassment, even sympathetic ones, even officers charged with enforcing the law, consistently bemoan its unsettled state. Linda Rubin and Sherry Borgers, for example, point out in their attempted synthesis of the psychological research on the topic during the 1980s that "a clear definition of sexual harassment has yet to be commonly accepted in the psychology research. The majority of studies conducted on sexual harassment have generated their own definitions and lists of specific behaviors identified as harassment."[41] William Woerner and Sharon Oswald point out in their analysis of sexual harassment and hostile environments in the law that "the years since *Barnes v. Train* (the initial sexual harassment case in 1974) have only served to add new terms and provide new angles, without defining the term itself. The decisions seem to overturn so regularly that the entire issue seems to be in a state of chaos."[42] This "chaos" leads critics to maintain that hostile environment extension to the campus is both bad law and bad social policy. Alan Charles Kors, a historian at the University of Pennsylvania, writes, "Whatever the problem of these harassment policies outside of the university, in the academy, and relating to academic life, they raise problems of a serious and disturbing nature."[43] Those who criticize the extension of hostile environment law to academe do not object to all Title VII applications to academe. Kors, for example, accepts policies that protect individuals from "all physical sexual coercion, all pressures to trade intimacy for better grades or job promotion, all molestation, and indeed from all invidious discrimination that evaluates their work and their careers by anything other than appropriate, in this case academic, standards."[44] But they insist, to quote a *New Republic* editorial, that "the solution to this mess is a definition of sexual harassment that excludes verbal harassment that has no other effect on its recipient than to create an unpleasant working environment."[45] Some critics, for example, Ellen Frankel Paul, a philosopher at the Social Philosophy and Policy Center at Bowling Green State University, even suggest that "a new tort of sexual harassment would handle [hostile environment] cases better. Only instances above a certain threshold of egregiousness or outrageousness would be actionable."[46] Naomi Levine, a Canadian lawyer, international sexual harassment consultant, and sexual harassment officer at the University of Winnipeg, has suggested that universities move toward "respectful workplace" policies rather than sexual harassment policies and points out that many legal remedies already exist within the law for combating sexual harassment that may in fact be more productive than EEOC investigations and prosecutions.[47] The question that remains, then, is: who is right? The arguments for and against campus hate speech regulations are now before us. A wide variety of hate speech incidents, histories, legal cases and decisions, and moral arguments have been introduced to assist us in judging the plausibility of various claims. Clearly, no policy will please everyone or satisfy every desirable criterion. Advocates do not agree on what the policies should say or what justifies them. Critics disagree about what speech is outside First Amendment protection and how various free speech doctrines apply in specific cases. What sense can be made of this chaos? In the next chapter, I summarize my findings and offer my own suggestions for you to consider.

# And the Verdict Is . . .

*Which matters are to be punished? Malfeasance and misfeasance, of course. Violence
and vandalism, certainly. But not heterodox opinions. The campus has no need for
policement of prejudice. Universities should confront offensive ideas by rebuttal, not by
suppression. John Milton, John Stuart Mill, and Oliver Wendell Holmes had it
right: truth doesn't need a stacked deck to be victorious.*

MARTIN GRUBERG, "How Should Campuses
Respond to Expressions Which Demean?"[1]

## HATE SPEECH LESSONS

The main theme of this book has been that campus hate speech (and its regulation) has been on trial both figuratively and literally in recent years. A wide
variety of campus hate speech codes have been proposed, debated, adopted,
and enforced, and in some cases legally challenged. Those who advocate campus speech codes appeal to important constitutional and moral values concerning racial and sexual equality and try to minimize the impact of their proposed
restrictions on campus speech, at least on the speech they think worthy of First
Amendment protection. On the other hand, those who criticize campus speech
codes appeal to different, yet also important, constitutional and moral values
concerning freedom of speech and expression and try to undermine speech
codes by pointing out their weaknesses and dangers.

In reaching a "verdict," one should be mindful of the importance of this
"trial" and its outcome. Its importance should be manifest to those in academia: we are the ones whose speech will be governed by any policy that is
adopted and enforced. But the "trial" and its outcome have significance outside
the academy as well. For example, if group libel defenders of campus speech
codes are correct about the justification for speech regulation, those same justifications may well apply to speech on the job, in the political arena, in the

movie theater, and so on. If Catharine MacKinnon is right about the egalitarian basis of speech restriction, not only would campus hate speech codes be justified, so too would bans on hard- and soft-core pornography (which is, in fact, her main concern in *Only Words*). On the other hand, if Kingsley Browne and the editors at the *New Republic* are correct, then hostile environment regulations would have to be dropped from the workplace as well as the campus. Edward J. Cleary was right: how we deal with hate speech helps define us as a nation. Hate speech is not a conceptually or practically isolated issue. What we decide here has ramifications for many other areas of our lives. Leon Friedman, a professor of civil liberties at Hofstra University and participant in a major academic conference on campus hate speech regulation, writes, "What is at stake is not merely a very significant constitutional law question—perhaps, indeed, the most important issue under our Constitution—but a crucial choice about how our society should be governed and how groups in our pluralistic society should confront and relate to one another."[2]

So what is the outcome? Where do things stand? I begin by suggesting five lessons we can draw from this study of campus hate speech codes.

First, the most plausible (and today most frequently used) basis for regulating campus hate speech is the Title VII hostile environment harassment approach. As we saw in Chapter 4, courts have repeatedly struck down both broad (as in the Michigan case) and narrow (as in the Stanford case) speech codes and regularly found for plaintiffs even in the absence of codes (as in the GMU case) when they are defended on fighting words, the intentional infliction of emotional distress, or group libel grounds, or a combination of those approaches, when they face First Amendment challenges. Since courts have upheld some university restrictions on speech based in hostile environment law (though not student codes per se), advocates continue to lobby on its behalf, while the other approaches wane.

It is worth noting that this basis for speech regulation is grounded in a liberal, individualistic conception of the community and rights rather than a "communitarian" conception of community and group rights. Many, though certainly not all, advocates of broad campus hate speech codes appeal to a moral and political communitarianism developed and defended by a group of scholars and activists[3] to ground their restrictions on speech; they frequently portray the campus as needing to be some kind of idyllic community, with uniform values held by equals in an atmosphere of civility and mutual respect.[4] This turn to communitarianism is not surprising, given the lack of success advocates of campus speech regulation had from an individualistic basis; however, communitarian attacks on individual rights (which the traditional view of free speech rests upon) that focus on the impact of policies on a social group as a "whole" (e.g., the impact of hate speech on blacks as a group of "second-class" citizens) must be viewed with considerable skepticism for several reasons.

First, communitarians (and those who adopt their rhetoric) have failed to clarify adequately the kind of community they are asking us to uphold. Kent Greenawalt identifies four lines of division among communitarian thinkers: (1) conservatives (dedicated to preserving traditional community values and practices) versus radicals (dedicated to upending traditional community values and practices), (2) nationalists (dedicated to federally enforced standards) versus localists (dedicated to local autonomy), (3) communitarians focused on the political community versus those who focus on some other community (church, clubs, unions, etc.), and (4) those who value community for its own sake versus those who value community because it nurtures individuals.[5] Again, Robert Post identifies three different views of the educational community: the "civic" ideal, in which the university stands as an instrument of community life and in which racist speech might be outlawed as uncivil and contrary to "shared" values; the "democratic" ideal, in which the university is to create autonomous citizens capable of fully participating in the rough-and-tumble world of public discourse; and the "critical" ideal, in which the university is simply to discover and disseminate knowledge through the unfettered pursuit of truth.[6] Until and unless advocates of campus speech codes clarify and defend their view of community, we cannot assess accurately the strengths and weaknesses of their community ideals in comparison to the individualist ideals currently dominating the academy.

Second, many communitarian criticisms do not hit home, and still others can be accommodated within a liberal framework.[7] Even Charles Taylor, one of the communitarians, has pointed out that communitarians and liberals are talking past one another on many issues.[8] Thus, when Charles Lawrence advocates universities without "masters and slaves" and Cass Sunstein defends a university community without "castes" and Laura Lederer and Richard Delgado call for a national town meeting (which they claim individualist free speechers oppose), they are merely pushing over straw men. But the biggest problem is that the communitarian ideal has never existed except at the expense of others, usually the very sorts of marginalized groups that speech code advocates want to protect. Derek Phillips has argued convincingly that (1) the realization of the communitarian ideal requires a common territory, a common history and shared values, participation in common activities, and solidarity (social interdependence and a feeling of belonging together), (2) these conditions have rarely been met (probably only in ancient Athens), and (3) the realization of these conditions is possible only through the exclusion of large numbers of people (unpropertied males, women, children, slaves, etc.).[9] This is clearly not the kind of community campus egalitarians seek. Again, Stephen Holmes points out that egalitarians should find little appealing about the communitarian ideal since (1) it is the ideology of anti-egalitarians, Nazis, and fascists and (2) the greatest threat to healthy communities arises not from individualism and its protection of individual rights but from collective passions, ideological conflict, and inherited rivalries between hostile factions.[10] In sum, campus speech code advocates who urge us to abandon or curtail well-defined individual rights to freedom of speech in favor of nebulous group rights and group-think fail to make their case. Advocates of campus hate speech codes are more likely to succeed in justifying their policies from an individualistic, rather than communitarian, perspective.

The second lesson is that an individualistic, rights-based Title VII hostile environment approach faces serious difficulties too. Courts have found it inappropriate for student speech in general (as in the Wisconsin case) and overbroad and unduly vague in regulating faculty speech (the Central Michigan and San Bernardino cases). Even defenders of campus speech codes have begun to recognize this flaw. John Wilson, for example, admits in his 1995 analysis that "some speech codes are badly written and others are badly enforced."[11] A study of the twenty largest public universities by Richard Kirk Page and Kay Hartwell Hunnicutt revealed that eight of the ten universities that had explicit speech regulations violated one or more of the thirty salient constitutional principles.[12] They conclude that

> until a new jurisprudence becomes more pervasive in the courts, rather than only in law schools . . . none of these laws can be applied readily to general harassment on campus. However, this change is not likely to occur without significant changes in the United States Constitution or the Supreme Court's interpretation of the Constitution. Until the law so changes, university administrators must work within established judicial guidelines to control harassment, taking into consideration the principles identified by the courts before adopting a policy that may impinge on speech.[13]

In other words, strict scrutiny of a campus hate speech code reveals clear violations of constitutional guarantees that courts will not abide. Robert Sedler, legal counsel for the plaintiffs in the *Doe* case, predicted in the wake of *R.A.V.* that any public university speech code challenged in court is likely to be declared unconstitutional.[14] So too Kent Greenawalt, one of our leading First Amendment scholars, and Tom Foley, the Ramsey County prosecutor who argued on St. Paul's behalf in the *R.A.V.* case, suggest that the *R.A.V.* majority may well have reached out the way it did partly in order to indicate disapproval of campus speech codes.[15] Their hypothesis appears to have been confirmed in the Central Michigan, Stanford, and San Bernardino cases.

Is it possible for advocates to develop a hostile environment speech code that avoids these problems?

The problem is that the hostile environment standard has not been defined with sufficient and defensible precision to provide people with fair notice. As we saw in Chapters 5 and 6, advocates and judges propose and apply very different standards. The "chaotic" condition of hostile environment law and its enforcement does not bode well for free and open discourse on campuses. The U.S. Supreme Court recognized forty years ago that

> the essentiality of freedom in the community of American universities is almost self-evident. No one should underestimate the vital role in a democracy that is played by those who guide and train our youth. To impose any strait jacket upon the intellectual leaders in our colleges and universities would imperil the future of our nation. . . . Scholarship cannot flourish in an atmosphere of suspicion and distrust. Teachers and students must always remain free to inquire, to study and to evaluate, to gain new maturity and understanding; otherwise our civilization will stagnate and die.[16]

The difficulties inherent in defining "words that wound" should persuade us to tread slowly. Thomas Emerson served us notice in his 1966 statement of the traditional ideal of free speech when he discussed the gap between the words prohibited and the harm caused.[17] Campus speech regulations seek to prevent and punish harms based on membership in protected classifications, but given the gap between words and their effects, the regulation will apply to expressions that do not cause harm as well as those that do. Many examples discussed in this book point directly to this fact. Blacklisting "hostile" or "abusive" words won't end bigoted attitudes or actions. And even in those cases where identifiable harm is caused, that harm has to be weighed against the benefits to the individual and society of permitting expression of offensive ideas. A strong commitment to free speech enables us to confront and combat, and in some cases correct, wrongheaded ideas; it reinforces the importance of tolerance in a pluralistic society; it reinforces the legitimacy and participatory nature of our constitutional democracy; it constrains the power of government and government agents to run our lives and force opinions on us; and more. Legal suppression of hostile environment hate speech on campuses will not empower minorities and women as much as will teaching people to value equality; to value racial, sexual, ethnic, religious "diversity"; to respond to hateful words with effective counterspeech. Robert O'Neil, director of the Thomas Jefferson Center for the Protection of Free Speech at the University of Virginia, writes:

> A faculty and administration that loudly condemn racial caricature and ethnic slur do not abridge a student's freedom of speech. An educational program, whether optional or required, designed to increase tolerance and eliminate bigotry, enhances free expression and inquiry. Inviting formal complaints from people aggrieved by demeaning speech violates no civil liberty as long as punishment reaches only conduct, not thought or words.[18]

The courts and critics have pointed out that punitive codes—whether grounded in fighting words or group defamation or hostile environment—are not necessary to advancing the interests of equality. To paraphrase Justice Scalia, universities have reasonable means at their disposal to fight incendiary speech without adding the First Amendment to the fire. To those who object on the grounds that university condemnations lacking sanctions are "mere" words, unable to affect bigots, we must point out if a university's speech is powerless, then so too is a bigot's. On the other hand, if the bigot's speech can effect harm, then so too must a university's speech be capable of good. There is no reason to suppose that only the speech of bigots has effects. To those who object that this leaves us out of the Western consensus supporting speech regulation, we must point out that Canadian and British anti-obscenity and hate speech rules have been used to punish the groups that egalitarian speech code advocates seek to protect. To those who object that official tolerance of hate speech amounts to endorsing it, we must point out that official tolerance of all kinds of dissident speech has not been seen as any kind of implicit endorsement. Do hate speech code advocates worry that our government is Communist because it permits university professors to defend Marx in the classroom? Do they suppose that our government is really anarchist because it permits anarchists to speak freely? Do they suppose our government supports right-wing militia groups because it allows them to publish their views?

Do you see now the contradiction this objection leads to?

Our third lesson is that campus speech regulations (whether Title VII–like or otherwise) are too often administered and enforced by individuals or groups whose institutional role is not to protect speech but to enforce personal opinions or a group-think ideology. It made no difference to the affirmative action officer at Central Michigan that the coach used the term and players heard his use of the term "nigger" in a positive manner. She knew better than they the harms of this word. It made no difference to the committee at New Hampshire that Silva was using an example also employed by Hemingway and other literary types to illustrate what a metaphor is. All they needed was a complaint to convict him. The list of abuses could go on, but what is more important to recognize, as Thomas Emerson did in his 1966 study of free speech, is that the apparatus of the administration and enforcement of speech regulations tends to encourage overzealousness as a means of career advancement and that even unsuccessful prosecution has a chilling effect on speech.[19] This is evident, Emerson points out, in every period of suppression: the Alien and Sedition Acts, local laws in the eighteenth and nineteenth centuries, the aftermath of World War I, and the McCarthy Era. What may begin as a well-intentioned effort to prevent harm can quickly become a weapon of speech czars. The only effective way to control a potential speech czar is to place strict limitations on speech regulations and have them administered by accountable and knowledgeable individuals or committees.

Our fourth lesson is that freedom of speech really is our first freedom and the greatest ally of equality. Pick your favorite dissident group pushing for its conception of equality—early 1900s labor union activists, 1960s civil rights advocates, 1970s Vietnam War protesters, animal rights extremists, radical feminists, liberation theologists, gay and lesbian studies advocates, Afrocentrists, anti–affirmative actionists, or any other group—and ask yourself whether or not the speech of members of such a group can create a "hostile" or "abusive" environment on the basis of race, color, sex, religion, and the like. Obviously, their speech can. In fact, civil rights demonstrators and anti-war demonstrators were arrested for inciting segregationists and "hawks" (even police) to violence. This is no mere historical curiosity. Complaints of hostile environment have been filed against professors who attack heterosexuality (e.g., in Texas) and universities that promote a gay and lesbian "agenda" (e.g., in Iowa). Without the right to use speech considered offensive, even abusive or harmful, by others, egalitarians of varying stripes will find their own speech subject to the same suppressive apparatus as anti-egalitarians. Equality needs free speech, and not just polite, sophisticated academic discourse; it needs Malcolm X, Lenny Bruce, Wayne Dick, and Archie Bunker.

It is true, as Richard Delgado has pointed out, that many such dissident groups also broke the law, sometimes conscientiously as a form of civil disobedience, to further their egalitarian agendas, and that sometimes the doctrines of free speech were used against them. But it doesn't follow that free speech is their enemy or that these causes would have been as successful as they were (or even more successful) in the absence of strong free speech protections. Martin Luther King Jr.'s letter from the Birmingham jail became a beacon for change when published in the mainstream press, and the historic March on Washington was able to go off as successfully as it did because of free speech rights. The ultimate "right" is not the right to peace (as Kenneth Lasson claims), for peace means little without a guarantee that if your peace is disturbed you will be able to voice opposition to its infringement.[20]

And our fifth and final lesson to be noted here is that universities should be bastions, not bastardizers, of free speech. The mission of a university is to disseminate ideas. This mission requires them to regulate ideas, as Cass Sunstein and many others have pointed out, by controlling classroom discussion in some ways (though not in any old way at all); by evaluating ideas in grading, hiring, and promotion, and so on (in accordance with standards of professional competence); and even by assessing professional competence (in accordance with consensus judgments). And part of this mission is to promote the (contested) ideal of equality. But, as the courts have repeatedly pointed out, promoting equality does not require speech codes when there are less restrictive means available. Free speech is special on the campus. The campus, of all places, is where ideas and lifestyles are explored and debated. Free speech near-absolutism is needed in a place where the good life must be pondered over and experimented upon, in a place where ideas must be discussed that will cause some people to be deeply offended. Free speech near-absolutism is needed in a community that values individual autonomy, that values "experiments in living" (to borrow a phrase from Robert Ladenson).[21] It is of more than passing interest that the psychologist whose work Delgado repeatedly cites to support his speech regulations, namely, Gordon Allport, surveys the efficacy of laws in dealing with racism and prejudice and concludes—contra Delgado—that they are best fought through restrictions on behavior, through education, and through the free flow of ideas, not through the restraint of speech.[22]

These five lessons imply great caution in the matter of campus hate speech codes and create a general presumption against campus hate speech regulation. Still, an important problem remains. As noted earlier, critics from every perspective, ranging from civil libertarians like former ACLU director Nadine Strossen and Nat Hentoff to conservative journalists like George Will and Dinesh D'Souza, accept restrictions on campus speech when it constitutes something more than mere "verbal harassment." Even Kingsley Browne, one of the most ardent critics of hostile environment harassment, admits that

> a conclusion that the current definition of hostile-environment harassment is unconstitutional does not sound the death knell for hostile environment theory. The truly egregious cases, such as *Hall v. Gus Construction Co.*,[23] will remain unaffected, because they typically rely little

on protected expression. Moreover, the analysis presented here does not impair the strength of hostile environment cases based upon unwanted sexual touching. Only the ability of a plaintiff to make out a hostile-environment case based [solely] upon expression is substantially affected.[24]

The problem we all face, then, is this: in the absence of any consensus or clear guidelines about what constitutes "something more than mere verbal harassment," universities are left between the proverbial Scylla and Charybdis. On the one hand, courts require universities to have policies on and punish those who create a hostile environment, on pain of an award of damages for engaging in (or permitting) sexual or racial discrimination. In order to protect themselves from lawsuits (and further their interest in equality, appease strident interest groups, etc.), universities have strong incentive to adopt and enforce broad speech policies. For example, Daphne Patai reports that in 1995 at the University of Massachusetts at Amherst, an "ombudsperson" speaking at a department meeting identified "leering, explicit jokes, offensive remarks and posters" as examples of hostile environment harassment and announced a new category of harassment called "general environmental harassment," which includes demeaning remarks, mean-spirited comments, and insensitive criticisms not related to race or gender.[25] Yet, on the other hand, courts require universities to protect "offensive" speech on pain of an award of damages for violating the First Amendment. In order to protect themselves from lawsuits (and further their interest in free speech, etc.), universities have strong incentive to respond to offensive speech with educative and counterspeech measures rather than punitive ones. So what are universities to do? By all appearances they are, in effect, damned if they do regulate hate speech and damned if they don't regulate hate speech. Courts have been willing to strike down hostile environment regulations at Central Michigan University and San Bernardino Valley College but have not offered anything in their place. How can, how should, a university distinguish genuine harassment from mere offensiveness?

## A MODEST PROPOSAL

In the present state of the art, there is no satisfying resolution to this dilemma. There simply is no philosophical, legal, political, or social scientific standard or standards that will put the issue to rest. But assuming the five lessons I drew in the previous section are on the right track, I propose the following framework.

First, universities should begin by recognizing that formal proceedings accompanied by sanctions (whether mandatory "reeducation" seminars, required apologies, suspensions, expulsions, etc.) must be a small part of the overall effort to ensure equal opportunity. If a university genuinely hopes to make progress in the fight for equality, it must focus on educational and economic measures. The sanctions imposed by a speech code, as even advocates realize, will do little by themselves to foster a concern for equality and respect for racial, religious, gender, and ethnic differences. Which is more effective in the long run: developing grassroots support for racial equality at Central Michigan or having a speech czar dictate that the word "nigger" cannot possibly have a positive meaning? A proactive educational and economic stance should yield better results in the long term than a reactive, punitive stance.

In fact, the short-term thinking represented by acceptance of makeshift punitive speech codes should be replaced by long-term thinking aiming at educating not just students, but the American population in general. Higher education has not been very successful at this, and it appears that the growing gap between higher education and the rest of society enabled some opportunists to mount a powerful attack on higher education in the 1990s. Too often these opportunists are able to exploit the fracture among university personnel caused by the hate speech debate and cast the privileged as browbeaten underdogs on American campuses. Universities must make stronger efforts to teach all Americans to understand and appreciate both equality and free speech. Instead of paying J. Donald Silva and his lawyers $230,000 for an illegal hostile environment prosecution, the University of New Hampshire could have funded a number of campus educational forums, community outreach programs, scholarships for minorities or women or the financially needy, and the like.

Second, universities should charge those responsible for enforcing any speech policy with scrupulously protecting free speech rights and not merely with vigorously promoting equality. This means, among other things, that universities must ensure that due process rights are protected. Proponents of equality will simply continue to draw the fire of many who would be their allies if they continue to encourage double standards, the presumption that the accused are guilty the moment a complaint is filed and the belief that consensual sex is "really" coerced or otherwise involuntary. An affirmative action officer, who typically has little or no training in free speech law or academic freedom, is probably not the best person to enforce a speech policy. Universities will continue to get hammered in the courts if their affirmative action officers and presidents go before the court and admit they have no principled way to distinguish illegal verbal harassment from merely offensive words, as in the Michigan and Central Michigan cases. Hopeful appeals to Title VII law will not help them escape this embarrassment. The trouble is, of course, that Title VII law is not settled: universities have no clear-cut paradigm on which to rest a hostile environment standard.

It is by virtue of this fact that I suggest, thirdly, that universities design policies that focus on conduct, not speech. In trying to get students to be more tolerant of different cultures and ideas, we set a poor example when we fail to tolerate different cultures and ideas! We must tolerate ideas that we hate (to paraphrase Justice Holmes), but we need not tolerate conduct that violates clear-cut rights. Mary Ellen Gale fails to recognize this point when she applies her Title VII–like code to various examples. Although I agree with her about the cases involving protected speech, including the demonstrations of a white supremacy group, the Beethoven poster, the tearing down of the poster, and the classroom discussion of theories positing sex- and race-based biological differences (they are all protected speech that can—and should—be addressed through education and counterspeech), we analyze her unprotected cases (numbers 5 through 8) differently. We both view cases 5 through 7 as subject to sanctions, although I would recommend formal proceedings not because of the discriminatory message, but because of the illegal conduct, and add that in accordance with *Wisconsin v. Mitchell*, universities can enhance penalties for illegal conduct when it is motivated by racial or sexual bias.[26] Case 5 (the case in which students invade a dorm room and write racist messages on a bathroom mirror) involves trespass and vandalism; case 6 (in which male students follow a female student around campus and threaten her with sexual assault) constitutes assault or stalking; and case 7 (in which a fraternity subjects a student to public ridicule) might well be acted on as a tort of emotional distress or libel. The discriminatory attitudes evidenced in these cases are offensive and should be combated through education and counterspeech, but the attitudes and the expression of those attitudes (in certain conditions) should not be held illegal. The illegality in these cases stems from their violation of rights to property, physical safety, and privacy. Compare: it is not illegal to desire a rich man's property; it is illegal to steal a rich man's property; and depicting or advocating the forcible confiscation of a rich man's property is regulated (e.g., a Communist's "manifesto" is protected speech, whereas a rioter's call to storm the fences is not: the difference, roughly speaking, is in the targeted nature and the harm caused). Again. it is not illegal to desire to have sex with a minor; it is illegal to engage in sex with minors; and depicting or advocating sex with minors is subject to regulation (e.g., novels and news reports generally are protected, whereas photographs of sex with minors are not: the difference, roughly speaking, is in the targeted nature and the harm caused). Ideas in and of themselves, however hateful, are protected; actions are not; and the expression of the idea is regulable under certain narrowly defined conditions.

The "accepted" view of free speech described in Chapter 4 still is, in spite of its many recent critics, the predominant view—as the six hate speech cases in Chapter 4 demonstrate. The line demarcating speech and conduct is not set in stone, but to abandon this distinction—that is, to treat all speech as conduct and all conduct as speech—is nonsensical. Since the First Amendment protects speech, if all conduct is really speech, then all conduct would be protected; yet, if all speech is really conduct, then the First Amendment protects nothing. The First Amendment becomes meaningless in either case. Edward Eberle notes in his analysis of *R.A.V.* that

> the difference between speech and conduct, sometimes stark, sometimes obscure, marks the emerging frontier of public discourse jurisprudence. Since one can view all words as "simultaneously communication and social action," the distinction between speech and conduct may be less intuitive than it seems. Still . . . in the end, we must make sense of our world. Thus, in First Amendment law, even though "every idea is an incitement to action," the Court ultimately has wisely decided that "the line between what is permissible and not subject to control and what may be subject to regulation is the line between ideas and overt acts."[27]

Thus it is that courts, in spite of their sympathy with the victims of hate speech and their acceptance of the goal of equality (conservative critics of equality correctly point out that equality has been and is enforced mostly by the judiciary), have not been convinced by the arguments of campus speech code advocates. Judge Cohn in *Doe*: "While the court is sympathetic to the University's obligation to ensure equal educational opportunities for all students, such efforts must not be at the expense of free speech."[28] Judge Warren in *UWM-Post*: "The problems of bigotry and discrimination sought to be addressed here are real and truly corrosive of the educational environment. But freedom of speech is almost absolute in our land."[29] And Justice Scalia in *R.A.V.*: "Let there be no mistake about our belief that burning a cross in someone's yard is reprehensible. But St. Paul has sufficient means at its disposal to prevent such behavior without adding the First Amendment to the fire."[30]

Nor should the courts be convinced by the arguments of campus speech code advocates. The first thing to suffer in American society when greater speech restrictions are accepted will be the effort to attain equality. The powers that be in society at large have little interest in greater equality. It does not take a lot of insight to see that enforcers of the status quo will turn any speech restrictions to their advantage. If egalitarians fear that anti-egalitarians have too loud a voice today, wait until broader speech restrictions are adopted. I have little doubt the speech of feminists, including Catharine MacKinnon, critical race theorists, homosexuals, "revisionist" historians, and other social critics will fare considerably worse if the doors are opened to greater censorship of ideas and their expression.

I am not suggesting that universities do not or should not regulate any speech. In fact, no one I know involved in the debate holds that position. I agree with Mary Becker that

> the boundaries of every academic conversation, as well as many assessments of academic quality, turn on questions of content, viewpoint, and ideology. More pointedly, unspoken rules and understandings about what speech is high quality permeate university life—and these turn on content and viewpoint. These assessments, grounded as they inevitably are in traditional notions of what a discipline is about, what counts as "truth," and what methods are valuable, hurt many newcomers to the university communities. . . . Indeed the value of their speech could lie precisely in its divergence from university standards. . . . Yet no court would entertain a constitutional challenge [to these speech regulations] under the free speech clause.[31]

The question is: why are these speech regulations permissible (generally speaking) while hate speech regulations are not permissible (generally speaking)? Becker maintains that it is purely a matter of tradition, but her analysis is too quick. The differences between the "regulations" she mentions and hate speech regulations are not obvious when you lump everything together; but when you examine them individually, relevant differences begin to appear. For example, although it is not hard to see how a university could avoid enforcing hate speech rules, it is impossible to see how a university could avoid any content or viewpoint judgments in hiring and firing decisions. Courts have balked at enforcing campus hate speech codes because there are other reasonable avenues (in particular, educational ones) for dealing with it. What is the alternative to hiring and firing on some kind of content and viewpoint? Even the most lazy and incompetent person could claim wrongful firing because the university would simply be "prejudiced" against the lazy and incompetent viewpoint. Should the university strive for neutrality in its hiring and firing decisions by using a coin? Heads you're hired, tails you're fired? That's not even neutral, I guess, because it is "dualistic" and punishes those who have a more pluralistic viewpoint. Is not being hired for a job because of content (they need a medievalist, he's a Far East scholar) really comparable to being suspended because one compares homosexuality to bestiality? Is Becker utterly ignoring academic freedom, the right of the professor to determine within professional standards which course materials are most appropriate, the right of a law school to hire more critical race theorists than racists? The freedom she implicitly attacks is the very freedom that enables her to publish her article in a book, attend academically sponsored conferences on her favored topics, and so on. Is Becker failing to address the distinctions Scalia makes when he addresses content-neutrality in *R.A.V.?*

Becker's argument takes an even more serious turn for the worse when she begins to attack binding judicial review (the right of courts to strike down legislation as unconstitutional without any recourse for the legislature to overturn the court's decision by, e.g., a supermajority vote).[32] Her reasoning is this: since the supporters of hate speech regulation have failed to convince judges of the justness of their cause, they should undermine the judge's ability to make binding law and work through legislatures to enact their hate speech codes. It is a turn for the worse for an obvious reason: if binding judicial review is undermined and legislatures are free to enact majoritarian desires, is it likely that the majority will enact the desires of critical race theorists, academic feminists, gay and lesbian radicals? To suppose this cuts against the very foundation of those views, in which each group sees itself as a victim of widespread social oppression. What is much more likely is that the backlash against egalitarians would be even more fierce—consider, for example, what has been happening with affirmative action in recent years. Those who regard it as an essential component of greater social equality do not have any majority willing to support them. Ira Glasser has put the point more succinctly:

> The attempt by minorities of any kind—racial, political, religious, sexual—to pass legal restrictions on speech creates a self-constructed trap. It is a trap because politically once you have such a restriction in place the most important questions to ask are: Who is going to enforce them? Who is going to interpret what they mean? Who is going to decide whom to target? The answer is: those in power. And what possible reason do minorities have to trust those in power?[33]

This is not to suggest that egalitarians should not try to influence legislators, city council representatives, and other officials. Rather, it is to say that they shouldn't put all their eggs in one basket. The best hope for egalitarians is education, political agitation, and recourse to the courts to enforce constitutional guarantees when necessary. To attack judicial review as a whole because it fails to deliver one desired outcome is shortsighted in ignoring the host of desirable outcomes it has delivered and continues to deliver. Becker's argument reveals the (implausible) lengths to which advocates of broad campus hate speech codes will go to attain their ends and shows in yet another way how some "liberal" advocates of broad campus speech codes draw upon old-line "conservative" arguments.[34] Thus, rather than put all speech restrictions into one basket or attack judicial review as Becker does in order to push for a broad hate speech code, I suggest that universities regulate only hate speech that targets a specific individual or individuals in a captive-audience context (regardless of the race, gender, religions, etc., of the speaker and hearer), is intended to cause harm to that individual or individuals, is clearly unrelated to any legitimate academic purpose, and is repeated (or, in an individual instance, sufficiently egregious) or done in conjunction with illegal conduct. Speech code advocates get a lot of mileage out of discussing cases that involve conduct violations. They characteristically mix in violent conduct with wounding words. But illegal conduct is not at issue in the hate speech debate. The hate speech debate cases strictly speaking involve only pure speech incidents. And those should be narrowly defined. Thus, a male student who yells "nice tits" to a female student across an open-air campus area (as in one of the Wisconsin cases) should not be hauled before a speech czar to face formal discipline, even if he intended to embarrass rather than compliment her. Instead, the woman, friends, and bystanders should express their disapproval of the remark. Resident directors should hold open forums to discuss the incident. Faculty should bring it up in relevant courses. Interested parties should write letters to the campus newspaper to express their opinions about the incident. The student newspaper, the faculty senate, the university president can voice an opinion. The ways this comment can be informally dealt with are limited only by the imagination. On the other hand, a male student who says "nice tits," "I want to fuck you," and other sexually explicit remarks to a female student every time he sees her before and after class, even after she has made clear that this attention is unwanted and has taken reasonable steps to avoid his harassment, and who is in fact interfering with her academic progress should be subject to some kind of sanctions. Targeted, intentional, repeated verbal abuse serving no legitimate academic purpose is identifiable, and its regulation is consistent with controlling court decisions.

A policy focused on conduct and targeted, intentional, repeated verbal abuse is unlikely to have any chilling effect on legitimate speech. Students should not have a hard time recognizing the difference between (a) vigorous, even heated, debates over sexual orientation, affirmative action, racism, welfare, belief in God, and other issues and (b) targeted, intentional, repeated verbal abuse. They will be free to pin up posters and invite onto campus speakers that other groups find highly offensive; but they will not be free to threaten or "feel up" people.

Faculty should not have a hard time recognizing the difference between (a) using a sexual example in a philosophy class to explain Plato's or J. S. Mill's distinction between qualitatively superior and inferior pleasures[35] and (b) using non-course-related sexual jokes and banter to discourage women from taking or succeeding in a required chemistry course. Faculty should be free to champion ideas hated by others and vigorously attack views cherished by others; but they should not be free to conduct campaigns of terror or intimidation or bar students from the classroom simply because the student disagrees with the professor's opinion, for example, that lesbians make the best parents.[36] Some extremists, perhaps Kingsley Browne, may object that my policy permits punishment of pure speech without any "conduct" elements. In assessing this objection, we must be cognizant of two points. First, regardless of my opinion or the extremist's opinion or anyone else's opinion about the punishment of pure speech without any conduct elements under the hostile environment standard, the Supreme Court's ruling in *Harris* permits this and is, at least for now, controlling precedent. Egregious pure speech cases must be dealt with by universities on pain of civil damages, at least in employment contexts. Second, the regulation of pure speech without any conduct elements accepted by the Court in *Harris* is essentially correct (even Antonin Scalia accepted the Court's position that conduct elements are not necessary where the speech is sufficiently egregious). The reason for this is that through the interpretation of our Constitution in dozens of court cases and enactment of many federal, state, county, and city laws, we have decided that an individual's equality rights and interests are important enough to his or her life prospects to deserve protection. The fact that the philosophical basis for this collective decision is not settled (nor ever likely to be settled) is not particularly troublesome to pragmatically minded folk, since the reality is that equality in the workplace is shaped by speech and not just by conduct, and any public policy that denies that is unrealistic. It doesn't follow, of course, that broad regulation of speech is therefore justified, since our speech interests must be attended to as well.

To my mind, the problem with *Harris* is not that it allows for regulation of pure speech in egregious cases; rather, it is the problem that Scalia notes in his separate concurrence: the Court needs to set clearer guidelines in place to help us distinguish legitimate from illegitimate claims of hostile environment. The task of clarifying these guidelines is what I have begun in this book in general and in this chapter in particular. For example, such policies must be content-neutral and provide enough clarity to avoid (minimize?) arbitrary enforcement. My policy is content-neutral in applying to all harassing speech, not merely such speech as applied to certain protected classes, and is unlikely to be arbitrarily enforced if monitored by a diverse committee governed by due process guidelines and educated in free speech doctrine. Campus policies and enforcement must be sensitive to these and many other concerns outlined in this book: captive-audience contexts, fair notice, due process, and more. I think Linda Seebach said it well: "Universities need to have harassment policies, of course, but they also need the backbone to tell complainants, gently but firmly, when they don't have a case."[37]

If the five lessons I have drawn are substantially correct, those who advocate a more restrictive or less restrictive code than the one I propose here have a heavy burden of argument to bear. A more restrictive code will run afoul of established free speech doctrines, and a less restrictive code will run afoul of established equality doctrines. It will be my pleasure, of course, to refine and correct this proposal in light of future developments.[38] One of the difficulties in taking a position in this debate is seeing clearly where the agreements and disagreements are, given how much the two sides seem to talk past one another. Yet there is perhaps less disagreement than one might suppose. Tom Foley, the Ramsey County prosecutor who argued on St. Paul's behalf in the *R.A.V.* case, later commented, "My position was that most speech is protected, but that if speech reaches the criminal threshold it is not. For instance, if the skinheads in *R.A.V.* had decided to march down the street in a parade burning a cross, I would have reluctantly agreed with the majority that this was protected speech. I argued that if there is a threat to a particular individual, then it is not protected."[39] I agree—and would add that R.A.V. was charged by the Justice Department under different statutes, convicted, and required to serve two years in a juvenile workhouse for his crime, not his speech. We must take hate crimes seriously and not dismiss all cases as innocuous pranks or overactive hormones or mere ignorance or isolated incidents. Howard Erlich and others have done extensive research documenting ethnoviolence. This plague must be addressed, and universities should not hesitate to impose available sanctions on hate criminals. We should also take hate speech seriously and not dismiss it as mere pranks, overactive hormones, or the like either. Universities should not hesitate to deal with serious hate speakers and provide solid educational strategies for fostering understanding. What they must not do is commit blunders that end up trivializing real harassment.

Before concluding, I want to address the criticism that my proposal is contradictory. On the one hand, I criticize speech codes and the hostile environment standard in drawing my "lessons," while on the other hand, I advocate a hostile environment speech code in my modest proposal. What gives? What gives is the contradiction. There is no contradiction in accepting two competing values (in this case, freedom and equality) and attempting to find a workable balance between them.[40] In fact, this is the very dilemma we all face in the hate speech debate, which I have tried to point out through this whole book—the tension all participants in the debate are faced with. Accepting the two propositions "freedom of speech is an important value" and "equality of opportunity is an important value" is not contradictory since there can be two important values, and rejecting broad campus speech codes while accepting a narrow one is not contradictory since there are clear reasons to reject the former but embrace the latter. The criticisms of speech codes and the hostile environment standard I endorse are not so weighty as to rule out every possible speech regulation. If they were, we would have to abandon all speech regulations, including those on child pornography, bribery, quid pro quo harassment, and such; and no serious participant in the hate speech debate believes all speech regulations must go. The criticisms are, however, weighty enough to require the careful qualifications I have outlined above. Rather than get caught up in debate about logical consistency here, we ought to focus on the relative value of the competing ideals and search for practical ways to resolve the tensions between them. This is what public policy analysis essentially is.

## CONCLUSION

In this chapter I have presented and briefly defended my own conclusions regarding campus hate speech codes through five lessons that emerge from the debate and a proposal for what hate speech a university ought to address with sanctions. The first lesson is that Title VII–like hostile environment harassment rules offer the most promising approach for universities to regulate campus hate speech. The second lesson is that despite this promise, the hostile environment approach faces serious issues that limit its appropriateness and effectiveness. To further the goal of equal opportunity, universities would do well to focus on educational and economic tactics and reforms rather than speech codes. The third lesson is that campus speech regulations need to be created and enforced by people who have the right training, knowledge, and skills to do so. Who enforces the rules is just as important, perhaps more important, than what the rules are. The fourth lesson is that freedom of speech has proven itself to be a more reliable asset than a liability to those who advocate equal opportunity and equal rights. The final lesson is that the primary mission of universities to create and disseminate knowledge is fundamentally at odds with broad campus speech regulations. In view of these lessons, I propose that universities design policies that focus on conduct rather than speech, limiting their speech restrictions to appropriately narrow and recognized legal categories, in particular, targeted, intentional, repeated, or egregious verbal abuse that lacks academic justification.

Although this is where my analysis and argumentation ended in the first edition of this book, the debate has not ended. New incidents and legal cases have arisen. New authors and arguments have entered the fray. Old arguments have been reworked. In the next chapter, I discuss the major additions to the debate over campus speech codes, deepening the reader's understanding of the issue and further defending the conclusions proposed in this chapter.

# 8

# The Debate: 1998–2008

*... it is conceivable that the goals and policies of a university, e.g., to promote respectful and reasoned discourse on issues of the moment, might be in direct conflict with rights protected by the First Amendment, which can entitle people, in some settings, to express themselves in unreasoned, disrespectful and intensely emotional ways. Thus a student might simultaneously behave in a manner that is patently inconsistent with SFSU's goals and policies but is protected under the First Amendment. It is with this dilemma that we wrestle in the pages that follow.*

JUDGE WAYNE D. BRAZIL, *College Republicans v. SFSU*

So what has changed about campus hate speech codes since 1998? Not the number or intensity of controversies. Consider just four examples. First, the Catholic League for Religious and Civil Rights demanded that administrators at the University of Minnesota–Morris "apply the appropriate sanctions to" (i.e., fire) a biology professor for harassment—his crime was to maintain a provocative atheist Web site displaying, among other things, sacrilegious actions.[1] Second, a lawsuit was filed against Citrus College in California for enacting a student speech code that restricted freedom of student speech to three small, remote "free speech areas" open from 8 a.m. to 6 p.m. Monday through Friday and that required students, in advance, to get official permission to use the area, alert campus security of their intended message, and provide authorities with any printed materials they wished to distribute.[2] Third, a crusade was launched by outraged students and citizens demanding sanctions against a University of Wisconsin–Madison law professor for allegedly anti-Hmong comments during class.[3] Fourth and finally, student members of the College Republicans at Georgia Tech sued the university for a "draconian" residence hall policy used to shut down their "affirmative action bake sale" and limiting their protests against "The Vagina Monologues."[4] The legal outcomes have not changed either: four more student speech code cases, four more judicial rejections of broad campus speech restrictions. Still, there is much to be learned from these events and the scholarly work being done on campus hate speech codes. In this new chapter, I address legal cases and scholarly work since 1998 involving the Deterrence Argument (from Chapter 1), hostile environment regulations (from Chapters 5 and 6), and the International Argument (implied but not developed in Chapter 1). However, before proceeding I want to offer a reminder and a terminological warning.

The reminder concerns what is at issue. First, the issue is not whether a university or college should have speech restrictions. Everyone agrees a campus should have some speech restrictions, for example, restrictions against plagiarism, genuine threats, quid pro quo harassment, and more. This is important to remember, as too many commentators still try to score points by characterizing opponents of broad speech codes as First Amendment/free speech "absolutists" opposed to all regulations on hate speech (a.k.a. hate propaganda, biased speech, racist speech, sexist speech, discriminatory speech, misethnic speech, etc.). The issue is whether a campus should have a broad speech code banning offensive expressions (whether or not these are based on race, ethnicity, religion, gender, or whatever other categories or persons are deemed to need protection) or should have only a narrow code. Whether these restrictions are called a "code" or not (usually they are not) is irrelevant. Even better, the question is: under what conditions and based on what reasons should a campus punish faculty or student speech? Second, our issue is not which causal factors were most significant in the adoption (or rejection) of broad (or narrow) campus speech codes, or what variables caused the codes to spread, or what causes them to continue to exist in spite of the legal decisions restricting their enforceable scope. The most comprehensive work to date on these empirical issues is *Speak No Evil* (2005), by law professor Jon Gould.[5] My concern in this book and chapter is the normative one: what campus speech regulations regarding hate speech are justifiable? Indeed, since broad hate speech regulations have proliferated and (Gould would say) even "triumphed" in the United States despite the legal decisions against them, and many of our democratic "cousins" around the world have broad hate speech regulations, the normative question is more important than ever.

My terminological warning concerns the phrase "hate speech." Hereafter, I shall more often use the term "offensive speech" than the term "hate speech" when writing in my own voice. To be sure, "hate speech" makes for a better headline and sound bite than "offensive speech," and it has been and remains the phrase of choice for most writers on the subject, but the truth of the matter is that the campus speech code debate is more about offensive speech than any truly hateful speech. Neither university policies nor legal decisions use the term "hate speech" in any meaningful way, and too often use of the term becomes a red herring. For example, a narrow focus on the term "hate speech" has led some university administrators (and others) to claim that they do not have a hate speech code even though their school had a verbal harassment policy banning offensive speech.[6] Again, emphasis on this term has contributed to the approval of bans on "hate speech" by 60 percent of Americans[7]—after all, what kind of person would *support* hate? Yet few of those who approve seem to have any clear understanding of the scope of the policies or their consequences. Canadian law professor Stefan Braun notes,

> In principle, [the idea of hate] is unambiguous. But in censorship practice, it is a socially malleable and politically pliable concept of public injury. Framing the cause against intolerance, ignorance, and prejudice in the language of hate as progressive censors do can become a straitjacket on more nuanced and balanced thinking. Once the problematic is successfully packaged in the socially singular and politically absolute language of hate, the case for censorship becomes almost self-evident. . . . This packaging . . . does not simply conceal the tensions and conflicts among censorship goals and the dilemmas they pose for the progressive cause. It masks the politically self-contradictory thinking and socially-self-defeating assumptions that underlie the progressive case for censorship.[8]

Even a brief study of the issue reveals a wide variety of definitions for hate speech, within national boundaries as well as across national boundaries.[9] And just how very long the arm of the law should be in the minds of many post-1998 speech code advocates will become evident as we examine specific proposals and examples. Moreover, as Harvey Silverglate and Greg Lukianoff note, "virtually none of the cases that FIRE [Foundation for Individual Rights in Education] has dealt with have followed the paradigm that 'hate speech codes' were supposedly crafted to combat: the intentional hurling of an epithet at a member of a racial or sexual minority."[10]

To be sure, you may wonder: how is the term "offensive speech" any better than "hate speech"? The reason it is better is that whatever legal category (fighting words, group libel or defamation, hostile environment harassment) or extralegal category was or is used by an actual or proposed university policy, in substantial measure the debate boils down to whether and how the policy restricts speech that some individuals may be offended by. In all of the relevant legal cases, a crucial issue has been whether the code restricted offensive yet legitimate speech. This fact has even been noticed outside the United States. German author Claudia Haupt writes,

Although the choice of free speech issues—campus speech codes, pornography, Holocaust revisionism, and the honor of German soldiers—seem unrelated at first sight, a comparable controversy is taking place in Germany and the United States in the area of free speech. The underlying question is whether free speech should be limited when the target of offensive speech is a group that has historically been discriminated against.[11]

The problem—regardless of the varied and primarily instrumental motives of the university administrators who enact and enforce the codes[12]—was and is that the language and enforcement of the policies restricted speech that clearly was protected by U.S. Supreme Court decisions. Thus, I shall tend to use the term "offensive speech code" or even just "speech code" when writing in my own voice and employ the term "hate speech code" only in limited contexts where it seems more appropriate or when explaining the views of commentators who use that term.

## THE DETERRENCE ARGUMENT REVISITED

In Chapter 1, I explained the three arguments regularly used in combination to support broad campus offensive speech codes. Although there have been no major developments in the First Amendment Argument or the University Mission Argument, we can profitably examine several contributions related to the Deterrence Argument.

Richard Delgado and his frequent co-author, Jean Stefancic, have attempted to strengthen the Deterrence Argument and the case for broad speech codes by bolstering the Harm Premise. In their 2004 book *Understanding Words That Wound*, they explain the harms of racist hate speech through three categories: harms to the individual, to the perpetrator, and to society as a whole.[13] Harms to the individual may include short-term physical harms such as rapid breathing, headaches, raised blood pressure, dizziness, rapid pulse rate, drug-taking, risk-taking behavior, and even suicide as well as long-term physical harms like depression, hypertension, hypertensive disease, and stroke. The individual may also suffer psychological harms such as damaged self-image, lowered aspirations, fear, nightmares, withdrawal, anger, lowered self-esteem, and life dissatisfaction. Further, the individual may suffer tangible and economic harms such as lowered GPAs and standardized test scores, decreased job performance, and decreased career options. Harms to the perpetrator include failing to develop a universal moral sense that extends to all persons and the potential to suffer from a "mildly paranoid mentality." Harms to society as a whole include a failure to live up to our ideal that "all men are created equal" and perpetuation of a class system opposed to American democracy. According to Delgado and Stefancic, not only are the harms of racist hate speech multifaceted and severe, but they are also pervasive. They write:

> The average black undergraduate at a white-dominated campus . . . experiences a racial remark or slur several times in a typical school year. If one counted the many code words, often spoken with a knowing expression or curled lip, that, like "you people" or "inner-city culture," carry heavily negative connotations, the frequency of exposure might approach one or more a day.[14]

They claim that social science shows hate speech is increasing, particularly, though not exclusively, on American campuses, and is likely to continue to increase for some years because of increased racial competition for resources.[15] According to Delgado and Stefancic, since the more overt institutional forms of racial segregation and domination (such as Jim Crow laws) have been eliminated, the constant depiction of the average person of color as inferior, stupid, dangerous, lazy, and morally debased must account for a substantial portion of the continued economic misfortunes of the average person of color.

Lisa Woodward provides a list of harms to victims of sexual harassment similar to the list of harms suffered by victims of racial harassment provided by Delgado and Stefancic: sexual harassment interferes with student emotional and physical well-being; lowers self-esteem; increases feelings of powerlessness, vulnerability, embarrassment, and self-blame; and can cause mental stress, depression, and anxiety leading to drug and alcohol addiction, sleeping and eating disorders, headaches, and ulcers.[16]

Based on the severity and pervasiveness of the harms of hate speech, Delgado and Stefancic recommend that a university enact a speech code punishing "severe personal insults" that is content-neutral (to be consistent with *R.A.V. v. City of St. Paul*) and has enhanced penalties for hate-motivated speech or crimes (which is permitted by *Wisconsin v. Mitchell*).[17] They describe (p. 116) two examples of insults covered by the policy and two tiers of penalties thus: "That way, the campus can end up punishing insults based on fatness or poor parking ('you idiot, why did you take up two spaces?') mildly, and ones based on race, gender, or sexual orientation ('you fag, you're going straight to hell') more severely." According to Delgado and Stefancic, the two tiers are necessary because the latter insults, most especially racial ones, attack an immutable feature of the individual and thus cause greater harm.

Although there is much to recommend in *Understanding Words That Wound*—in particular its moral appeal to oppose both overt and subtle discriminatory expression—its proposal concerning a campus speech policy is not one of its stronger points. Although the authors (p. 11) chastise those who use the term "hate speech" loosely, since it can be direct or indirect, veiled or overt, single or repeated, backed by authority and power or not, targeted at an individual, small group, or whole class of people, spoken or manifested in a symbol, accompanied by threats or assault, and varies according to who is doing the speaking, they fail to follow their own advice. For example, although the proposal appears limited to speech targeted at an individual, it does not appear to take into account who is doing the speaking (student? faculty? invited speaker? campus visitor?), where the speech is occurring (classroom? parking lot? dormitory room? a campus public sidewalk?), or whether it is intended to cause harm or not.

Although their proposal takes into account two Supreme Court cases that were not campus speech cases—*R.A.V.* struck down a city ordinance applied to a cross burning and *Mitchell* upheld a state statute applied to an aggravated assault—it does not take into account the numerous federal circuit and appellate court cases directly ruling on campus speech cases based on Supreme Court decisions about protected speech. Of course it is no accident that they ignore the lower court decisions: to take those decisions into account would reveal the stunning overbreadth and vagueness of their proposal. Further, the *Mitchell* decision was reached by the Supreme Court because it viewed the statute as applying to conduct, not to a pure speech/expression case. Most importantly, there is no speech category recognized by the Supreme Court that would justify either of the two examples that Delgado and Stefancic offer. There is no specific speech category of illegal "insults" in the United States (unlike Germany, which is discussed below), and neither example they provide would be severe enough to meet the tests for fighting words, verbal harassment, incitement, individual libel, true threats (including some forms of intimidation recognized in *Virginia v. Black*, 538 U.S. 343 [2003]), and so on.[18] Nor should any court uphold a policy that inflicts state-authorized punishment on anyone, much less students, faculty, staff, or visitors to campus merely for asserting "you idiot, why did you park in two spaces?" In fact, it does not take much imagination to think of a case in which this speech would be justified—for example, the person has taken up two parking spots five days in a row. Thus, what Delgado and Stefancic call "severe personal insults" really translates into most any personal insult: readers who do not pay close attention or do not know better may well fail to notice the sizable amount of speech they hope to restrict and punish. However, to equate calling a parking hog an "idiot" with a true threat or a pervasively discriminatory work environment or a racial epithet used during an assault or rape or murder is to succumb to the very "analytical unclarity and policy disaster" they decry.

Alexander Tsesis adds an even more ominous element to the Harm Premise in the course of defending a general criminal statute punishing "misethnic speech" in his 2006 book *Destructive Messages*, arguing that hate speech paves the way for genocide.[19] Since his proposed criminal statute would apply to the campus context, his argument deserves our attention. Schematically, his argument is this:

1. Past and present experience (including but not limited to American slavery and the removal of Native Americans, as well as their lingering effects; Nazi Germany's anti-Semitism; and contemporary slavery in Mauritania) prove that misethnic speech is a necessary (though not sufficient) condition for great social, political, and personal evils.
2. These evils pose a genuine and unjustifiable threat to fundamental human rights and the long-term survival of any legitimate democracy. Thus,
3. In order to protect the fundamental human rights undergirding legitimate democracy, we have a positive obligation to enact laws banning misethnic speech. Further,
4. Current U.S. free speech law limiting misethnic speech regulation to incitements to immediate violence prevents us from fulfilling this duty. Thus,
5. We should enact a new law penalizing misethnic speech.

Tsesis (pp. 207, 208) proposes that this law target misethnic expression that is an incitement to discriminate, persecute, or oppress members of an identifiable group (especially, historically persecuted "outgroups") where there is a substantial probability, based on the content and context of the message, that it will elicit such acts and where the speaker intended the message to promote such acts, except if the statement was uttered as an expression of opinion on a neutral scientific, academic, or religious subject and/or the statement was made to eliminate the incidence of hatred toward an identifiable group.

Although Tsesis refers to his law as a "narrow" one, it really must be anything but narrow, since his statute aims to "prevent disparaging stereotypes from ingraining themselves in the social conscience" (p. 198) and to prohibit charismatic leaders from "harnessing racist, xenophobic, and anti-Semitic ideologies to further discrimination and achieve ruinous objectives" (p. 203) regardless of whether or not these expressions posed any direct or immediate threat of harm. It is not misethnic epithets that he seeks primarily to eradicate but rather the promotion of misethnic ideologies. His intention, in essence, is to eliminate the stains of misethnic violence and discrimination by cleansing our minds of misethnic ideologies and thoughts.

However, this can be accomplished only by criminalizing a very broad and ill-defined spectrum of misethnic expression, and for many reasons such a broad proposal is an untenable one.[20] First, as indicated throughout this book, there are good reasons to doubt that our government should be entrusted with such broad and ill-defined power and that our government would use it to protect vulnerable "outgroups." Second, the fact that misethnic speech is a logically necessary condition for genocide (though true) does not single out misethnic speech for punitive legal action, since there are other necessary conditions for genocide. Why target misethnic speech for legal sanctions rather than the other necessary conditions? Presumably we should ban the condition or conditions most "responsible" for genocide—but Tsesis does not make that argument. The gap between misethnic speech being merely a logically necessary condition and its being "responsible" for genocide leads to a significant disconnect between many examples of misethnic speech "paving the way for genocide" that Tsesis provides in the chapters prior to his statutory proposal and his actual proposed statute with its intent requirement and neutral theory exception. For example, he notes that Wilhelm Marr, the man who coined the term "anti-Semitic," called on his fellow Germans to "Elect no Jews" during the 1879 elections (pp. 14–15); and Thomas Cooper of South Carolina College published a manuscript arguing that slavery was justified because the Bible did not condemn it (p. 41). Would his statute apply to these examples? If it does not, then his proposal is far too narrow to prevent misethnic speech from "paving the way" for genocide; yet if it does apply to these examples, his statute is far broader than he admits. Perhaps most importantly, Tsesis does not discuss religious or social or political or legal institutions or practices that mitigate and/or marginalize misethnic speech even in the absence of hate propaganda laws. For example, Richard Abel, an opponent of broad speech codes, notes that:

> If progress [toward equality] is fitful and costly, it is important to recall how many forms of status degradation long taken for granted have been delegitimated. Racist, anti-Semitic, and sexist slurs that routinely infected daily discourse have been banished to the margins of deviance. . . . In most Western nations hegemonic religion has yielded to pluralistic tolerance. Public disapproval is curtailing sexual harassment. The differently abled, long forced to hide, beg or display themselves as 'freaks,' have gained greater access to public life. Even homophobia is in retreat.[21]

This being so, we can observe that even if misethnic speech is a necessary condition for genocide, misethnic speech laws are not a necessary condition to avoid genocide, and this fact rather dulls the cutting edge of Tsesis's argument.

Since the Canadian approach to hate speech is much admired by advocates of broad campus speech codes, it is worth noting that Canadian law professor Stefan Braun makes similar criticisms of Canadian "hate propaganda" laws in his 2004 book *Democracy off Balance*.[22] Braun observes that one of the stated goals of broad speech restrictions is to punish expression beyond the reach of ordinary police powers; but he adds that they result in a "coerced, muted public discourse [that] will not serve well the need for robust debate and self-expression in a modern, diverse, pluralistic democracy" (a fact frequently mentioned in U.S. court decisions). Braun notes that a second goal of broad hate speech regulation is to protect multiculturalism and the psychological self-sufficiency of historically disadvantaged groups; however, in this case broad speech codes fail because they do not take context sufficiently into account and necessarily end up punishing speech that does not cause the requisite harm. A third goal of such regulation addressed by Braun is the desire to ensure inclusiveness; but broad speech codes fail to ensure inclusiveness because other laws that regulate discriminatory conduct are already increasing "visible" inclusiveness and no law can reach "invisible" exclusion. Finally, Braun argues that if the goal is to prevent political or social disintegration or conflagration, then broad speech codes fail because "history suggests that building a politically less fragile democracy on the strength of more open, probing, and self-knowing publics—rather than artificially guaranteeing political stability by quieting discursive public conflicts and papering over determined differences—is the better way to do it."[23]

Like Delgado, Stefancic, and Tsesis, law professor Richard Abel seeks to reduce or eliminate the harms of hate speech. However, like Braun, he also rejects broad offensive speech regulations in his 1998 book *Speaking Respect, Respecting Speech*. So what is his angle? Abel's contribution to the debate is to argue that although the broad speech code is too clumsy, the civil libertarian approach is too limited to deal adequately with the political competition for respect and status that underlies the hate speech debate.[24] Using an abundance of examples to illustrate the complexity of the issue and the importance of context in analyzing speech, Abel proposes a two-part solution. First, we should pursue both governmental and nongovernmental proactive strategies that equalize cultural capital in symbolic spaces by creating a social environment that screens and modifies (censors) disrespectful speech.[25] Second, we should develop social mechanisms for redressing speech harms when they occur. Abel writes:

I agree that the best antidote to degrading speech is more speech, but of a particular kind: only an apology can rectify the status inequality constructed by harmful words. To achieve this, the social settings within which respect is conferred should encourage victims to complain through an informal process that evaluates speech in context and makes offenders render an apology acceptable to both victim and community.[26]

When the proactive social environment fails to "screen and modify" (censor) disrespectful messages and disrespectful speech is used, communities should help subordinated individuals and groups challenge the disrespectful speech (in order to overcome the social disincentives to complain) and provide for a structured conversation between victims and their offenders in which the goal is to equalize status, not resolve conflicts or settle disputes, and have victims decide when offenders have been rehabilitated.[27] These apologies must include reciting the offensive acts and accepting full responsibility for the acts and their motives, must be commensurate to the offense, and must provide material redress where appropriate. In sum, Abel's view is that the harms of hate speech are real but best dealt with through the nonlegal mechanism of social pressure to apologize.

Although one can admire Abel's argument for a more respectful speech environment, there are several important questions he leaves unanswered. For example, at what point does disrespectful speech cross the line from being merely a social issue to being a legal issue? When should a university or college take legally enforceable action against an instructor or student? More fundamentally, what exactly is "disrespectful" speech and how does an individual or community decide what it is? How exactly does a community get offenders to offer the kind of apology Abel demands of them? What social pressure would convince a member of the Ku Klux Klan or the homophobic Westboro Baptist Church of Topeka, Kansas, to apologize to their victims? Further, Abel himself notes that many "victims" do not seek or accept such apologies.[28] And what "community" is it that will enforce respectful speech and apologies? The United States is far more diverse and divided culturally than either Germany or France, two cultures commonly praised for their enforcement of respect and civility. Moreover, James Q. Whitman has explained how the social and legal mechanisms in Germany and France that enforce civility and respect rely on cultural traditions and institutions absent from the United States.[29] Finally, one worries that Abel's scheme, if successful, could lead to a social (as opposed to legal) "tyranny of the majority" that compels members to self-censor anything others might find offensive and coerces public recantations whenever anyone feels their dignity has been impugned.

## THE HOSTILE ENVIRONMENT
## ARGUMENT REVISITED

In Chapters 2 and 3, I explained why two of the major proposed legal categories offered to justify campus offensive speech codes—namely, the fighting words and group libel/defamation doctrines—are too narrow to support broad campus speech codes and in Chapter 5 that this led to a reliance on Title VII–type hostile environment harassment regulations. As there have been no new developments in regard to the fighting words and group libel doctrines, except to cast an even deeper shadow over their ability to justify any meaningful campus speech regulations,[30] I shall address here only developments regarding the hostile environment approach to campus offensive speech codes.

In Chapter 6, I explained the two major arguments against the hostile environment approach, namely, the Title VII–like codes are Unlawful Argument and the Title VII–like codes are Wrongheaded Argument; and in Chapter 7, I argued that in view of the problems raised by these arguments, a university ought to avoid a broad hostile environment approach and instead take a narrow approach focusing on educational rather than punitive methods, punishing illegal conduct rather than offensive speech, having First Amendment–trained personnel in charge of campus speech policies that focus on (in addition to standard legal categories such as obscenity, libel, threats, and so on) targeted speech in captive audience contexts that lacks academic justification and is pervasive or egregious. However, some legal analysts continue to oppose all hostile environment speech restrictions whether in the workplace or education.[31] Since a full-scale defense of narrow hostile environment speech restrictions is beyond this single chapter, my remarks here must be limited to the most salient points raised by critics. For the sake of convenience, we can view the critics' argument through the lens of a 2001 law review article by Richard Allen Olmstead.[32]

The primary objection to hostile environment speech regulations is the "demarcation problem" (to borrow a phrase from Mane Hajden[33]). For example, Olmstead claims that the court-adopted definition of hostile environment harassment is unduly vague since it "gives absolutely zero guidance as to what speech or conduct is prohibited."[34] It thereby threatens constitutionally protected political and religious speech such as "David Duke for President" posters, criticisms of the Catholic Church by a Jewish worker, burning a flag in your work cubicle, and religious proselytizing. He criticizes the decision of the Texas Court of Criminal Appeals upholding the state statute in *Sanchez v. Texas*, 995 S.W.2d 677 (Tex. Crim. App. 1999). According to Olmstead, in overruling the decision of the lower court that the statute was unduly vague, the appellate court erred in relying on an irrelevant precedent: it based its decision on the enhanced penalties case *Wisconsin v. Mitchell*, but that case was not a harassment case and was challenged for overbreadth, not vagueness. Thus, the effect of the Texas decision was to uphold a law that necessarily has a chilling effect on legitimate speech, since employers will impose more severe restrictions on employee speech than the Constitution permits to minimize their liability in harassment litigation. In regard to overbreadth, Olmstead (quoting Browne's 1992 article) notes that the legal definition of speech creating a hostile environment is overbroad in three ways: (1) it permits constitutionally protected speech to be used as evidence of a hostile environment in a case in which speech not protected by the Constitution would be insufficient; (2) it presents the risk that constitutionally protected speech will be used by the trier of fact in its holding, even when there is sufficient evidence provided by unconstitutionally protected speech; and (3) in reaching any constitutionally protected speech, it loses its claim on restricting only unprotected expression. To support his overbreadth claim further, Olmstead offers the Washington supreme court decision in *City of Bellevue v. Lorang*, 992 P.2d 496 (Wash. 2000). In this case the court held that a state phone harassment law was overbroad because it banned (among other things) "profane" speech, and since constitutionally protected speech critical of religion might be considered "profane," the statute was overbroad on its face.

Critics also argue that there is no principled way to limit the expansion of hostile environment restrictions to every area of life. Olmstead explains four directions in which this expansion can occur, and has occurred.[35] First, since every place is a workplace there is nothing in principle to stop their application to places like the classroom (the teacher's workplace), the open street (the construction worker's workplace), or the theater (the theater manager's workplace). Second, since the workplace includes patrons as well as co-workers and supervisors, their application cannot be limited to the speech of co-workers or supervisors, and thus some courts have upheld hostile environment claims based on the speech of patrons.[36] Third, the restrictions apply to legitimate businesses that may create hostile work environments for some employees by the very nature of the business, for example, a bookstore that carries racist or erotic materials. Fourth (and most relevant to the campus speech code debate), Olmstead maintains that there is no principled way to stop the regulations from restricting legitimate academic speech, for example, the comment by the student in *Doe v. Michigan* that "homosexuality is a sickness and all gays should be ashamed." Olmstead claims, in sum, that Title VII has become what it was never meant to be, namely, a "clean language act," since so many sources define sexual harassment broadly to encompass any sexual comments, jokes, gestures or looks, and compliments about clothing.[37]

Although the demarcation problem carries substantial weight against a broad hostile environment speech code, it is considerably less problematic for the narrow version I propose. First, unless one wishes to delegitimize all law, one has to accept some level of imperfect specification as adequately informing the public as to what is and is not permitted. Both judges and legal commentators have pointed out that some degree of legal uncertainty is a fact of life, since no area of U.S. law is 100 percent internally consistent and no legal rule or decision can anticipate every possible future case. And even if the law were 100 percent consistent and anticipated every case, it is still possible (indeed likely) that a court would overturn precedent in some cases by creating a new rationale or reinterpreting an old rationale.[38] Second, in numerous legal precedents—for example, in *Faragher v. City of Boca Raton*, 524 U.S. 775, 788 (1998)—the Supreme Court has explicitly held that mere offense, even the sporadic use of abusive language or gender-related jokes, does not constitute harassment. This suggests that the narrow approach I advocate is not "unduly" vague and is sensitive to context and the facts as such regulations should be. So it is false to say that narrow guidelines provide "zero" guidance. Miranda Oshige McGowan remarks, "There are few (if any) actual cases that have allowed complaints based on overheard comments or jokes or displayed images to proceed to trial, and few cases in which complaints based on comments or discussion about current affairs, religion, or politics (broadly construed) have made it past summary judgment."[39] Many cases posed as counterexamples were dismissed, involved facts far more serious than critics describe, or pre-dated relevant Supreme Court decisions. Similarly, John Wirenius observes:

> The courts have been grudging in watering down the requisite levels of severity or of pervasiveness, resisting almost instinctively the standard's inherent flexibility. As a result, plaintiffs have been required to show a concrete impact, which has the effect of altering the victim's relationship with management and co-workers in a manner that is both objectively perceivable and subjectively recognized—the same terms and conditions of the employment contract do not apply. These courts have sometimes gone embarrassingly out of their way to emphasize that speech, however offensive, that does not have this impact cannot create a hostile work environment. Thus, where an employee participates in sexual banter, or complains about general workplace offensiveness that does not exclude her, no hostile work environment can be established. By contrast, where concrete impact can be shown, and traced to the discriminatory animus, a hostile work environment can be shown.[40]

Using a legal distinction between verbal behavior that is treated by the courts as "conduct" and verbal behavior that is treated as "speech," Oshige McGowan suggests that the fatal flaw in the view of the extremist hostile environment critics can be understood through their concession that banning quid pro quo harassment is legitimate, since it is "speech" that is treated by the courts as "conduct" because it is a "regulable performative."[41] If so, it would follow logically that punishing hostile environment harassment is legitimate where the factual circumstances support a finding that the "speech" creating the hostile environment harassment similarly constitutes "conduct."

Even if I am right that the demarcation problem can be reasonably minimized, critics maintain that all hostile environment speech restrictions are objectionable, since they are a form of content and viewpoint discrimination. Recall that, for example, a law that bans all fighting words or all true threats—which *Virginia v. Black*, 538 U.S. 343 (2003) held includes some "intimidating" words—is content- and viewpoint-neutral, whereas a law that banned only fighting words or intimidation expressed through cross burning would discriminate on the basis of content and a law that banned only fighting words or intimidation directed at Protestants would discriminate on the basis of viewpoint. If, as critics of hostile environment law maintain, a law that discriminates on the basis of content or viewpoint is considered facially invalid, then hostile environment restrictions, whether narrow or broad, are facially invalid since they restrict the content (sex-based harassment is banned but not, for example, weight-based harassment) and point of view expressed (sexist harassment is banned but not anti-sexist harassment).

One problem with this argument is that the U.S. Supreme Court has repeatedly upheld hostile environment speech restrictions and does not consider them invalid forms of content or viewpoint discrimination. Although Justice White (in his concurring *R.A.V.* opinion) and numerous legal commentators have suggested that Scalia's reasoning in *R.A.V.* would make verbal sexual harassment law unconstitutional, the U.S. Supreme Court has had numerous opportunities to reach such a conclusion and has not. Moreover, many legal scholars have pointed out that the Supreme Court does not regard content-neutrality or viewpoint neutrality as constitutional absolutes, nor should it.[42] For example, the Court upheld content-discrimination in *Lehman v. Shaker Heights*, 418 U.S. 298 (1974), ruling that a city may permit commercial advertising on city buses but ban political advertising, and in *Morales v. Transworld Airlines*, 504 U.S., 374 (1992), ruling that government may regulate airline advertising but not bus advertising. Again, *Watts v. United States*, 394 U.S. 705 (1969), held that threats against the president of the United States have a different legal status than threats against other individuals and *Burson v. Freeman*, 504 U.S. 191 (1992), held that even core political speech can be banned within 100 feet of a polling place the day of an election. In the 2003 *Virginia v. Black* cross burning case, the state cross burning statute was found unconstitutionally overbroad, but Justice Sandra Day O'Connor, writing for the Court majority, explicitly noted (p. 362) that a content-based state statute that banned only intimidation through cross burning rather than all intimidating words would be constitutional. Further, the Court has upheld viewpoint discrimination in permitting advertising against cigarettes but banning advertisements for cigarettes, and in banning favorable comments about a company in proxy statements while permitting unfavorable ones.[43] Moreover, many legal scholars have pointed out that education necessarily discriminates on the basis of viewpoint: a professor of ethics can flunk a student whose essays are filled with false major claims or based entirely on fallacious reasoning, and a meteorology department can reject a job candidate who plans to teach students how to forecast the weather using astrology. In some educational contexts, some content and some viewpoints can be and should be rejected. Of course, I am not suggesting that universities have unlimited authority to discriminate on the basis of content or viewpoint. For example, if the ethics student's fallacious and misinformed essays were published as editorials in the student newspaper, the professor and university should take no punitive action. In sum, since the Supreme Court does not view content or viewpoint neutrality as constitutional absolutes and does not view Title VII–type harassment policies in particular as an unconstitutional form of content or viewpoint discrimination, and education necessarily involves some forms of content and viewpoint discrimination, it would appear the burden is on critics to provide stronger evidence demonstrating that the kind of viewpoint discrimination specifically involved in narrow hostile environment regulations lacks normative justification.

Critics of hostile environment regulations also object to the "captive audience" doctrine invoked by defenders of narrow Title VII–type regulations. In their view, the captive audience doctrine only applies to the home, not to the workplace or education. For example, Olmstead argues that the two major Supreme Court cases employing the doctrine—namely, *Rowan v. U.S. Post Office*, 397 U.S. 728 (1970), and *FCC v. Pacifica Foundation*, 438 U.S. 726 (1978)—relied on the fact that the audiences were in their home, and that in the one major case in which the audience was not at home (*Lehman v. Shaker Heights*, 418 U.S. 298 [1974], involved passengers on a city bus), the use of the expression "captive audience" (by only one justice) was not in its technical legal sense, but rather, an informal expression inveighing against the right of government to impose its favored ideas upon citizens.[44] One might add that the captive audience doctrine also was invoked in two subsequent labor picketing cases in residential areas, *Carey v. Brown*, 447 U.S. 455 (1980), and *Frisby v. Schultz*, 487 U.S. 474 (1988).

One problem with this objection is that courts have employed the captive audience rationale in nonhome settings. Columbia University law professor Michael Dorf writes:

> The captive audience concept applies only in special *places*. Clearly the home counts as one such place. Are there others? Yes, there are plenty. . . . At one time or another, lower courts have also relied on the captive audience rationale to uphold restrictions on expression at military induction centers and outside abortion clinics, as well as to uphold restrictions on panhandling in the New York City subways.[45]

Again, Professor Njeri Mathis Rutledge observes that "the Supreme Court has . . . exhibited a willingness to apply the captive audience doctrine outside the context of residential privacy, particularly when the interests of the unwilling listener are at stake."[46] For example, in *Madsen v. Women's Health Center, Inc.*, 512 U.S. 753, 768 (1994), the Supreme Court held that "the State's strong interest in residential privacy, acknowledged in *Frisby v. Schultz*, applied by analogy to medical privacy." In *Hill v. Colorado*, 530 U.S. 703, 717 (2000), the Court explained that "the right to avoid unwelcome speech has special force in the privacy of the home . . . but can also be protected in confrontational settings." Moreover, the captive audience doctrine was used in the workplace harassment cases *Robinson v. Jacksonville Shipyards*, 760 F. Supp. 1486, 1534–37 (M.D. Fla. 1991), and *Aguilar v. Avis Rent-a-Car*, 980 P.2d 846, 871–73 (Cal. 1999). Finally, numerous courts have emphasized that the classroom is not a traditional public forum and some courts have specifically invoked the captive audience doctrine in education cases. Three such K–12 cases include *Bethel School District v. Fraser*, 478 U.S. 675, 684 (1986), *Miles v. Denver Public Schools*, 944 F.2d 773, 776 (10th Cir. 1991), and *Saxe v. State College Area School District*, 240 F.3d 200, 210 (3d Cir. 2001). It also has been applied to the classroom speech of university instructors in *Martin v. Parish*, 805 F.2d 583 (5th Cir. 1995), and *Bonnell v. Lorenzo*, 241 F.3d 800, 811 (6th Cir. 2001), discussed below.

To be sure, the captive audience doctrine has greater force when applied to a personal residence (including student dormitory rooms) than to the workplace or classroom. For example, William E. Lee uses the 1978 *Cohen v. California* "Fuck the Draft" jacket decision to note that, "outside the home, a different set of considerations [normally] apply; citizens have to absorb the 'first blow' of offensive speech before they turn away and the fact that some individuals would prefer to avoid any exposure whatsoever is irrelevant."[47]

In the workplace and education contexts, this means that the verbal harassment normally must be pervasive, not a single incident or even sporadic, and targeted (see, e.g., *Frisby v. Schultz* at 486). However, in other factual circumstances, it is the severity rather than pervasiveness that is relevant. Arguably, the legal origin of the captive audience rationale lies not in the 1970s cases critics cite, but rather in *Kovacs v. Cooper*, 336 U.S. 77, 86–87 (1949),[48] in which the Supreme Court upheld a city ordinance banning loud noises from sound trucks:

> The unwilling listener is not like the passer-by who may be offered a pamphlet in the street but cannot be made to take it. In his home or on the street he is practically helpless to escape this interference with his privacy by loud speakers except through the protection of the municipality.

Here the court did not differentiate the home from the street in its rationale and emphasized the severity (loudness) rather than the pervasiveness of the noise. Certainly we must be careful to avoid extending the captive audience doctrine too far, but the mere fact that the speech occurs in a nonresidential place does not negate the truth that in a limited set of factual circumstances, government should protect students who are unable reasonably to avoid unwelcome messages forced upon them in places in which they are pursuing an important and legitimate purpose.

Finally, critics of hostile environment restrictions might appeal to Judge Warren's ruling in the 1991 University of Wisconsin-System case that Title VII restrictions apply to university employees in the campus workplace but not to nonemployee students or to educational contexts on campus.

But how different are the employment and educational contexts? First, just as Title VII aims to provide equal opportunity and prevent discrimination in the workplace, Title IX aims to provide equal opportunity and prevent discrimination in education. Thus, as Ellen Lange observed in her 1990 paper, any difference between the two seems to be "in degree more than [in] kind."[49] Numerous scholars have pointed out that both the workplace and educational environment also are alike in being places in which the denial of equal opportunity affects tangible future benefits, places in which an employee and student interact with the same set of people on a regular basis, places in which people share and pursue both individual and collective goals, and places in which people have limited avenues of retreat from harassing speech; furthermore, both are discrete, definable experiences.[50] In view of these similarities, courts have held both Title VII and Title IX standards applicable to university cases involving quid pro quo offers of a tangible academic benefit in exchange for sexual favors and university cases involving hostile environment claims based primarily in unwelcome sexual conduct and/or unwelcome targeted sexual comments or advances.[51]

Of course there are considerations of academic freedom that require campus speech regulations to be even more narrow than workplace ones; but academic freedom does not offer blanket protection for all professorial speech in the classroom. For example, in *Bonnell v. Lorenzo*, 241 F.3d 800 (6th Cir. 2001), the federal appeals court upheld university sanctions for a community college professor. John Bonnell, a professor of English at Macomb Community College since 1967, was held to have created a hostile environment in his classroom based on his constant use of profanities such as "fuck," "cunt," and "pussy"; sexually explicit comments; and stories with sexual innuendo. The court held (at 811) that

> [Bonnell] does not have a constitutional right to use . . . [profane and vulgar] language in a classroom setting where they are not germane to the subject matter, in contravention of the College's sexual harassment policy. . . . This is particularly so when one considers the unique context in which the speech is conveyed—the classroom where a professor is speaking to a captive audience.

The decision relied on *Martin v. Parrish*, 805 F. 2d 583, 584–85 (5th Cir. 1995), which held that classroom profanity by a professor (in this case, denigrating students for their "poor attitude") did not enjoy constitutional protection since it did not address a matter of public concern and held that students were a captive audience in the classroom. Similarly, the *Bonnell* court (at 816) distinguished the gratuitous use of obscenities in the classroom (legally unprotected) from his use of such terms in a matter of public concern, namely, his published "Apology" (which did qualify for, but in the court's opinion lost, the relevant balancing test). What matters is not merely the word(s) used, but their germaneness; hence it is important that university speech policies take into account whether or not the speech has an academic justification.

But here we must note a more general problem: the concept of academic freedom lacks any clear or consistent definition or justification in current law.[52] For example, Todd A. DeMitchell and Vincent J. Connelly write,

> The academic freedom of professors and teachers is much discussed, but its borders remain stubbornly indistinct and blurred. It is a constitutional

right claimed by educators in schools and colleges but not consistently proclaimed by the courts. The courts' view of academic freedom impacts policy-making and practice, yet the impact is inconsistent and not easily discerned.[53]

R. George Wright states, "Academic freedom is largely unanalyzed, undefined, and unguided by principled application, leading to its inconsistent and skeptical or questioned invocation."[54] Thus it was that the Macomb CC vice president for human resources stated in a rather ominous warning to Bonnell prior to the sanctions that

> the principle of academic freedom under the First Amendment serves to protect the utterances only if they are germane to course content as measured by professional teaching standards. Since the precise frontier between academic freedom and sexual harassment remains to be defined by the courts case by case, a teacher . . . may be able to find safety and comfort under the [First] Amendment only if the words uttered are found in appropriate textual materials and the utterances are pertinent to discussion of those materials. Beyond this point, the teacher enters uncharted territory and proceeds at his or her own risk of being found guilty of sexual harassment.[55]

What this means is that the problem of determining what instructor speech is protected and what instructor speech is not protected is not exclusively or primarily or even necessarily due to any problems in hostile environment regulations. Consider, for example, *Vega v. Miller*, 273 F.3d 460 (2d Cir. 2001). In the summer of 1994, Professor Edward Vega led a free association exercise called "clustering" that was designed to help students avoid repetition in their essays during a six-week composition class at New York Maritime College. On July 21, students chose "sex" as their topic for the exercise and began by offering "safe" examples like "marriage," "children," and "wedding ring" but soon were calling out "penis," "vagina," "fellatio," and "cunnilingus" and then "cluster fuck," "slamhole," "studded rubbers," and more. Vega did not attempt to stop the exercise, but he also did not write all examples on the blackboard and cautioned the students that the vulgar terms should not be used at all or used rarely, only when essential to enlighten and persuade the reader. No students complained about the exercise, and it came to the attention of the university as it investigated a separate complaint. Vega was then informed without any hearing or opportunity to explain or defend himself that he would not be reappointed, and he sued for a violation of his First Amendment right to freedom of speech. Although the appellate court found his pedagogy legitimate (without specifically ruling that it was fully protected or that the college's harassment policy was constitutional), the court reversed the district court's ruling in holding that Vega was not entitled to damages, since the college officials had qualified immunity under the law. Qualified immunity means the school administrators can be held liable only if they act unreasonably contrary to clearly established law. So the court ruled that the state of the law in 1994 was such that school administrators could reasonably believe they were within their rights in terminating Vega's employment. So even if Vega's speech was constitutionally protected, the university did no wrong in not reappointing him.

Judge José Cabranes argued in dissent that the *Vega* majority erred in not ruling on Vega's claims that the college's sexual harassment policy was both vague and overbroad and that its enforcement failed to meet standards of due process, a claim Cabranes (rightly) saw Vega winning. He also disputed the court's finding that the conduct of the officials was reasonable at the time since both *Doe v. Michigan* in 1989 and *UWM-Post v. Board of Regents* in 1991 had struck down similar campus speech rules. Thus, he writes (at 477), "The defendants failed to realize that their sexual harassment policy was vague and overbroad because of their own inadequate training and judgment, not because the law on the subject was unclear."

Further, Cabranes argued that Vega's actions were clearly within the legal bounds of academic freedom at the time (as announced in *Hazelwood v. Kuhlmeier*, 484 U.S. 260 (1988), since his actions were suitable for the age and sophistication of the students and constituted a teaching method reasonably related to a valid teaching objective; also, he stated, the presentation had a suitable context and manner. Cabranes writes (at 480), "In sum, the simple fact that sexually-explicit terms were used by students in a ten-minute classroom exercise is not sufficient to show that Vega exceeded the clearly-established bounds of academic freedom protected by the First Amendment." Thus, Cabranes reasoned that the qualified immunity defense did not apply since the college administrators' actions were objectively unreasonable.

Perhaps the reader will not be surprised to learn that I agree with Judge Cabranes. By 1994, an objectively reasonable legal observer would have known through case law at least (1) that the accused is entitled to due process; (2) that the harassment had to be severe or pervasive enough to materially change the conditions of education for some student(s); and (3) that due consideration had to be given to Vega's First Amendment rights, including the age and sophistication of the students and the legitimacy of his pedagogy. The factual record indicates the college officials did not provide due process; did not attempt to determine whether anyone was sexually harassed, much less whether the harassment was severe or pervasive; and took no account either of the age and sophistication of the students or Vega's pedagogical purposes. Rather, the college officials simply heard tell of the event and summarily determined that Vega was guilty not of actual harassment, but of putting the school at risk of a sexual harassment lawsuit. In all these ways, the *Vega* case is strikingly different from the *Bonnell* case—numerous students had complained about Bonnell over a period of years, the university gave Bonnell opportunity for rebuttal and change before proceeding to discipline, and the university relied on relevant First Amendment law. College instructors deserve better treatment from college officials and better judicial opinions than Vega got.

## STUDENT SPEECH CODES AND THEIR VICTIMS

Beyond the speech of instructors in college classrooms, there have been important post-1998 judicial decisions about campus offensive speech restrictions on the expression of students. These cases are important, not because the courts arrived at unexpected decisions or invoked novel justifications for their decisions, but because they evidence the continuing judicial rejection of campus speech codes when they reach merely offensive speech, while leaving the door open to narrower, more carefully drawn restrictions along the lines I recommend. Before continuing, it must be noted that since 1998 a significant organization has emerged specifically to combat unconstitutional campus speech policies as well as improper enforcement of constitutional policies. In the wake of their 1998 book *The Shadow University*, Alan Charles Kors and Harvey Silverglate (and others) founded the Foundation for Individual Rights in Education (FIRE). To be sure, FIRE has its share of supporters and critics, and it is only one among many other organizations—such as the ACLU, the Center for Campus Free Speech, the Thomas Jefferson Center for the Protection of Free Expression, the American Center for Law and Justice, the Christian Legal Society, Feminists for Free Expression, the Student Press Law Center, Students for Academic Freedom, Collegefreedom.org, and the Alliance Defense Fund— carefully watching speech restrictions on U.S. campuses, but certainly it has been the most aggressive agent challenging student speech codes.

In April 2003 Walter Bair and Ellen Wray, two students at Shippensburg University in Pennsylvania, filed suit alleging that Shippensburg's student speech policies were overbroad and unduly vague and had a chilling effect on their rights to engage in discussions of theories, ideas, and political and/or religious beliefs. The university argued that their fears were not objectively reasonable and that the policies were "aspirational" rather than punitive, that the policies fostered free speech rather than discouraged it, and that the language in the policies was acceptable since it used language from Title VII policies. However, in *Bair v. Shippensburg University*, 280 F. Supp. 2d 357 (M.D. Pa. 2003), the court rejected all of the university's arguments. The student fears of prosecution were legitimate since "the loss of First Amendment freedoms, for even minimal periods of time, unquestionably constitutes irreparable injury"[56] and the policies had punitive force at least because one was part of the student code of conduct and another addressed which student groups would be chartered and funded. Although the policies were intended to foster free speech, the court ruled (at 367) that "this sword has two edges. Certainly during President Ceddia's tenure the Speech Code has not been used, and likely will not be used, to punish students for exercising their First Amendment rights. However, given that this is a facial challenge, our inquiry must assume not the best of intentions, but the worst." The court (at 371–372) rejected the appeal to Title VII–like language because "while the University's objective of preventing forms of discrimination against these protected classes of individuals is certainly laudable, this ambition still runs afoul of First Amendment concerns if discrimination policies have the effect of prohibiting protected forms of expression. Simply utilizing buzzwords applicable to anti-discrimination legislation does not cure this deficiency." But what specific language in the policies was overbroad or unduly vague? The court agreed with plaintiffs that banning "inflammatory or harmful" or "intolerant" expression in the university catalog and limiting speech to expression that does not "provoke, harass, intimidate, or harm" another—as provided in the student code of conduct—is overbroad, since the U.S. Supreme Court has repeatedly held that speech regulations cannot ban expression simply because it is provocative or offensive. Since no limiting construction can save this language, and Shippensburg did not provide any evidence that such language would cause any material disruption to the educational environment, the university was enjoined from enforcing those provisions and was restricted to regulating student conduct and speech based on other provisions of the code, local ordinances, the criminal laws of the Commonwealth of Pennsylvania, and applicable federal anti-discrimination laws.

In 2003 Jason Roberts, a law student at Texas Tech University, sought to give a speech and distribute literature expressing his view that "homosexuality is a sinful, immoral, and unhealthy lifestyle." Although he was free to use the designated "free speech area" in a gazebo near the student union without any prior university permission, he submitted a request on May 23 to speak at another campus location on June 5. Through a series of e-mails, Roberts was given permission to speak at another location, but on June 6 he notified school officials that he declined to speak for personal reasons. On June 12, Roberts sued the university, alleging that its policy was facially unconstitutional.[57] In *Roberts v. Haragan*, 346 F. Supp. 2d 853 (N.D. Tex. 2004), the court ruled that the university's speech policy as applied to areas that constitute a "traditional public forum" (such as sidewalks, parks, and other common areas) was subject to strict scrutiny, not the reasonableness standard applied to limited public forums. Thus, the "prior permission" the university required for student expression in campus public forums must be shown by the university to be necessary to serve its significant interests (said to be preserving an environment suitable for classroom instruction and library study, avoiding scheduling conflicts, and the safety of pedestrian and vehicular traffic). However, the court held (at 870) that the permission requirement "sweeps too broadly in imposing a burden on a substantial amount of expression that does not interfere with significant interests of the university." Further, the court held (at 872) that the university ban on insults, epithets, ridicule, or personal attacks (whether words or printed materials) in public forums was overbroad since it "would suppress substantially more than threats, 'fighting words,' or libelous statements that may be considered constitutionally unprotected speech, to include speech that, no matter how offensive, is not proscribed by the First Amendment."

On October 17, 2006, members of the San Francisco State University (SFSU) College Republicans held an "Anti-Terrorism Rally" at the campus's Malcolm X Plaza. During the rally they stomped on butcher-paper replicas of the flags of Hamas and Hezbollah, which include the Arabic script for "Allah." When some observers protested, the College Republicans allowed objectors to mark out the word "Allah" on both flags and permitted one objector to take the Hamas flag away. Throughout the rally, members of the College Republicans and objectors engaged in heated debate, but university police in attendance did not need to intervene. However, a week later a student filed a complaint against the College Republicans for failing to act "civil" during their rally as required by the SFSU "Standards for Student Conduct." During the process following the complaint, more students complained about the rally and the matter was forwarded by a school administrator to formal proceedings held by the Student Organization Hearing Panel.

Although the panel dismissed the complaint, the College Republicans sued SFSU, alleging that the student policies requiring "civility" and banning "intimidation" and "harassment" and other behaviors "inconsistent with SF State goals, principles and policies" were overbroad and unduly vague. SFSU argued that the civility provision was merely "aspirational" and that the other provisions applied in a viewpoint-neutral way only to conduct, not to speech. Since the relevant policies actually were promulgated by the California State University Board of Trustees and applied statewide to all California State University campuses, the lawsuit was highly publicized. Specifically citing *Bair*, *Roberts*, and *Doe v. Michigan*, the court held in *College Republicans v. Reed*, 523 F. Supp. 2d 1005 (N.D. Ca. 2007), that the speech regulations were not merely "aspirational," since they were included in a student code of conduct that set forth requirements for student behavior and were subject to "corrective actions" that in fact prompted a disciplinary hearing; that they were overbroad, since the term "civil" is "broad and elastic" and undefined by the policy and reached protected political speech in a classic public forum that was merely thought disrespectful and offensive by some observers; and that the civility requirement cannot be saved by the university's suggested narrowed construction.[58] However, the court did not grant the plaintiff's motion for a preliminary injunction against the portion of the policy banning "intimidation" or "harassment," since the text suggested these were limited to actions ("conduct" not "speech") that threatened or endangered the health or safety of any person.[59]

Christian DeJohn, a member of the Pennsylvania Army National Guard, was enrolled in the MA program in Military and American History at Temple University. In 2006, during his last semester in the program, DeJohn filed suit against the university, alleging that its verbal sexual harassment policy was overbroad, specifically, that it inhibited his expression of his views concerning women in combat and women in the military. Three weeks prior to the deadline for filing dispositive motions, Temple voluntarily modified its policy and urged the district court to quash the suit. However, the district court issued a permanent injunction against the policy due to its overbreadth and awarded one dollar in damages to DeJohn. The appellate court upheld the decision in *DeJohn v. Temple University*, Case No. 07–2220, 2008 U.S. App. LEXIS 16463 (3d Cir. August 4, 2008). Since there is no "harassment exception" to the First Amendment, where pure expression is involved the university policy must not run afoul of First Amendment requirements. The first problem was that *Tinker v. Des Moines* requires a school to show that the speech will cause actual material disruption of the educational environment before prohibiting it, and the Temple harassment policy permitted punishment for harassing speech based solely on the speaker's intention rather than its having any actual effect. Judge Smith wrote (at 41–42),

> Under the language of Temple's Policy, a student who sets out to interfere with another student's work, educational performance, or status, or to create a hostile environment would be subject to sanctions regardless of

whether these actions and motives had their intended effect. . . . As such, the focus on motive is contrary to *Tinker's* requirement that speech cannot be prohibited in the absence of a tenable threat of disruption.

Second, the policy failed to require the speech to be severe or pervasive, and thus its restrictions could be applied to punish offensive speech that is protected by the First Amendment. Judge Smith wrote (at 42–43),

> Further, the policy's use of "hostile," "offensive," and "gender-motivated" is, on its face, sufficiently overbroad and subjective that they "could conceivably be applied to cover any speech" of a "gender-motivated" nature the content of which offends someone." . . . This could include "core" political and religious speech, such as gender politics and sexual morality. . . . Absent any requirement akin to the showing of severity or pervasiveness . . . the policy provides no shelter for core protected speech.

We have then a set of judicial decisions extending from the 1989 *Doe v. Michigan* case to the 2008 *DeJohn v. Temple* case consistently rejecting broad university and college student speech codes. In all four of these more recent cases, school administrators defended clearly illegal codes—so clearly illegal on their face that courts granted preliminary injunctions. A staff editorial in the *Washington Times* commented,

> Colleges and universities generally know the game is up. Indeed, Temple saw the ruling coming and tried to pre-empt it by throwing out the offending sections of the speech code early in the proceedings. Before a lower court, Temple tried to argue that the voluntary removal of these sections solved the problem and should close the case. Both courts disagreed. Nothing would stop Temple or another school from simply reinstating these sections at some future date, the appellate court reasoned. Perhaps the Temple dons should enroll in their own constitutional law offerings.[60]

Given Gould's observation that administrators are moved primarily by instrumental reasons, perhaps holding administrators personally liable by a stricter standard would give them a strong enough instrumental reason to get rid of the unconstitutional policies and correctly apply constitutional policies.

The consistency of the legal decisions has also enabled free speech advocacy organizations to bring moral pressure to bear successfully in some cases in which a campus speech policy either on its face or in its application violated student rights to free expression. These moral challenges are critical. As Judge Avern Cohn (of the *Doe v. Michigan* case) notes in his review of *The Shadow University* by Kors and Silverglate,

> Both experienced lawyers and long-serving judges can attest to the fact that a case in court should never be looked upon as a profit center, and is a poor, very expensive, and seldom successful way to achieve worthwhile social change. Although at times there is no alternative to litigation, we certainly do not need to duplicate the road from *Plessy v. Ferguson* to *Brown v. Board of Education* to achieve a balance of evils in college and university policies and practices today regarding speech codes, discipline, and efforts to achieve diversity and assure appropriate multicultural programming.[61]

The most convenient place to find information on many nonlitigated university cases is FIRE's website, www.thefire.org. FIRE was active in many, though not all, of the cases discussed there.

One of the side debates arising from the continued enforcement of overreaching campus speech codes concerns the "victims" of these unconstitutional policies. From the earliest stages of the controversy, many commentators saw the heavy hand of left-wing "thought police" at work, and many observers continue to claim that political conservatives suffer the brunt of broad university speech restrictions in the United States.[62] Consider, for example, the recent work of University of Wisconsin political scientist Donald Downs.[63] Downs abandoned his support for broad speech codes based on the group libel approach (discussed in Chapter 2) in the mid-1990s, when he saw how campus speech codes actually functioned, and he has become a leading critic of such codes as well as an advocate of political mobilization against them. Downs now emphasizes the need for campuses to accept freedom of speech for all sides based on mutual self-interest ("interest group liberalism"), or even better, for its own sake (the "citizenship" model).[64] Downs, like others before him—in particular, Alan Charles Kors and Harvey Silverglate, authors of the polemical and influential *Shadow University* and co-founders of FIRE—believes that the main obstacle to free expression on American campuses since the late 1980s has been the rise of a Herbert Marcuse–inspired progressive censorship aimed at promoting a particular conception of social justice and equality.[65] Downs supports his contention with extended discussions about selected high-profile campuses, including his own campus, UW-Madison.

On the other side, Richard Delgado and Jean Stefancic maintain that allegations of conservative victimization ring hollow since (1) hate speech directed at minorities on campus has grown in frequency and severity, whether of the vulgar or sophisticated kind, and (2) "white thought, ideas, and power" are in little danger of being suppressed.[66] Putting aside the apparent hasty generalization equating conservative political thought with "white thought, ideas, and power," their point seems to be this: any chilling effects or other harms that campus conservatives endure as a result of broad campus speech codes are dwarfed by the continuing substantial chilling effects and harms suffered by campus minorities.

A second complaint urged against those who emphasize the plight of political conservatives on American campuses is that they ignore or underemphasize conservative censorship of liberal expression. For example, Jon Gould has accused FIRE (and vocal supporters like Downs) of exaggerating the extent of the problem and having its own biased agenda because it champions conservative victims of private university censorship but ignores liberal victims of private university censorship.[67] Robert O'Neil, director of the Thomas Jefferson Center for Free Expression, has also expressed numerous reservations about FIRE's claims and tactics.[68]

Of course, one should expect that different organizations will pursue some different free speech cases, while also pursuing some common cases—the 2008 *DeJohn* case brought FIRE together with the ACLU of Pennsylvania, the Christian Legal Society, Collegefreedom.org, Feminists for Free Expression, the Individual Rights Foundation, Students for Academic Freedom, and the Student Press Law Center. Moreover, some of Gould's own research findings suggest the problem of anti-conservative hate speech regulation has spread beyond campus to the mainstream media. In response to David Horowitz's advertisement against reparations for slavery that provoked an outpouring of conservative criticism of campus newspapers that refused the ad, Gould and a student researcher developed a procedure for sending three mock ads concerning the legacy of the 9/11 attacks (one neutral, one highly liberal, one ultra conservative) to 113 major newspapers.[69] The result? Every newspaper that received the neutral ad agreed to publish it, and there was no relationship between the newspaper's own political orientation and its willingness to run one of the two partisan ads when the editorial staff focused on the overall message; however, when editors focused on specific language in the ad, the conservative ad was rejected, since nearly half the newspapers had a policy against publishing hate speech and the conservative ad was thought to contain hate speech.

Lacking reliable empirical evidence about these matters, I shall leave it to the reader to form his or her own opinion about the side debates. My own impression is that there are not mobs of left-wing "progressive censors" running rampant in U.S. universities silencing conservatives, although certainly there are some left-wingers who attempt to silence conservatives and advance their own agenda—just as there also are right-wingers attempting to silence liberals and advance their own cause.[70] Moreover, Gould's limited but useful research suggests that university and college speech regulations are usually enacted by administrators for instrumental rather than partisan reasons and that the percentage of schools with overbroad speech policies is under 15 percent.[71] Finally, we should keep in mind that in two of the student legal cases (Stanford and Texas Tech), no one at all had been disciplined for speech under the overbroad policy. Perhaps Judge Cohn has it right:

> If one wants to work the Internet long and hard enough, one can put together a succession of incidents that would appear to create the impression of a pattern and practice of wrongdoing and little positive response in almost any area of public life. However, if one is willing to take the time to personally inquire and cull the websites of, for example, The Chronicle of Higher Education, Justice on Campus, National Association of State Universities and Land-Grant Colleges, National Association of College and University Attorneys, and American Association of University Professors, one will come away with [the impression that] by and large, college and university administrations are doing rather well at their tasks, and college and university students, for the most part, are trying to equip themselves to make a good living when they get out in the world.[72]

In this vein, Robert Sedler has suggested that the existence of unenforced overbroad codes is not particularly worrisome.[73] Although I share Sedler's confidence that any broad campus speech code would not withstand judicial scrutiny, I am less confident that faculty and students understand their rights well enough to know if a particular enforcement of a campus speech code against them is legal or not, or that they have the resources or strength of will to contest the legality of the enforcement. The problem continues to be that too many people believe that they are justified in punishing others or in demanding punishment for others for merely provocative or offensive expression and that the continued existence of broad codes and their ideological support provides them some degree of cover and eventual success. And this leads us to a discussion of an increasingly popular argument for broad campus speech codes: they are justified because they are consistent with the international consensus against hate speech.

## THE INTERNATIONAL ARGUMENT

Strictly speaking, the appeal to an international consensus against racist speech is not new: it goes back at least to Kenneth Lasson's 1985 law review article discussed in Chapter 2. However, since 1998 the argument has become increasingly common in both the scholarly literature and popular media, and since I did not explicitly state or evaluate the argument in Chapter 2, it deserves our attention here. Even Anthony Lewis, the widely published journalist and career-long defender of robust freedom of speech, has retreated from the strict *Brandenburg* imminence standard to a standard that allows punishment for speech that "urges terrorist violence to an audience some of whose members are ready to act on the urging" due to his loss of faith in the nearly unique American protections of, for example, Holocaust denials.[74] Although Lewis's sympathies lie with a far narrower proposal than those of Tsesis or Delgado, it is noteworthy that so stalwart a defender of robust free speech as Lewis should find strict imminence "inappropriate" for certain contexts—such as Muslim imams urging their congregations to bomb civilians. Schematically, the International Argument is this:[75]

1. Most individual democratic nations as well as major international agreements have adopted broad hate speech restrictions.
2. These restrictions are effective.
3. These restrictions protect (or even enhance) overall freedom of speech. Thus,
4. The U.S. ought to adopt hate speech restrictions similar to the rest of the world.

*Premise (1): Most individual democratic nations as well as international agreements have adopted broad hate speech restrictions.* Numerous legal scholars have suggested (some sympathetically, some unsympathetically) that the United States is an exception to the current trend by governments and international bodies to adopt broad bans on offensive speech.[76] European democracies such as Austria, Belgium, Cyprus, Great Britain, France, Germany, Italy, Netherlands, and Switzerland as well as Canada, India, South Africa, New Zealand, and many Caribbean nations enforce laws protecting freedom of expression but specifying that this does not extend to speech that may incite racial or ethnic hostility or social disharmony.[77] Claudia Haupt notes that "comparing the U.S. approach with the approaches taken in Germany and various other European countries is a popular academic exercise in which German hate speech regulation is often cited favorably, even admiringly."[78] Advocates approvingly discuss restrictions on racist speech endorsed by Article 10 of the European Convention for the Protection of Human Rights and Fundamental Freedoms (ECHR) and Article 4 of the International Convention on the Elimination of All Forms of Racial Discrimination (CERD). Winfried Brugger gives this hypothetical example of a person waving a placard to illustrate the basic difference, noting that the expression would be protected on the steps of the U.S. Capitol but not on the steps of the German Reichstag:

> Wake up, you tired masses. I have four messages that you had better listen to, understand, and share! First, our president is a pig! I have painted two pictures to demonstrate my point. Here is one showing our clearly recognizable president as a pig engaged in sexual conduct with another pig in a judge's robe, and here is another, showing our President having a sexual encounter with his mother in an outhouse. Second, all our soldiers are murderers. Third, the Holocaust never happened. Fourth, African Americans use the slavery lie to extort money from the American government in the same way Jews use the Holocaust to extort money from Germany. Something should be done about this.[79]

Although Article 5 of the German Constitution—like American judicial interpretations of our Constitution—explicitly protects "worthless" and "dangerous" speech, sections of the German Federal Criminal Code—lacking any U.S. equivalents—penalize verbal and nonverbal expression that incites hatred or attacks human dignity (and specifically penalizes Holocaust denials, lies, or approvals) as well as insults and defamation that attack the honor of another person.[80] Although the details of the laws and their enforcement vary from country to country, it is common for nations and international bodies to adopt broader restrictions on hate speech than the United States permits.

*Premise (2): These restrictions are effective.* Alexander Tsesis claims misethnic speech laws could decrease hate speech and deter hate crimes, just as the Thirteenth, Fourteenth, and Fifteenth Amendments to the U.S. Constitution have significantly reduced unequal treatment in housing, employment, and voting rights, since legislation can be an effective agent in changing attitudes through its preventative and instructive nature. Therefore, Tsesis contends, "The potential that today's fringe groups will gain political ascendancy through sustained ideological dissemination calls for legislative vigilance."[81] Delgado and Stefancic write, "At a minimum, [these laws] enable monitoring commissions to compile statistics, issue progress reports, and coordinate the work of different nations. They also provide the basis for occasional prosecution of notorious hatemongers, all of which presumably has some deterrent effect."[82]

Further, Tsesis argues that even if such laws are not effective, they are still justified—just as laws prohibiting murder or theft are justified even if they do not reduce the number of murders or thefts. Regardless of the consequences of such laws, misethnic speech must be banned since it violates the fundamental human rights necessary to a legitimate democracy. Tsesis writes, "In a constitutional democracy each person's rights must be respected as intrinsically valuable . . . repudiating someone's personhood [as misethnic speech does] is in effect denying that reciprocal [moral] duty of humanity and the imperative to empathetic treatment are at all applicable to him or her."[83] In sum, hate speech does not deserve First Amendment protection because it has no legitimate expressive value; on the contrary, it is intended to and actually does chill legitimate expressive speech and legitimate expressive values.

*Premise (3): These restrictions protect (or even enhance) overall freedom of speech.* Delgado and Stefancic claim that in spite of the broad hate speech restrictions, the Canadian and European presses are "feistier," more "independent" of government influence, and "less beholden to corporate interests" than the U.S. media.[84] Delgado claims in a 1998 article that free speech has not suffered in Western democracies that have enacted hate speech laws.[85] Advocates also suggest (implicitly or explicitly) that such restrictions silencing the intimidating and hostile speech of members of the "in-group" would empower members of "out-groups" to exercise their right to free speech and thereby enhance overall freedom of speech.

*Conclusion: The U.S. ought to adopt hate speech restrictions similar to the rest of the world.* For these reasons, advocates of broad campus speech codes see the United States as an international "outlier" mistakenly clinging to an extremist conception of free speech. We need to "get with the game" and recognize that broad speech policies should be implemented to protect civil discourse and human dignity, the cornerstones of modern democracy.

In analyzing the International Argument, we must first note that the mere fact of some, many, most or even all other democracies having adopted law X or law Y does not by itself constitute a moral or legal reason for us to adopt law X or Y. To adopt such regulations merely because others have is to commit the so-called *argumentum ad populum* or "bandwagon fallacy." What must be shown is that there are better reasons for law X than there are reasons against it. Are these laws effective in combating offensive speech? If they are not effective, are they still justified? If they are effective, do their benefits outweigh their costs? In fact, do they protect (or even enhance) overall freedom of speech? I suggest there are good reasons to doubt affirmative answers to these questions.

First, the existence of broad offensive speech laws in the past did not prevent great evils from happening. The German Weimar Republic had a law much like the one proposed by Tsesis; this law, however, did not prevent the Nazis from coming to power and perpetrating their evil. The censor-friendly "bad tendency" speech test in the United States did not prevent the misethnic speech that Tsesis claims paved the way for slavery or the removal of the indigenous peoples. It is no mystery why this is so: the majority of people interpreting and enforcing these laws were part of the in-group/establishment prejudiced against the out-group. Sharing the prejudices of other insiders, they denied protections to outsiders.

Will it turn out differently today? Will the new censors be more enlightened than their predecessors? Certainly there is no guarantee that the enforcers will act always as advocates of broad codes recommend, since there can be no guarantee that the enforcers will share the views of broad code advocates. Thus, Steven Gey has noted that postmodern, critical race theorists like Delgado who support broad speech restrictions cannot guarantee their interpretation (even if we assume it is the correct or best interpretation) will prevail.[86] Indeed, it seems unlikely their interpretation would prevail, given that the majority of Americans—whether we consider the class of citizens in general or the subset of academics or politicians or judges or lawyers—do not subscribe to postmodern, critical race theory.

Skepticism about the International Argument also is supported by a brief review of how foreign nations actually apply their broad offensive speech laws. Certainly some nasty characters have been punished, but is it accurate to say—as supporters of the International Argument claim—that legitimate speech is not threatened? The facts suggest otherwise. Steven Gey cites numerous examples from Great Britain, Canada, and France to support his claim that "even a brief glance at how hate-speech [and pornography] laws have actually been enforced in Western democracies unencumbered by the First Amendment exposes a much more troublesome reality." Just a few of his examples include the author Roger Garaudy, convicted in France, not for denying the Holocaust, but for calling the killings "pogroms" or "massacres" rather than "genocide" or a "Holocaust"; Princeton professor Bernard Lewis, convicted in France for arguing that the Turkish massacre of Armenians in 1915 did not constitute "genocide" per se because it was not a "deliberate, planned attempted extermination of a people"; and the seizure by Canadian authorities of Salman Rushdie's *Satanic Verses* after a complaint from the Islamic Society of North America, as well as a film sympathetic to Nelson Mandela since it "stirred ill feelings against white South Africans."[87] Consider a few more examples. Canadian authorities also seized a newsletter published by the Ayn Rand Institute titled "In Moral Defense of Israel," which contained numerous articles published in mainstream U.S. newspapers. An outraged Jewish leader subsequently remarked, "It stuns the mind that an official at [Canada Customs and Review Authority] would even remotely consider the need, much less the propriety of examining this pamphlet. . . . Is it incompetence, madness, mischief, or something more malign?"[88] Mark Steyn, author of the best-selling *America Alone*, which laments the ostensible decline of the Western world, and Ezra Levant, publisher of the Canadian journal *Western Standard*, which reprinted cartoons depicting Muhammad from a Danish newspaper, were hauled before a Canadian Human Rights Commission (CHRC) to answer to charges of hate speech. Alan Borovoy, one of the originators of the CHRC, commented, "It never occurred to us that this instrument, which we intended to deal with discrimination in housing, employment and the provision of goods and services, would be used to muzzle the expression of opinion." On the other hand, Dean Steacy, a CHRC investigator, when asked under oath what value he attached to freedom of speech, replied disdainfully, "Freedom of speech is an American concept, so I don't give it any value."[89]

Actress and animal rights activist Brigitte Bardot was fined $23,000 in France for criticizing a Muslim ritual that involves the slaughter of sheep.[90] Journalist Oriana Fallaci was indicted in Italy for "vilification" of a "religion acknowledged by the state" for her criticisms of Islam and bemoaning what she believed was the Islamization of Europe. (Fallaci died before going to trial.)[91] In his extensive analysis of Canadian hate propaganda law, Stefan Braun concludes,

> Even in the relatively short life of hate law, there are already numerous illustrations of such dilemmas in censorship practice. Hate law tends to become whatever those with the power to threaten or enforce it think it is in the particular circumstances. In practice, it may be stretched, narrowed, even redefined, depending on the prevailing social times and changing political climates, without a single word [of the law] being changed.[92]

Braun also notes that contrary to claims made by advocates of the International Argument, the "America [sic] media establishment is larger and more diverse than it is in Canada. It has shown itself more conscious of its independence and more willing to challenge attempts by established authority to trespass upon it."[93] The *National Post*, a major Canadian newspaper founded in 1998 specifically to combat the perceived liberal bias in the Canadian media, ran an editorial on "Press Freedom Day" in 2004 bemoaning the "backsliding" of freedom of the press in Canada (ranked twenty-third in the world by Freedom House, tied with Malta) and other developed democracies due to vaguely worded laws concerning hate propaganda and their over-enforcement.[94] Claudia Haupt notes that the German system admired by advocates of the International Argument "has a number of problems that are often overlooked. . . ."[95] For example, through its decisions, the German Constitutional Court (their version of our U.S. Supreme Court) has failed to establish any clear hate speech rule balancing the various competing values, shifting from initial strong protections of offensive speech in the 1958 Luth case to a weakening in the 1971 Mephisto and 1987 and 1990 Strau [beta] cases and adopting conflicting approaches in the more recent Holocaust Denial (weighing in favor of human dignity) and Soldiers Are Murderers (weighing in favor of free speech) cases.[96] James Q. Whitman notes that the German preference for respect and honor over free speech extends to everyday discourse and can even punish forms of rudeness like "the finger" or calling someone a "jerk" and argues that German and French hate speech laws must be understood through their cultural and legal acceptance of an aristocratic conception of personal honor and social hierarchy from the eighteenth and nineteenth centuries.[97] Whitman also discusses how the German laws do not protect women from even "spectacular" sexual insults or affronts, including bosom-groping and attempted rape, and treats anti-Turk speech, for example, differently than anti–German Jewish speech.[98] Winfried Brugger, one of the few German academics to question the German approach, suggests the German legal system has failed to address critical issues regarding the exact nature of the different treatment of speech, the extent to which a divergence from the usual doctrine is appropriate, and the time frame during which such a divergence should be acceptable.[99] Such considerations suggest we exercise great caution before climbing aboard the international offensive speech code bandwagon.

Indeed, thoughtful—as opposed to naïve—comparative analysts are careful to warn that there is no universal legal solution to the problem of discriminatory speech: different countries must take different approaches given their different cultural, political, religious, and legal traditions. For example, Friedrich Kubler writes, "The widely differing solutions found in each of these opinions are not intended to serve as models or examples to be strictly followed by other countries. It is not the intention of this Article to advocate for or recommend identical rules and results for all legal systems. Even within Europe this would not work."[100] More pointedly, Kevin Boyle, a native Irishman teaching law in England and practicing in European courts, maintains that "the United States is to be criticized not because of the First Amendment but rather over its failure to do more to reverse the effects of past discrimination."[101] Some comparative analysts are blunt: Haupt writes, "Given the fundamental differences between the two approaches to free speech and consequently to hate speech regulation, the result of comparing the U.S. approach and the German approach should not be to call for the implementation of the German system or its elements in the United States."[102] International comparisons are problematic because political and legal systems are relatively insular and there are profound differences in national histories, cultural assumptions, political and legal traditions, and philosophical underpinnings. For example, European democracies accept greater speech restrictions than the United States in general, not just in regard to hate speech. Why? Brugger notes that unlike the U.S. Constitution, the German Constitution explicitly puts competing values ahead of free speech in both its text (free speech comes in Article 5, whereas respect for human dignity is in Article 1, the right to personality in Article 2, and the right to personal honor in Article 5) and practice.[103] Haupt explains that they were "founded on different philosophical premises; they also offer different interpretations of historical events that led to diverging responses in the legal framework concerning the value of free speech."[104] More specifically, she believes that our more Lockean individualistic approach contrasts sharply with the more aristocratic approach of Germany and other European democracies in which remnants of the feudal experience and (more recently) the Kantian approach giving human dignity precedence over all other values has led to extensive restrictions on both anti-democratic and uncivil speech.[105] The American mindset tends to distrust government, oppose aristocracy, and believe good ideas will triumph over evil ideas; the European mindset tends to trust government as a normative agent, to accept that "we are all aristocrats now," and to recognize how the triumph of evil ideas can result in the worst kinds of atrocities.[106] Steven Gey notes that "European countries have never institutionalized the uniquely American belief that citizens can sort out truth and falsehood for themselves, and likewise can recognize and respond appropriately to hatred when they hear it."[107] Differences in history and culture rightly influence the law of a nation. Thus, when Anthony Lewis poses the rhetorical question, "Should we in America who have avoided such tragedies [as the 1994 Hutu massacre of 500,000 Tutsis and moderate Hutus] tell Rwandans that it is wrong for them thus to limit freedom of speech?"[108] the answer, of course, is "No"; but the (dis)analogy works both ways: the same answer should be given to the question, "Should Rwandans who have experienced such tragedies tell Americans who have not that it is right for them to limit freedom of speech?"

Indeed, the differences between nations in laws regarding hate speech are strong enough that it is a long stretch to claim there exists some clear international norm prohibiting hate speech. Winfried Brugger observes, "On the whole, neither modern constitutional law nor international law consistently permits or consistently prohibits hate speech. In the world community, such speech is sometimes prohibited, and sometimes not."[109] Whitman notes that whereas German personal honor law barely recognizes any component of free speech, French personal honor law is explicitly balanced against free speech, with honor weighing the more in several areas—principally, regarding government officials and, in particular, police officers—but rarely enforced in casual, private encounters.[110] Ronald Krotoszynski Jr. offers the most extensive and current international comparisons and discussion of their value in his 2006 book *The First Amendment in Cross-Cultural Perspective*.[111] Krotoszynski examines the five factors of text, structure, history, precedent, and national experience while documenting numerous differences in the approaches of Canada, Germany, Japan, and the United Kingdom as compared to the United States regarding fundamental issues. These include the extent of and basis for judicial review of legislation, the values that are in competition with free speech as well as their relative weight in the balancing equation, the legitimacy of state action to prevent private harms, and the specific provisions in and enforcement of hate speech laws. For example, Canada has weighed equality over free speech, whereas the German approach is based in the precedence of human dignity and personal honor; Japan has explicitly embraced Alexander Meiklejohn's theory of free speech grounded in democratic self-governance; and the United Kingdom has delegated to the European Court of Human Rights the nature and extent of its free speech protections. All these differences in approach lead to differences in application. Thus, although it can be said in the abstract that many democratic nations seek to protect free speech while also combating hate speech, they all do so in their own ways according to their own lights. Roger Alford notes,

> The great gift of Krotoszynski's book is to turn our attention to a knottier subject on which there is far less agreement. If modern democracies disagree about the essentials of free speech theory and practice, there is little basis for shaming an outlier. Of course, one can try to play that game by analyzing a particular free speech variant—say, defamation or hate speech—comparing the United States' practice to a few select countries based on one or two contextual factors, and simplistically declaring the United States a "freedom of expression outlier." But such dimensionality reductions ignore the reality that a careful examination of multiple free speech variants in multiple countries using multiple contextual factors suggests something quite different. Each country is different from the United States, but each country is also different from one another.[112]

That is to say, not only is the U.S exceptional, but all nations are exceptional: there is no international consensus on the nature or value of free speech in general or hate speech in particular, except in a very abstract way that sees different applications within the constraints of each nation's legal texts, structure, history, precedent, and national experience. This complexity or dimensionality seriously undermines the international argument, for then its advocates must address questions they have not, and most likely cannot, answer: Whose hate speech restrictions have proven most effective? Whose have best protected (or even enhanced) overall free speech, and by whose standard will we judge whether broad offensive speech laws have positively or negatively impacted overall freedom of speech? That of Germany? Japan? Canada? the United States? More fundamentally, why suppose there is a uniquely best answer to the problem of hate speech or that all countries should employ the same means to maximize free speech while minimizing hate speech? As Brugger and other scholars note, American confidence in free speech is based on our progressive history and belief that good opinions will overcome bad ones, that offensive speech has had liberating effects, that we should not trust government to mandate our opinions, and that even dangerous and hurtful speech can address legitimate matters of public concern.[113]

## CONCLUSION

In April 2008, three University of Wisconsin–Stout students died in a tragic off-campus apartment fire. Just five days later, members of the extremist anti-homosexual Westboro Baptist Church of Topeka, Kansas (an independent, unaffiliated church notorious for protesting at gay pride events and the funerals of soldiers killed in Iraq), came to demonstrate at UW-Stout, not because any of the students were homosexual, but rather because the church also preaches that students are drunks and whores and their deaths are God's punishment for sins. (They also planned to conduct a demonstration at the funeral of one of the fire victims.[114]) The church notified university officials that they intended to stage a demonstration on public university property, and officials notified campus members via a mass e-mail in which officials recommended that the campus ignore the demonstration. However, students quickly organized a counterdemonstration to support the memory of the students and protest the views of the church. Thus, the next morning, three Westboro Church members paraded their signs on the campus quad amid an estimated crowd of 500 emotionally charged counterdemonstrators (mostly students), some of whom silently held up their own counterspeech signs, some of whom shouted obscenities, some of whom milled about in the background. One student grabbed a sign from a church demonstrator and ran, but was quickly arrested by a plain-clothes police officer. Although they had planned to demonstrate from 7:45 a.m. to 8:30 a.m., the church members left after about 15 minutes. The demonstration and counterdemonstration got considerable campus and local media attention; students learned how to lawfully protest; and many people learned that the Westboro Baptist Church is a tiny clan that hates gays, Catholics, Jews, Muslims, Chinese, Swedes, Canadians, Irish, British, and Mexicans, regards non-WBC members as bound for hell, and travels the country picketing, hoping its rights are trampled so it can win lawsuits to fund its activities.

Now suppose that instead of permitting the offensive, even hateful, speech of the demonstrators and some students, UW-Stout had a broad campus speech policy like the one proposed by Delgado and Stefancic, or by Tsesis. Would the church have been denied the opportunity to demonstrate in the first place—banned from campus as many people would have liked? Would they have been allowed to demonstrate but then cited as soon as their speech crossed "the line"? Did their speech cross "the line"? According to Delgado and Stefancic, it is over the line to use a "severe personal insult" such as "you idiot" or "you fag, you are going straight to hell." So presumably, the church members would have been subject to sanctions for their "God Hates Fags" signs along with the students shouting insulting obscenities at the church members. According to Tsesis, it is over the line to incite misethnic discrimination or violence that will occur at some indefinite future time. How would a typical campus cop or college administrator (or anyone else) decide this?

With other proponents of narrow campus speech policies, I suggest it is better on balance for UW-Stout to permit the demonstration and counterdemonstration rather than silence the church and/or students. The best legal and moral course for American public (and most private) universities to pursue in regard to hate speech, hate propaganda, biased speech, discriminatory speech, misethnic speech, offensive speech, or whatever we wish to call it, is to focus on eliminating illegal conduct, provide anti-discrimination education, and employ First Amendment–trained staff to enforce a narrow policy concentrating on (in addition to true threats, individual libels, true incitements, and so on) targeted harassment in a captive audience context that lacks academic justification and is repeated, egregious, or in conjunction with illegal conduct. At the end of the day, permitting offensive speech under the bright sunshine of free speech is preferable to banning offensive speech under the cold, dark cloud of censorship.

# NOTES

## CHAPTER ONE. INTRODUCTION

1. National Institute Against Prejudice and Violence, *Campus Ethnoviolence . . . and the Policy Options* (Baltimore: National Institute Against Prejudice and Violence, 1990). This study, headed by Howard Erhlich, was redone in 1995, reported in the *Higher Education Extension Service Review* 6:2, and is available on the Web at http://www.review.org/issues/vol6no2.html. Ehrlich's statistics should be viewed in light of (1) the study being done by an advocacy group and (2) the inherent difficulty of obtaining reliable data on such social "facts."

2. See Richard Delgado, "Words That Wound: A Tort Action for Racial Insults, Epithets, and Name-Calling," 17 *Harvard Civil Rights–Civil Liberties Law Review* 133 (1982); and Mari Matsuda, "Public Response to Racist Speech: Considering the Victim's Story," 87 *Michigan Law Review* 2320 (1989). Both rely especially on Gordon Allport, *The Nature of Prejudice* (Cambridge, Mass.: Addison-Wesley, 1954); and Harry Kitano, *Race Relations* (Englewood Cliffs, N.J.: Prentice-Hall, 1974).

3. Charles R. Lawrence III, "If He Hollers Let Him Go: Regulating Racist Speech on Campus," 1990 *Duke Law Journal* 431, 481 (1990).

4. Michael Olivas of the University of Houston Law Center, quoted in Nat Hentoff, *Free Speech for Me—But Not for Thee* (New York: HarperCollins, 1992), 30. *USA Today* set the number at more than two hundred in an October 15, 1992, article. John Wilson has pointed out that it is difficult to set a very precise number, since the term "hate speech code" is not well defined and many universities were merely updating earlier speech regulations. See John K. Wilson, *The Myth of Political Correctness: The Conservative Attack on Higher Education* (Durham, N.C., and London: Duke University Press, 1995), 92.

5. Hentoff, *Free Speech for Me*, ch. 4.

6. *Chronicle of Higher Education* (Nov. 24, 1993), A10.

7. Nadine Strossen, "Regulating Racist Speech on Campus: A Modest Proposal?" *Duke Law Journal* 484, 489 (1990).

8. In addition to dozens of popular and academic articles, five important books were published in the wake of the Nazis-in-Skokie incident. Two were firsthand accounts written by ACLU participants: ACLU executive director Aryeh Neier's *Defending My Enemy: American Nazis, the Skokie Case, and the Risks of Freedom* (New York: Dutton, 1979); and ACLU lawyer Mark Hamlin's *Nazi-Skokie Conflict* (Boston: Beacon Press, 1980). Two were academic treatises: Donald A. Downs, *Nazis in Skokie: Freedom, Com-*

*munity, and the First Amendment* (Notre Dame, Ind.: Notre Dame University Press, 1985); and James L. Gibson and Richard D. Bingham, *Civil Liberties and Nazis: The Skokie Free Speech Controversy* (New York: Praeger, 1985). One was a major reexamination of the First Amendment: Lee Bollinger, *The Tolerant Society* (New York: Oxford University Press, 1986).

9. The United States has fewer restrictions on racist speech than many other democracies. See, e.g., Kenneth Lasson, "Racial Defamation as Free Speech: Abusing the First Amendment," 17 *Columbia Human Rights Law Review* 11, 50–53 (1985); and Matsuda, "Public Response," 2341–2348. See Chapter 8, "The International Argument," for further discussion on the comparison of U.S. law on hate speech to the law of other nations.

10. See Plato's *Republic*, Books 2 and 3, for his account of the preliminary education of the "guardians," and Book 7 for the education of the "philosopher-kings." He addresses the poets in Book 10.

11. Liva Baker provides an excellent overview of Holmes's life and jurisprudence in *The Justice from Beacon Hill* (New York: HarperCollins, 1991).

12. Samuel Walker, *Hate Speech: The History of an American Controversy* (Lincoln and London: University of Nebraska Press, 1994).

13. Edward J. Cleary, *Beyond the Burning Cross: The First Amendment and the Landmark R.A.V. Case* (New York: Random House, 1994), ch. 6.

14. George Will, "Academic Liberal's Brand of Censorship," *San Francisco Chronicle* (Nov. 7, 1989), A22, and "In Praise of Censure," *Time* (July 31, 1989), 71–72; and Dinesh D'Souza, "Illiberal Education," *Atlantic* (March 1991), 51.

15. Wilson, *Myth of Political Correctness*, 100.

16. See, e.g., Brooke Noel Moore and Richard Parker, *Critical Thinking*, 4th ed. (Mountain View, Calif.: Mayfield, 1995), chs. 5 and 6.

17. Walker, *Hate Speech*, 2.

18. Hentoff, *Free Speech for Me*, 166.

19. William Rehnquist, "The Notion of a Living Constitution," 54 *Texas Law Review* 693 (1978).

20. Rodney Smolla, *Free Speech in an Open Society* (New York: Knopf, 1992), 151.

21. Strossen, "Regulating Racist Speech on Campus," 503.

22. Christopher Shea, "A Sweeping New Code," *Chronicle of Higher Education* (Nov. 17, 1995), A37.

23. Robin Wilson, "Whose Rights Are Protected?" *Chronicle of Higher Education* (Sept. 8, 1995), A25–A26.

24. Cleary, *Beyond the Burning Cross*, 24.

25. For example, the United States was the first (and for many years, the only) nation to guarantee freedom of speech in a constitution or federal law. And to this day our reputation for freedom of speech is internationally envied, and not just by academics or politicians. George Weah, the European, African, and World Soccer Player of the Year in 1996, who suffered the consequences of expressing his opinion that the United States should take over Liberia until its civil unrest was calmed, said, "In Africa there is no freedom of speech. I wish I were in America." *Soccer America* (July 22, 1996), 7.

26. See Catharine MacKinnon, *Only Words* (Cambridge, Mass.: Harvard University Press, 1993).

27. See Richard Delgado, "Campus Antiracism Rules: Constitutional Narratives in Collision," 85 *Northwestern Law Review* 343 (1991).

28. See Kingsley R. Browne, "Title VII as Censorship: Hostile Environment Harassment and the First Amendment," 52 *Ohio State Law Journal* 481 (1991).

29. Free speech controversies and the views informing the participants at the founding of our country are carefully outlined by Leonard Levy, *Freedom of Speech and Press in Early America: A Legacy of Suppression* (New York: Harper and Row, 1963), and *Emergence of a Free Press* (New York: Oxford University Press, 1985). Later controversies are addressed in Zecariah Chafee Jr.'s classic work, *Free Speech in the United States* (Cambridge, Mass.: Harvard University Press, 1941), and Walker's *Hate Speech*.

## CHAPTER TWO. BAN IT!: THE INITIAL ARGUMENTS FOR CAMPUS SPEECH CODES

1. In a footnote to his addendum, Judge Cohn expresses frustration at not having an opportunity to read Matsuda's article prior to reaching his decision, writing: "An earlier awareness of Professor Matsuda's paper certainly would have sharpened the Court's view of the issues." *Doe v. University of Michigan*, 721 F. Supp. 852, 869 (E.D. Mich. 1989).

2. See, e.g., Richard Delgado, "Words That Wound: A Tort Action for Racial Insults, Epithets, and Name-Calling," 17 *Harvard Civil Rights-Civil Liberties Law Review* 133 (1982); Martin Denis, "Race Harassment Discrimination: A Problem That Won't Go Away?" 10 *Employee Relations Law Journal* 415 (1984); Catherine MacKinnon, *Only Words* (Cambridge, Mass.: Harvard University Press, 1993); and Howard Erhlich, *Campus Ethnoviolence . . . and the Policy Options* (Baltimore: National Institute Against Prejudice and Violence, 1990).

3. Kent Greenawalt, *Fighting Words* (Princeton, N.J.: Princeton University Press, 1995).

4. He said, "Racism has no place in this day and age. . . . [The subcommittee] will make their decision [on appropriations for the university] during their budget discussions of the next few weeks. . . . Some things have to change. . . . Holding up funds as a club may be part of our response, but they will predicate on how the university responds." Quoted in Robin Hulshizer, "Securing Freedom from Harassment without Reducing Freedom of Speech: *Doe v. University of Michigan*," 76 *Iowa Law Review* 383, 387 n. 27 (1991).

5. Patricia Hodulik, "Racist Speech on Campus," 37 *Wayne State Law Review* 1433 (1991).

6. Ibid., 1443.

7. Samuel Walker, *Hate Speech: The History of an American Controversy* (Lincoln and London: University of Nebraska Press, 1994), 133–136.

8. Oliver Wendell Holmes Jr., *Northern Securities Co. v. United States*, 193 U.S. 197, 400–401 (1904).

9. Mari Matsuda, "Public Response to Racist Speech: Considering the Victim's Story," 87 *Michigan Law Review* 2320, 2323.

10. Delgado, "Words that Wound," n. 32, 135.

11. Ibid., n. 32, 136–149.

12. A short list of Delgado's sources on the harms of hate speech includes Gordon Allport, *The Nature of Prejudice* (Cambridge, Mass.: Addison-Wesley, 1954); Philip Mason, *Race Relations* (Oxford: Oxford University Press, 1970); Oliver Cox, *Caste,*

*Class, and Race* (New York: Doubleday, 1948); Kenneth Clark, *Dark Ghetto* (New York: Harper & Row, 1965); Joel Kovel, *White Racism: A Psychohistory* (New York: Pantheon, 1970); John Howard Griffin, *Black Like Me* (New York: Signet, 1970); and Harburg, Erfurt, Hawenstein et al., "Socioecological Stress, Suppressed Hostility, Skin Color, and Black and White Male Blood Pressure: Detroit," 35 *Psychosomatic Medicine* 76 (1973).

13. See, e.g., Richard Delgado, "Campus Antiracism Rules: Constitutional Narratives in Collision," 85 *Northwestern Law Review* 343 (1991); "First Amendment Formalism Is Giving Way to First Amendment Legal Realism," 29 *Harvard Civil Rights–Civil Liberties Law Review* 169 (1994); Delgado and Jean Stefancic, "Overcoming Legal Barriers to Regulating Hate Speech on Campus," *Chronicle of Higher Education* (Aug. 11, 1993), B1–B3; and Delgado and David Yun, "The Neoconservative Case against Hate-Speech Regulation—Lively, D'Souza, Gates, Carter, and the Toughlove Crowd," 47 *Vanderbilt Law Review* 1807 (1994), and "Pressure Values and Bloodied Chickens: An Analysis of Paternalistic Objections to Hate Speech Regulation," 82 *California Law Review* 871 (1994).

14. Matsuda, "Public Response," 2331–2341.

15. Ibid., 2336.

16. Ibid., 2340 and 2371.

17. Ibid., 2341–2348.

18. Ibid., 2348.

19. For useful contrasts between the U.S. and Canadian legal analyses of hate speech, see MacKinnon, *Only Words*, ch. 3; and Greenawalt, *Fighting Words*, 64–70.

20. Kant's *Grundlegung Zur Metaphyzik der Sitten* (1785) has been translated many times. I use Kant, *Ethical Philosophy* (Indianapolis, Ind.: Hackett Publishing, 1983).

21. Ibid., 31. This is what Kant seems to have in mind when discussing the "lying promise" example.

22. Ibid., 36.

23. Charles R. Lawrence III, "Good Speech, Bad Speech—Yes," 42 *Stanford Lawyer* 6 (1990); reprinted in David M. Adams (ed.), *Philosophical Problems in the Law* (Belmont, Calif: Wadsworth, 1992), 266.

24. See, e.g., Marcus Singer, "Golden Rule," in Paul Edwards (ed.), *Encyclopedia of Philosophy*, vol. 3 (New York: Macmillan, 1967), 365–367; and Harvey K. McArthur, "Golden Rule," in James F. Childress and John Macquarrie (eds.), *Westminster Dictionary of Christian Ethics* (Philadelphia: Westminster Press, 1986).

25. Ronald Dworkin, *Taking Rights Seriously* (Cambridge, Mass.: Harvard University Press, 1978), 182.

26. Molefi Kete Asante, "Unraveling the Edges of Free Speech," *Phi Kappa Phi Journal* (Spring 1995), 12.

27. John Leo, "Our Misguided Speech Police," *U.S. News and World Report* (Apr. 8, 1991), 25.

28. Andrew Altman, "Liberalism and Campus Hate Speech: A Philosophical Examination," 103 *Ethics* 302 (1993).

29. Ibid., 310.

30. Gerald Gunther, "Good Speech, Bad Speech—No," 42 *Stanford Lawyer* 7 (1990); reprinted in Adams, *Philosophical Problems*, 266.

31. Delgado, "Campus Antiracism Rules," 348–358.

32. Hulshizer, "Securing Freedom from Harassment," 384.

33. Charles Jones, "Equality, Dignity, and Harm: The Constitutionality of Regulat-

ing American Campus Ethnoviolence," 37 *Wayne State Law Review* 1383, 1389–1390 (1991).

34. Christina Bodinger–de Uriate of Phi Kappa Delta's Center for Evaluation, Development, and Research provides an illuminating report on hate crime in that organization's *Research Bulletin* (Dec. 1991), no. 10.

35. Nat Hentoff, *Free Speech for Me—But Not for Thee* (New York: HarperCollins, 1992), 164.

36. Jones, "Equality, Dignity, and Harm," 1391.

37. Charles R. Lawrence III, "If He Hollers Let Him Go: Regulating Racist Speech on Campus," 1990 *Duke Law Journal* 431, 462 (1990).

38. Ibid., 467.

39. *Capital Times* (Wis.) editorial, *Wisconsin State Journal* (Mar. 15, 1992).

40. Patricia Gunn, a dean at Duke University, quoted in the University of Wisconsin–Stout student newspaper, *Stoutonia* (Nov. 12, 1991).

41. Hodulik, "Racist Speech on Campus," 1445.

42. James E. Sulton, letter to the editor, "No 'Holy War' by UW against Free Speech," *Wisconsin State Journal* (May 25, 1991), 24.

43. Matsuda has argued that hate speech should constitute its own category of unprotected speech. See Matsuda, "Public Response," 2357ff. This approach has little plausibility given the American experience. Some others have considered the intentional infliction of emotional distress as a basis for regulating speech. This approach is discussed in Chapter 4. Still others have argued that hate speech should be understood through the hostile environment harassment model. This is addressed in Chapters 5 and 6.

44. Cass Sunstein, *Democracy and the Problem of Free Speech* (New York: Free Press, 1993), 188–193.

45. Greenawalt, *Fighting Words*, and "Insults and Epithets: Are They Protected Speech?" 42 *Rutgers Law Review* 287, 306–307 (1990).

46. Walker, *Hate Speech*, 71.

47. Thomas C. Grey, "Civil Rights vs. Civil Liberties: The Case of Discriminatory Verbal Harassment," *Social Philosophy and Policy* 8, no. 2 (1991), 91.

48. Ibid., 94.

49. John K. Wilson, *The Myth of Political Correctness: The Conservative Attack on Higher Education* (Durham and London: Duke University Press, 1995), 98.

50. Walker, *Hate Speech*, ch. 5, "The Curious Rise and Fall of Group Libel in America: 1942–1952."

51. Donald A. Downs, *Nazis in Skokie: Freedom, Community, and the First Amendment* (Notre Dame, Ind.: Notre Dame University Press, 1985).

52. Kenneth Lasson, "Racial Defamation as Free Speech: Abusing the First Amendment," 17 *Columbia Human Rights Law Review* 11 (1985).

53. Delgado, "Campus Antiracism Rules," 376–380.

54. Rhonda G. Hartman, "Revitalizing Group Defamation as a Remedy for Hate Speech on Campus," 71 *Oregon Law Review* 853 (1993).

55. Downs, *Nazis in Skokie*, 4–5.

56. Ibid., 156.

57. Lasson, "Racial Defamation," 35.

58. Ibid., 33.

59. Ibid., 39.

60. Ibid., 45.

61. Ibid., 43.

62. Ibid., 53.

63. Delgado, "Campus Antiracism Rules," 343.

64. Hartman, "Revitalizing Group Defamation," 351.

65. UW Regent Lee Dreyfus, commenting on an attempt to redraft UW-17 after it was struck down in federal court, *Wisconsin State Journal* (Mar. 7, 1992).

66. Robert O'Neil, director of the Thomas Jefferson Center for the Protection of Free Speech, commenting on the effort to revive UW-17 after the federal court struck it down, *Wisconsin State Journal* (May 18, 1992).

67. Delgado, "Campus Antiracism Rules," 381.

68. Isabel Wilkerson reports that at the University of Maryland, a study found that two-thirds of white students had not heard of racist incidents, while four-fifths of African American students had. Wilkerson, "Campus Blacks Feel Racism's Nuances," *New York Times* (Apr. 17, 1988), 1, 34.

69. Lawrence, "If He Hollers," 470–472.

70. Sunstein, *Democracy*, 199.

71. Willmore Kendall, "The 'Open Society' and Its Fallacies," *American Political Science Review* 54 (1960), 973.

72. Walter Berns, *Freedom, Virtue, and the First Amendment* (Baton Rouge: Louisiana State University Press, 1957).

73. William R. Harbour, *The Foundations of Conservative Thought* (Notre Dame, Ind.: Notre Dame University Press, 1982), esp. 99–112.

74. Matsuda, "Public Response," 2371.

75. Wilson, *Myth of Political Correctness*, 107.

76. Carnegie Fund for the Advancement of Teaching, *Campus Life* (New York: Carnegie Fund, 1990).

77. Lawrence, "If He Hollers," 459.

78. Arati Korwar, *War of Words: Speech Codes at Public Colleges and Universities* (Nashville, Tenn.: Freedom Forum First Amendment Center, 1994), 32.


CHAPTER THREE. WAYNE DICK'S PLEA:
THE CRITICS FIGHT BACK

1. Nat Hentoff, *Free Speech for Me—But Not for Thee* (New York: HarperCollins, 1992), 122.

2. Ibid., 124–125.

3. See ibid., 99–118, for a discussion of earlier incidents at Yale and the development of the Woodward Report.

4. Donna Shalala, quoted in the *Oshkosh Northwestern* (May 7, 1992).

5. Nadine Strossen, "Regulating Racist Speech on Campus: A Modest Proposal?" 1990 *Duke Law Journal* 484 (1990).

6. Arthur Terminiello, an active anti-Semitic, quasi-fascist organizer and suspended Catholic priest, delivered a racist speech to a large audience in a Chicago meetinghouse. About one thousand angry protestors milled about outside protesting his speech, and when Terminiello denounced them, they threw rocks through the windows of the building. Police then entered the building and arrested Terminiello for his "fighting

words." Brandenburg, a Ku Klux Klansman, vented his racist views at a rally outside Cincinnati, urging the return of blacks to Africa and Jews to Israel, by violent means if necessary.

7. Strossen cites a series of "companion" cases from 1972 (*Brown v. Oklahoma*, 408 U.S. 914 [1972]; *Lewis v. New Orleans*, 408 U.S. 913 [1972]; *Rosenfeld v. New Jersey*, 408 U.S. 901 [1972]); and from 1974 (*Karlan v. Cincinnati*, 416 U.S. 924 [1974]; *Rosen v. California*, 461 U.S. 924 [1974]; *Lucas v. Arkansas*, 416 U.S. 919 [1974]; and *Kelly v. Ohio*, 416 U.S. 923 [1974]).

8. Strossen, "Regulating Racist Speech on Campus," 510.

9. Reported in Hentoff, *Free Speech for Me*, 188–192.

10. In March 1991, Jeffrey Gerson, like so many other defenders of free speech, found himself the target of censorship and public outrage when he tried to show in a direct fashion what he thought the real meaning of the First Amendment is by burning a small replica of an American flag during a class discussion of free speech.

11. Strossen, "Regulating Racist Speech on Campus," 519.

12. *Beauharnais v. Illinois*, 343 U.S. 250, 274 (1951).

13. Quoted in Edward J. Cleary, *Beyond the Burning Cross: The First Amendment and the Landmark R.A.V. Case* (New York: Random House, 1994), 49.

14. Alan Charles Kors, "Harassment Policies in the University," *Society* 28, no. 4 (1991), reprinted in Edmund Wall (ed.), *Sexual Harassment: Confrontations and Decisions* (Buffalo, N.Y.: Prometheus Books, 1992), 46–47.

15. Strossen, "Regulating Racist Speech on Campus," 490.

16. D'Souza, during the *MacNeil-Lehrer Newshour*, transcript in Paul Berman (ed.), *Debating PC: The Controversy over Political Correctness on College Campuses* (New York: Dell, 1992), 35.

17. George Will, "The Pollution of Politics," *Newsweek* (Nov. 6, 1989), 92.

18. *Report of the President's Ad Hoc Committee on Racial Harassment*, University of Texas at Austin (Nov. 27, 1989).

19. Charles J. Sykes and Brad Miner, "Sense and Sensitivity," *National Review* (Mar. 18, 1991), 31.

20. Kathyrn Marie Dessayer and Arthur J. Burke, "Leaving Them Speechless: A Critique of Speech Restrictions on Campus," 14 *Harvard Journal of Law and Public Policy* 565, 580 (1991).

21. Ibid., 580.

22. Scott Jaschik, "First Amendment Carries Most Weight in 2 Race-Harassment Rulings," *Chronicle of Higher Education* (Apr. 21, 1995), A38.

23. *Chronicle of Higher Education* (Sept. 28, 1994), A22.

24. Dessayer and Burke, "Leaving Them Speechless," 580.

25. Leonard Jeffries of CUNY.

26. David F. McGowan and Ragesh K. Tangri, "A Libertarian Critique of University Restrictions of Offensive Speech," 79 *California Law Review* 825, 907 (1991).

27. Hentoff, *Free Speech for Me*, 155.

28. Robert Bork, "That Delicate Balance: Our Bill of Rights, the First Amendment, and Hate Speech," panel discussion at Columbia University, PBS video, 1992.

29. Benno Schmidt, quoted in "Abolish the Speech Codes," editorial, *Wall Street Journal* (June 11, 1990), A10.

30. Gunther, "Good Speech, Bad Speech—No," 7.

31. McGowan and Tangri, "A Libertarian Critique," 838.

32. Patrick Garry, "Censorship by the Free Speech Generation," *Phi Kappa Phi Journal* (Spring 1995), 30.

33. Liva Baker, *The Justice from Beacon Hill* (New York: HarperCollins, 1991), 536–538.

34. Margaret Blanchard, *Revolutionary Sparks: Freedom of Expression in Modern America* (New York: Oxford University Press, 1992), 487.

35. Arati Korwar, *War of Words: Speech Codes at Public Colleges and Universities* (Nashville, Tenn.: Freedom Forum First Amendment Center, 1994, 1995), 12.

36. Theodore Simon, "Fighting Racism: Hate Speech Detours," 26 *Indiana Law Review* 411, 432 (1993).

37. Dinesh D'Souza, *Illiberal Education* (New York: Free Press, 1991), 140–155; Stephen Carter, *Reflections of an Affirmative Action Baby* (New York: Basic Books, 1992), 77, 180–181; Henry Louis Gates Jr., "Let Them Talk," *New Republic* (Sept. 23 and 27, 1993), 37, 43, 47–49; and Donald Lively, "Reformist Myopia and the Imperative of Progress: Lessons for the Post-Brown Era," 46 *Vanderbilt Law Review* 865 (1993).

38. Hentoff, *Free Speech for Me*, 100.

39. Hirsch, quoted in *Oshkosh Northwestern* (Mar. 7, 1992).

40. Quoted in Dessayer and Burke, "Leaving Them Speechless," 578.

41. Gunther, "Good Speech, Bad Speech—No," 267–268.

42. Hentoff, *Free Speech for Me*, 151.

43. Marcia Pally, *Sex and Sensibility: Reflections on Forbidden Mirrors and the Will to Censor* (Hopewell, N.J.: Ecco Press, 1994), 158.

44. Hentoff, *Free Speech for Me*, 162.

45. Cleary, *Beyond the Burning Cross*, 105.

46. Garry, "Censorship by the Free Speech Generation," 30–31.

47. Charles Calleros, "Reconciliation of Civil Rights and Civil Liberties after *R.A.V. v. City of St. Paul*: Free Speech, Antiharassment Policies, Multicultural Education, and Political Correctness at Arizona State University," 1992 *Utah Law Review* 1205 (1992).

48. Simon, "Fighting Racism," 429.

49. Rodney Smolla, *Free Speech in an Open Society* (New York: Knopf, 1992), 169.

50. Hentoff, *Free Speech for Me*, 1.

CHAPTER FOUR. SEE YOU IN COURT:
THE CAMPUS HATE SPEECH CASES

1. *Doe v. University of Michigan*, 721 F. Supp. 852, 853 (E.D. Mich. 1989).

2. Ibid., 863.

3. Ibid., 866.

4. Ibid., 867.

5. Ibid.

6. "Tufts Drops Speech Restrictions Policy, Saying It Was Open to Challenge," *Boston Globe* (Oct. 5, 1989), 44.

7. *UWM-Post v. Board of Regents*, 774 F. Supp. 1163, 1171 (E.D. Wis. 1991).

8. Ibid., 1174.

9. Ibid., 1181.

10. *Iota Xi v. George Mason*, 773 F. Supp 792, 795 (E.D. Va. 1991).

11. *Matter of Welfare of R.A.V.*, 464 N.W.2d 507, 508 (Minn. 1991).

12. Ibid., 511 (quoting *Cantrell v. Connecticut*, 310 U.S. 296, 309–10 [1940]).

13. *R.A.V. v. City of St. Paul*, 505 U.S. 377, 387–388(1992).

14. Ibid., 392. "Marquis of Queensbury Rules" is a reference to the eighth Marquess of Queensbury (1844–1900), who supervised ca. 1867 the formulation of the basic rules of modern boxing (e.g., use of gloves, division into rounds, no hitting below the belt, etc.).

15. Ibid., 394.

16. Ibid., 396.

17. Gregory Heiser and Lawrence Rossow, "Hate Speech or Free Speech: Can Broad College Hate Speech Rules Survive Current Judicial Reasoning?" 22 *Journal of Law and Education* 134, 151 (1993).

18. Edward Eberle, "Hate Speech, Offensive Speech, and Public Discussion in America," 29 *Wake Forest Law Review* 1135, 1158–59 (1994).

19. Arati Korwar, *War of Words: Speech Codes at Public Colleges and Universities* (Nashville, Tenn.: Freedom Forum First Amendment Center, 1994, 1995), 20.

20. Ibid., 20. Jeff Carr, Memorandum to Chancellor Joseph Wyan, April 13, 1994.

21. Dambrot also sued for defamation, but the court dropped that cause of action.

22. *Dambrot v. Central Michigan*, 839 F. Supp. 477, 481 (E.D. Mich. 1993). The decision was upheld in full by the Sixth Court of Appeals, *Dambrot v. Central Michigan University*, 55 F.3d 1177 (6th Cir. 1995).

23. Ibid., 484.

24. Ibid., 482.

25. Ibid., 482, n. 7.

26. Ibid., 483.

27. Ibid., 483–484.

28. Thomas C. Grey, "Civil Rights vs. Civil Liberties: The Case of Discriminatory Verbal Harassment," *Social Philosophy and Policy* 8, no. 2 (1991), 106–107.

29. *Corry, et al. v. Stanford*, Santa Clara Superior Court, case no. 740309, February 27, 1995, 9.

30. Ibid., 19.

31. Ibid., 25.

32. Stanford argued that the Leonard Law violated its First Amendment rights by (a) compelling it to provide access to racists, (b) being content-based, (c) prohibiting Stanford's free expression, and (d) interfering with Stanford's right of association. Judge Stone ruled that the Leonard Law (a) merely ensures constitutionally protected speech is not restricted by schools like Stanford, that it does not compel Stanford to approve of illegal fighting words or illegal conduct; (b) does not restrict speech for its content because it promotes more speech, i.e., the fact that it strikes down Stanford's content-based policy does not make it content-based itself; (c) does not prevent Stanford from expressing any views at all, but only prevents Stanford from punishing the constitutionally protected speech of its students; and (d) does not interfere with Stanford's right of association, since the law does not substantially alter the group's activities, i.e., its membership is not coextensive with any message it may wish to convey, and it may continue to express its official view while admitting "undesired" members who dissent from that official view.

33. John K. Wilson, *The Myth of Political Correctness: The Conservative Attack on Higher Education* (Durham, N.C., and London: Duke University Press, 1995), 92.

34. Ibid., 99.

35. *University of Chicago Student Information Manual* (Chicago: University of Chicago, 1993–1994), 30.

36. Wilson, *Myth of Political Correctness*, 96.

37. Ibid., 99.

38. Ibid., 101.

39. Justice Brennan, writing for the majority, found the Texas statute unconstitutional by focusing on the communicative elements involved in the flag burning and the legal precedents barring government from punishing offensive speech, insisting that all that is special about the flag can continue to be expressed and felt by patriots. Brennan writes, "We do not consecrate the flag by punishing its desecration, for in doing so we dilute the freedom that this cherished emblem represents." Chief Justice Rehnquist, joined by Byron White and Sandra Day O'Connor in dissent, found the Texas statute constitutional by focusing on the unique status of the flag and the noncommunicative elements of the act, characterizing it as "the equivalent of an inarticulate grunt or roar." Rehnquist writes, "Surely one of the high purposes of a democratic society is to legislate against conduct that is regarded as evil and profoundly offensive to the majority of people—whether it be murder, embezzlement, pollution, or flag-burning."

40. J. S. Mill's *On Liberty*, originally published as articles in a magazine in 1859, has been published in book form many times. I use Mill, *On Liberty*, ed. Currin V. Shields (Indianapolis, Ind.: Bobbs-Merrill, 1956).

41. Zechariah Chafee Jr., *Free Speech in the United States* (Cambridge, Mass.: Harvard University Press, 1941.)

42. Alexander Meiklejohn, *Free Speech and Its Relation to Self-Government* (New York: Harper and Brothers, 1948).

43. Thomas I. Emerson, *Toward a General Theory of the First Amendment* (New York: Random House, 1966), 15.

44. Ibid., 6.

45. Ibid., 8.

46. Ibid., 6.

47. Ronald Dworkin, "The Coming Battles over Free Speech," *New York Review of Books* (June 11, 1992), 56.

48. Stanley Fish, *There's No Such Thing as Free Speech: And It's a Good Thing, Too* (New York: Oxford University Press, 1994), 14.

49. Thomas Scanlon, "A Theory of Freedom of Expression," *Philosophy and Public Affairs* 1, no. 2 (1972), 204–226.

50. Joseph Raz, *The Morality of Freedom* (Oxford: Clarendon Press, 1986); and "Free Expression and Personal Identification," in W. J. Waluchnow (ed.), *Free Expression* (Oxford: Clarendon Press, 1992), 1–29.

51. Raz, *Morality of Freedom*, 200ff.

52. Lee Bollinger, *The Tolerant Society* (New York: Oxford University Press, 1986).

53. David A. J. Richards, "Free Speech as Toleration," in Waluchnow (ed.), *Free Expression*, 31–57.

54. Ibid., 38–39.

55. For example, Meiklejohn writes in *Free Speech and Its Relation to Self-Government*, 17, "The phrase 'Congress shall make no law . . . abridging freedom of speech' is unqualified. It admits of no exceptions." Yet, on the very next page (!) he writes, "No one can doubt that, in any well-governed society, the legislature has both the right and the duty

to prohibit certain forms of speech." Justice Black, famous for his dictum that "no law means no law," also wrote, "It is a myth to say any person has a constitutional right to say what he pleases, where he pleases, and when he pleases." *Tinker v. Des Moines School District*, 393 U.S. 503, 576 (1969). And Justice Douglas wrote, "Freedom of speech, though not absolute . . . is nevertheless protected against censorship or punishment, unless shown likely to produce a clear and present danger of a serious substantive evil that rises far above public inconvenience, annoyance, or unrest." *Terminiello v. Chicago*, 337 U.S. 1, 4 (1949).

56. Emerson, *Toward a General Theory*, 59 and 19.

57. Cass Sunstein, *Democracy and the Problem of Free Speech* (New York: Free Press, 1993).

58. Ibid., 34–37.

59. Ibid., 188–193.

60. Ibid., 130, 163.

61. Walter Williams, "Race, Scholarship, and Affirmative Action," *National Review* (May 5, 1989), 36.

62. Robin Wilson, "College's Anti-Harassment Policies Bring Controversy over Free Speech Issues," *Chronicle of Higher Education* (Oct. 4, 1989), A1, A38.

63. Anti-Defamation League of B'nai B'rith, *Combating Bigotry on Campus* (New York: Anti-Defamation League of B'nai B'rith, 1989), 2.

64. Strossen, "Regulating Hate Speech on Campus," 490, 496–501, and Appendix.

65. *R.A.V.*, at 389.

66. Hentoff, "Free Speech: Are There Limits?" *Progressive* (May 1993), 16.

## CHAPTER FIVE. HOSTILE ENVIRONMENT TAKES A FRONT SEAT

1. Catharine MacKinnon, *Sexual Harassment of Working Women: A Case of Sex Discrimination* (New Haven, Conn.: Yale University Press, 1979).

2. Ellen E. Lange, "Racist Speech on Campus: A Title VII Solution to a First Amendment Problem," 64 *Southern California Law Review* 105 (1990).

3. John T. Shapiro, "The Call for Campus Conduct Policies: Censorship or Constitutionally Permissable Limitations on Speech?" 75 *Minnesota Law Review* 201 (1990).

4. Mary Ellen Gale, "Reimagining the First Amendment: Racist Speech and Equal Liberty," 65 *St. John's Law Review* 119 (1991).

5. For a good review of early court decisions, see William L. Woerner and Sharon L. Oswald, "Sexual Harassment in the Workplace: A View through the Eyes of the Courts," *Labor Law Journal* (Nov. 1990), reprinted in Edmund Wall (ed.), *Sexual Harassment: Confrontations and Decisions* (Buffalo, N.Y.: Prometheus Books, 1992).

6. See *Barnes v. Train*, 13 FEP 123 (D.C. Dist. of Col. 1974); *Corne v. Bausch and Lomb, Inc.*, 390 F. Supp. 1639 EPD Par. 10,093.

7. *Tomkins v. Public Service Electric and Gas Co.*, 422 F. Supp. 553 (D.C. N.J. 1976).

8. J. B. Attanasio, "Equal Justice under Chaos: The Developing Law of Sexual Harassment," 51 *Cincinnati Law Review* 1 (1982).

9. Gale, "Reimagining the First Amendment," 164.

10. Ibid., 174.

11. Lange, "Racist Speech on Campus," 125.

12. Ibid., 127.

13. Catharine MacKinnon, *Only Words* (Cambridge, Mass.: Harvard University Press, 1993), 30.

14. Ibid., 12ff.

15. Ibid., 107.

16. Ibid., 77.

17. Ibid., 17.

18. Linda S. Greene, "Racial Discourse, Hate Speech, and Political Correctness," *Phi Kappa Phi Journal* (Spring 1995), 34.

19. Courts have upheld university sanctions regarding sexual harassment in many cases. See, e.g., *Cockburn v. Santa Monica Community College*, 207 Cal. Rptr. 589 (Ct. App. 2d Dis. 1984); *Korf v. Ball State University*, 726 F.2d 1222 (7th Cir. 1984); *Naragon v. Wharton*, 737 F.2d 1403 (5th Cir. 1984); and *Levitt v. University of Texas at El Paso*, 759 F.2d 1724 (5th Cir. 1984).

20. Greene, "Racial Discourse," 35.

21. John K. Wilson, *The Myth of Political Correctness: The Conservative Attack on Higher Education* (Durham, N.C., and London: Duke University Press, 1995), 101.

22. Cass Sunstein, *Democracy and the Problem of Free Speech* (New York: Free Press, 1993), 196.

23. Arati Korwar, *War of Words: Speech Codes at Public Colleges and Universities* (Nashville, Tenn.: Freedom Forum First Amendment Center, 1994, 1995), 32, table 1.

24. Gale, "Reimagining the First Amendment," 182–183.

25. Lange, "Racist Speech on Campus," 128.

26. Ibid.

27. Ibid., 129–130.

28. Shapiro, "The Call for Campus Conduct Policies," 230–231.

29. See, e.g., Nancy Tuana, "Sexual Harassment in Academe: Issues of Power and Coercion," *College Teaching* 33, no. 2 (1985), 53–57, 61–63; reprinted in Wall (ed.), *Sexual Harassment* (1992), 49–60.

30. Gale, "Reimagining the First Amendment," 176–182.

31. Wilson, *Myth of Political Correctness*, 91, 95, and 103.

32. See Leonard Levy, *Freedom of Speech and Press in Early America: A Legacy of Suppression* (New York: Harper and Row, 1963).

33. See Kent Greenawalt, *Fighting Words* (Princeton, N.J.: Princeton University Press, 1995), ch. 5, "Campus Speech Codes and Workplace Harassment," esp. 96–98.

34. Richard Delgado and David Yun, "Pressure Valves and Bloodied Chickens: An Analysis of Paternalistic Objections to Hate Speech Regulation," 82 *California Law Review* 871, 886–887 (1994).

35. See, e.g., Richard Delgado, "First Amendment Formalism Is Giving Way to First Amendment Legal Realism," 29 *Harvard Civil Rights–Civil Liberties Law Review* 169 (1994); Delgado and Yun, "Pressure Values and Bloodied Chickens"; Delgado and Yun, "The Neoconservative Case against Hate-Speech Regulation: Lively, D'Souza, Gates, Carter and the Toughlove Crowd," 47 *Vanderbilt Law Review* 1807 (1994); Delgado and Jean Stefancic, "Hateful Speech, Loving Communities: Why Our Notion of a 'Just Balance' Changes So Slowly," 82 *California Law Review* 851 (1994); Laura Lederer and Richard Delgado (eds.), *The Price We Pay: The Case against Racist Speech, Hate Propaganda and Pornography* (New York: Hill and Wang, 1994).

36. Delgado and Yun, "The Neoconservative Case," 1816.

37. Ibid., 1819.

38. Laura Lederer, "'Freedom of Hate Speech' Too Costly," *Minneapolis Star-Tribune* (May 31, 1995).

39. Nadine Strossen, "Regulating Racist Speech on Campus: A Modest Proposal?" 1990 *Duke Law Journal* 484, 498 (1990).

CHAPTER SIX. THE ATTACK ON
HOSTILE ENVIRONMENT

1. Nat Hentoff, *Free Speech for Me—But Not for Thee* (New York: HarperCollins, 1992),160.

2. Jonathan Rauch, "In Defense of Prejudice," *Harper's Magazine* (May 1995), 38. Also see Rauch, *Kindly Inquisitors: The New Attacks on Free Thought* (Chicago: University of Chicago Press, 1993).

3. *UWM-Post v. Board of Regents*, 774 F. Supp. 1163, 1177 (E.D. Wis. 1991).

4. Courtney Leatherman, "Court Finds College Violated First Amendment," *Chronicle of Higher Education* (Sept. 6, 1996), A16.

5. *UWM-Post*, at 1177.

6. Ibid.

7. Ibid.

8. Kingsley R. Browne, "Title VII as Censorship: Hostile Environment Harassment and the First Amendment," 52 *Ohio State Law Journal* 481, 538 (1991), 502–503.

9. *Harris v. Forklift Systems*, 510 U.S. 17, 21 (1993).

10. Hentoff, *Free Speech for Me*, 169.

11. Rauch, "In Defense of Prejudice," 38.

12. Browne, "Title VII as Censorship," 543.

13. Ibid., 546.

14. Ibid., 517.

15. Ibid., 518 and 519, n225.

16. Ibid., 546.

17. Martha Minow, "Looking Ahead to the 1990's: Constitutional Law and American Colleges and Universities," reprinted in Thomas P. Hustoles and Walter B. Connolly, Jr. (eds.), *Regulating Racial Harassment on Campus: A Legal Compendium* (Washington, D.C.: National Association of College and University Attorneys, 1990), 208–209, 210, 214–215.

18. *Dube*, quoting *Keyishian v. Board of Regents*, 385 U.S. 589,603 (1967).

19. Browne, "Title VII as Censorship," 545–546.

20. Ibid., 542–543.

21. Courtney Leatherman, "Free Speech or Harassment?" *Chronicle of Higher Education* (Sept. 28, 1994), A22.

22. Hentoff, *Free Speech for Me*, 168.

23. Rauch, "In Defense of Prejudice," 43.

24. Ibid., 46.

25. Browne, "Title VII as Censorship," 550.

26. Ibid., 540–544.

27. *UWM-Post*, at 1175.

28. John Stuart Mill, *On Liberty* (edited with an introduction by Currin V. Shields) (Indianapolis, Ind.: Bobbs-Merrill, 1956), 64.

29. Rauch, "In Defense of Prejudice," 38.

30. Ibid., 39.

31. Ibid., 46.

32. Browne, "Title VII as Censorship," 524.

33. The cartoon ran in newspapers on May 19, 1991.

34. Richard Delgado and David Yun, "Pressure Valves and Bloodied Chickens: An Analysis of Paternalistic Objections to Hate Speech Regulation," 82 *California Law Review* 871, 881 (1994).

35. William B. Rubenstein, "Since When Is the Fourteenth Amendment Our Route to Equality?: Some Reflections on the Constitution of the 'Hate Speech' Debate from a Lesbian/Gay Perspective," in Gates et al., *Speaking of Race, Speaking of Sex* (New York: New York University Press, 1994), 280–299.

36. Browne, "Title VII as Censorship," 536ff.

37. Ibid., 537–538.

38. Robert C. Post, "Racist Speech, Democracy, and the First Amendment," 32 *William and Mary Law Review* 267 (1991), reprinted with some revisions in Gates et al., *Speaking of Race*, 115–180.

39. "Report of the Subcommittee on Academic Freedom and Sexual Harassment," *Academe* (Sept.–Oct. 1994), 64–68.

40. Ibid., 65.

41. Linda J. Rubin and Sherry B. Borgers, "Sexual Harassment in Universities during the 1980s," *Sex Roles*, 23, nos. 7–8 (1990), reprinted in Edmund Wall (ed.), *Sexual Harassment: Confrontations and Decisions* (Buffalo, N.Y.: Prometheus Books, 1992), 25–40.

42. William L. Woerner and Sharon L. Oswald, "Sexual Harassment in the Workplace: A View through the Eyes of the Law," *Labor Law Journal* (Nov. 1990), reprinted in Wall (ed.), *Sexual Harassment*, 180.

43. Alan Charles Kors, "Harassment Policies in the University," *Society* 28, no. 4 (1991), reprinted in Wall (ed.), *Sexual Harassment*, 44.

44. Ibid., 45.

45. The Editors, "Talking Dirty," *New Republic* (1991), reprinted in Wall (ed.), *Sexual Harassment*, 225–228.

46. Ellen Frankel Paul, "Bared Buttocks and Federal Cases," *Society* 28, no. 4 (1991), reprinted in Wall (ed.), *Sexual Harassment*, 155.

47. During her plenary session, "The Progress and Pitfalls in Sexual Harassment Procedures" at the 6th International Sexual Assault and Sexual Harassment on Campus Conference, Nov. 2–4, 1996, Levine mentioned breach of (implied) contract, breach of fiduciary relationship, constructive dismissal, wrongful dismissal, the tort of intentional (or negligent) infliction of emotional distress, negligent hiring, negligent firing, and negligent retention as specific legal tools a good lawyer can use to get after sexual harassers.

CHAPTER SEVEN. AND THE VERDICT IS . . .

1. *AAUP Wisconsin Conference Newsletter* (Fall 1993), 2.

2. Leon Friedman, "Freedom of Speech: Should It Be Available to Pornographers,

Nazis, and the Klan?" in Monroe H. Freedman and Eric M. Freedman (eds.), *Group Defamation and Freedom of Speech: The Relationship between Language and Violence* (Westport, Conn.: Greenwood Press, 1995), 307–308.

3. Influential communitarian works include Michael J. Sandel, *Liberalism and the Limits of Justice* (Cambridge: Cambridge University Press, 1982), and "Morality and the Liberal Ideal," *New Republic* (May 7, 1984), 15–17; Charles Taylor, "Atomism," in *Philosophy and the Human Sciences* (Cambridge: Cambridge University Press, 1985); Alasdair MacIntyre, *After Virtue*, 2nd ed. (Notre Dame, Ind.: University of Notre Dame Press, 1984), and *Whose Justice? Whose Reason?* (Notre Dame, Ind.: University of Notre Dame Press, 1988); Roberto Unger, *Knowledge and Politics* (New York: Free Press, 1975), and *Politics: A Work in Constructive Social Theory* (Cambridge: Cambridge University Press, 1987); Robert Bellah et al., *Habits of the Heart: Individualism and Commitment in American Life* (New York: Harper and Row, 1985); Elizabeth H. Wolgast, *The Grammar of Justice* (Ithaca, N.Y.: Cornell University Press, 1987), esp. ch. 1. See Robert Booth Fowler, *The Dance with Community: The Contemporary Debate in American Thought* (Lawrence: University Press of Kansas, 1991), for an insightful overview of contemporary and historical movements in communitarianism.

4. The group libel approach addressed in Chapters 2 and 3 is most clearly connected to communitarianism; see, e.g., Note, "A Communitarian Defense of Group Libel Laws," 101 *Harvard Law Review* 682 (1988). However, the group-rights, group-think ideals of communitarian philosophy also are adopted or implied in other ways, e.g., those who use "anti-subordination" and "caste" rhetoric; see, e.g., Charles R. Lawrence III, "Cross-Burning and the Sound of Silence: Anti-Subordination Theory and the First Amendment," in Laura J. Lederer and Richard Delgado (eds.), *The Price We Pay: The Case against Racist Speech, Hate Propaganda, and Pornography* (New York: Hill and Wang, 1994), 114–121, and Cass Sunstein, "Words, Conduct, Caste," in ibid., 266–271.

5. Kent Greenawalt, *Fighting Words* (Princeton, N.J.: Princeton University Press, 1995), 8–10.

6. Robert C. Post, "Racist Speech, Democracy, and the First Amendment," 32 *William and Mary Law Review* 267 (1991); reprinted in Henry Louis Gates Jr. et al., *Speaking of Race, Speaking of Sex* (New York and London: New York University Press), 115–180.

7. See esp. John Rawls, "Justice as Fairness: Political not Metaphysical," *Philosophy and Public Affairs* 14 (Summer 1985), 223–251; Allan Buchanan, "Assessing the Communitarian Critique of Liberalism," *Ethics* 99 (July 1989), 852–882; Amy Gutmann, "Communitarian Critiques of Liberalism," *Philosophy and Public Affairs* (Summer 1985), 308–322; and John Wallach, "Liberals, Communitarians, and the Tasks of Political Theory," *Political Theory* 15 (Nov. 1987), 581–611.

8. Charles Taylor, "Cross Purposes: The Liberal-Communitarian Debate," in Nancy L. Rosenblum (ed.), *Liberalism and the Moral Life* (Cambridge, Mass.: Harvard University Press, 1989), 159–182.

9. Derek Phillips, *Looking Backward: A Critical Appraisal of Communitarian Thought* (Princeton, N.J.: Princeton University Press, 1993).

10. Stephen Holmes, "The Permanent Structure of Antiliberal Thought," in Rosenblum (ed.), *Liberalism and the Moral Life*, 227–253.

11. John K. Wilson, *The Myth of Political Correctness: The Conservative Attack on Higher Education* (Durham, N.C., and London: Duke University Press, 1995), 93.

12. Richard Kirk Page and Kay Hartwell Hunnicutt, "Freedom for the Thought That We Hate: Speech Regulation at America's Twenty Largest Public Universities," 21 *Journal of College and University Law* 1 (1994).

13. Ibid., 29.

14. Robert A. Sedler, "The Unconstitutionality of Campus Bans on 'Racist Speech': The View from Without and Within," 53 *University of Pittsburgh Law Review* 61 (1992).

15. Greenawalt, *Fighting Words*, 76. Greenawalt sees Justice Blackmun suggesting as much in his dissent at 2561. Foley, in Lederer and Delgado (eds.), *Price We Pay*, 197.

16. *Sweeney v. New Hampshire*, 354 U.S. 234, 250 (1957).

17. Thomas I. Emerson, *Toward a General Theory of the First Amendment* (New York: Random House, 1966), 20.

18. Robert O'Neil, "The Pitfalls of Stifling Campus Speech," *AGB Reports* (Jan.–Feb. 1990), 12.

19. Emerson, *Toward a General Theory*, 20–21.

20. Richard Delgado and David Yun, "Pressure Valves and Bloodied Chickens: An Analysis of Paternalistic Objections to Hate Speech Regulations," 82 *California Law Review* 871, 882 (1994); Kenneth Lasson, "Racist Defamation as Free Speech: Abusing the First Amendment," 17 *Columbia Human Rights Law Review* 11 (1985): 53.

21. Robert Ladenson, "Is the Right of Free Speech Special?" paper presented at the Pacific Division Meeting of the American Philosophical Association, April 4, 1996.

22. Gordon Allport, *The Nature of Prejudice* (Cambridge, Mass.: Addison-Wesley, 1954), ch. 29.

23. 842 F.2d 1010 (8th Cir. 1988). Co-workers inflicted daily verbal abuse; demanded sexual favors; wrote obscene remarks in the dust on her vehicle; engaged in unwelcome physical contact such as rubbing her legs, thighs, and breasts, including one incident in which Hall was involuntarily held by one employee so others could fondle her; pulled down their pants to "moon" Hall; exposed themselves to her; flashed pictures of couples engaged in oral sex in her face; urinated in her water bottle and gas tank; and prevented her from using her vehicle to go to town to use the bathroom, then watching through surveying equipment as she relieved herself in the ditch.

24. Kingsley R. Browne, "Title VII as Censorship: Hostile Environment Harassment and the First Amendment," 52 *Ohio State Law Journal* 481, 544 (1991).

25. Daphne Patai, "What Price Utopia?" *Chronicle of Higher Education* (Oct. 27, 1995), A56.

26. *Wisconsin v. Mitchell*, 113 S. Ct. 2194 (1993).

27. Edward J. Eberle, "Hate Speech, Offensive Speech, and Public Discourse in America," 29 *Wake Forest Law Review* 1135, 1193–94 (1994).

28. *Doe v. University of Michigan*, 721 F. Supp. 852, 868 (E.D. Mich. 1989).

29. *UWM-Post v. Board of Regents*, 774 F. Supp. 1163, 1181 (E.D. Wis. 1991).

30. *R.A.V. v. City of St. Paul*, 505 U.S. 377, 396 (1992).

31. Mary Becker, "The Legitimacy of Judicial Review in Speech Cases," in Lederer and Delgado (eds.), *Price We Pay*, 208–215.

32. Ibid., 210–211.

33. Ira Glasser, Introduction, in Gates et al., *Speaking of Race*, 7.

34. Social conservatives have long argued that democratically enacted laws (such as those banning flag burning or pornography) should not be struck down by "liberal, activist" judges. See, e.g., former judge Robert Bork's *The Tempting of America: The Political Seduction of the Law* (New York: Macmillan, 1990), and the scholar Walter Berns,

"Government by Lawyers and Judges," *Commentary* (June 1987), 17. (These conservatives rarely object when "activist" judges strike down democratically enacted "liberal" laws.) Many commentators on both sides of the line view *Brown v. Board of Education* as the landmark "activist" case that initiated court-decreed "social engineering."

35. In *The Republic*, Plato argues that physical pleasures are not real pleasures because they are preceded by pain. In class, then, I often use eating and sex as examples: The pleasure of eating, being preceded by the "pain" of hunger, is not real pleasure since it merely relieves stomach pangs. So too the pleasure of sex, being preceded by aching or agitation in the sex organ, is not real pleasure since orgasm merely relieves the aching or agitation.

36. An incident at the University of Washington reported in Charles J. Sykes and Brad Miner, "Sense and Sensitivity," *National Review* (Mar. 18, 1991), 30–31.

37. Linda Seebach, "Colleges Shouldn't Guarantee Right Not to Be Offended," *Los Angeles Daily News*; reprinted in *Eau Claire Leader-Telegram* (Dec. 17, 1994), 11A.

38. For example, Akhil R. Amar argues that the Thirteenth Amendment provides a better foundation for campus hate speech codes than the Fourteenth. Amar, Comment, "The Case of the Missing Amendments: *R.A.V. v. City of St. Paul*," 106 *Harvard Law Review* 124 (1992). Again, Frederick Schauer argues that the costs of hate speech should be shifted from the victims to "consumers" in the marketplace of ideas at large through publicly subsidized libel insurance. Schauer, "Uncoupling Free Speech," in Lederer and Delgado (eds.), *The Price We Pay*, 262; reprinted from 92 *Columbia Law Review* 1321 (1992).

39. Thomas Foley, in an interview with Laura Lederer, in Lederer and Delgado (eds.), *Price We Pay*, 197.

40. Ken Kress makes a similar point in his response to Critical Legal Studies scholars who maintain the existence of a fundamental contradiction in the law. See Kress, "Legal Indeterminacy," 77 *California Law Review* 283, 305–307 (1989).

## CHAPTER 8. THE DEBATE: 1998–2008

1. Scott Jaschik, "Crusade against a Crusader," *Inside Higher Education* (July 28, 2008).

2. Harvey Silverglate and Greg Lukianoff, "Speech Codes: Alive and Well at Colleges . . ." *Chronicle of Higher Education Review* (Aug. 1, 2003), B8.

3. Scott Jaschik, "What the Professor Said," *Inside Higher Education* (Mar. 7, 2006).

4. Doug Lederman, "Freer Speech at Georgia Tech," *Inside Higher Education* (Aug. 16, 2006).

5. Jon B. Gould, *Speak No Evil: The Triumph of Hate Speech Regulation* (Chicago and London: Chicago University Press, 2005).

6. For example, when I spoke at a Division I midwestern state university some years ago, a university official questioned my claim that his school had a hate speech code. To his surprise (and annoyance) I then read verbatim their very broadly worded hostile environment verbal harassment policy. See also the Harvard example in Silverglate and Lukianoff, "Speech Codes," B7.

7. Gould, *Speak No Evil*, 177–178.

8. Stefan Braun, *Democracy off Balance: Freedom of Expression and Hate Propaganda Law in Canada* (Toronto: University of Toronto Press, 2004), 8.

9. For an account of changes in the meaning of hate speech in the United States, see Samuel Walker, *Hate Speech: The History of an American Controversy* (Lincoln and London: University of Nebraska Press, 1990). Ronald Krotszynski Jr. examines the different definitions of hate speech in the United States, Germany, Japan, Canada, and the United Kingdom in *The First Amendment in Cross-Cultural Perspective: A Comparative Legal Analysis of the Freedom of Speech* (New York: New York University Press, 2006). For a discussion of several philosophical definitions of hate speech, see J. Angelo Corlett and Robert Francescotti, "Foundations of a Theory of Hate Speech." 48 *Wayne State Law Review* 1071 (Fall 2002).

10. Silverglate and Lukianoff, "Speech Codes," B8.

11. Claudia Haupt, "Regulating Hate Speech—Damned If You Do and Damned If You Don't: Lessons Learned from Comparing the German and U.S. Approaches," 23 *Boston University International Law Journal* 299, 300 (Fall 2005).

12. Gould, *Speak No Evil*, 117–122.

13. Richard Delgado and Jean Stefancic, *Understanding Words That Wound* (Boulder, Colo.: Westview Press, 2004), 11–18. For an alternative categorization of the harms of hate speech, see Catherine Johnson, "Stopping Hate without Stifling Speech," 27 *Fordham Urban Law Journal* 1821, 1844–1849. Johnson presents the harms in terms of four arguments: "The Irreparable Harm of Hate Speech," "Assaultive Speech Lands a Blistering Blow," "Tolerance of Hate Speech Perpetuates a Social Reality of Subordination," and "Hate Speech Denies Equal Educational Opportunity."

14. Delgado and Stefancic, *Understanding Words That Wound*, 23.

15. Ibid., 21–27.

16. Lisa Woodward, "Collision in the Classroom: Is Academic Freedom a License for Sexual Harassment?" 27 *Capital University Law Review* 667 (1999), 673–674.

17. Delgado and Stefancic, *Understanding Words That Wound*, 114–118.

18. For a detailed discussion of the philosophy of insults, including its fit or lack thereof with various areas of U.S. speech law, see Jerome Neu, *Sticks and Stones: The Philosophy of Insults* (Oxford: Oxford University Press, 2008). Neu addresses insults in the campus hate speech context (pp. 153–164) and concludes that the solution is "more speech" rather than legal bans.

19. Alexander Tsesis, *Destructive Messages: How Hate Speech Paves the Way for Harmful Social Movements* (New York: New York University Press, 2002). See also George Anastaplo, *Campus Hate-Speech Codes, Natural Rights, and Twentieth Century Atrocities*, rev. ed. (Lewiston, N.Y.: Edwin Mellen Press, 1999), and George Frederickson, *Racism: A Short History* (Princeton, N.J.: Princeton University Press, 2002).

20. For more depth on these and further criticisms of *Destructive Messages*, see Anuj C. Desai, "Attacking *Brandenburg* with History: Does the Long-Term Harm of Biased Speech Justify a Criminal Statute Suppressing It?" 55 *Federal Communications Law Journal* 353 (March 2003); and W. Bradley Wendel, "The Banality of Evil and the First Amendment," 102 *Michigan Law Review* 1404 (May 2004).

21. Richard L. Abel, *Speaking Respect, Respecting Speech* (Chicago and London: University of Chicago Press, 1998), 282.

22. Braun, *Democracy off Balance*, ch. 3, "Functions and Assumptions of Hate Propaganda Law," 62–86.

23. Ibid., 86.

24. See Abel, *Speaking Respect, Respecting Speech*, ch. 5, "The Poverty of Civil Liber-

tarianism," for his critique of narrow regulations, and ch. 6, "The Excesses of State Regulation," for his critique of broad regulations.

25. Ibid., 250–253.

26. Ibid., 245–246.

27. Ibid., 261–273.

28. Ibid., ch. 4, "The Politics of Respect."

29. James Q. Whitman, "Enforcing Civility and Respect: Three Societies," 109 *Yale Law Journal* 1279 (Apr. 2000).

30. See, e.g., Lee Ann Rabe's withering analysis of the fighting words approach, "Sticks and Stones: The First Amendment and Campus Speech Codes," 37 *John Marshall Law Review* 205 (Fall 2003), 206–212. Regarding the continuing weakness of the individual and/or group libel approach, see, e.g., Neu, *Sticks and Stones*, 171–188.

31. See, e.g., Kingsley Browne, "Zero Tolerance for the First Amendment: Title VII's Regulation of Employee Speech," 27 *Ohio Northern University Law Review* 563 (2001); Mark Oring and S. D. Hampton, "When Rights Collide: Hostile Work Environment vs. First Amendment Free Speech," 31 *University of West Los Angeles Law Review* 135 (2000); and Mane Hajdin, *The Law of Sexual Harassment* (Selinsgrove, Pa.: Susquehanna University Press, 2002). See the Bibliography for a list of publications by the prolific critics David E. Bernstein and Eugene Volokh. For a discussion of the problems facing hostile environment rules in an expressive workplace, see Jonathan Segal, "The Expressive Workplace Doctrine: Protecting the Public Discourse from Hostile Work Environment Actions," 15 *UCLA Entertainment Law Review* 1 (Winter 2008), and Mariejoy Mendoza, "Making Friends: Sexual Harassment in the Workplace, Free Speech, and *Lyle v. Warner Bros.*," 40 *University of California Davis Law Review* 1963 (June 2007). For a critical discussion of the California Supreme Court *Aguilar* decision, see Irina V. Nirshberg, "Prior Restraint on Speech and Workplace Discrimination: The Clashing of Two Fundamental Rights," 34 *Suffolk University Law Review* 577 (2001).

32. Richard Allen Olmstead, "In Defense of the Indefensible: Title VII Hostile Environment Claims Unconstitutionally Restrict Free Speech," 27 *Ohio Northern Univ. Law Review* 691 (2001).

33. In addition to the demarcation problem, Hajdin also offers the usual objections involving viewpoint bias and the problem of "two tiers." His more fundamental criticism of current sexual harassment law as not being a form of sexual discrimination is beyond the scope of this chapter.

34. Olmstead, "In Defense of the Indefensible," 697–700.

35. Ibid., 719–723.

36. *Crist v. Focus Homes, Inc.*, 122 F. 3d 1107 (8th Cir. 1997), and *Folkerson v. Circus Circus Enter. Inc.*, 107 F. 3d 754 (9th Cir. 1997).

37. Olmstead, "In Defense of the Indefensible," 721–723.

38. One good example is *Barnette v. West Virginia Board of Education*, 319 U.S. 624 (1943), which overturned *Minersville School District v. Gobitis*, 310 U.S. 586 (1940). In an 8–1 vote, *Minersville* upheld a Pennsylvania law requiring students to salute the flag and say the Pledge of Allegiance even when the students (specifically, Jehovah's Witnesses) had religious objections. Just three years later in a 6–3 vote, *Barnette* held that such a law violated the free speech clause.

39. Miranda Oshige McGowan, "Certain Illusions about Free Speech: Why the Free

Speech Critique of Hostile Work Environment Harassment Is Wrong," 19 *Constitutional Commentary* 391, 432 (Summer 2002).

40. John Wirenius, "Actions as Words, Words as Actions: Sexual Harassment Law, the First Amendment and Verbal Acts," 28 *Whittier Law Review* 905 (Spring 2007).

41. Oshige McGowan, "Certain Illusions about Free Speech," 398–403.

42. See, e.g., Johnson, "Stopping Hate Speech without Stifling Speech," 1852–1854.

43. Cass Sunstein, "Half-Truths about the First Amendment," 1993 *U. Chicago Legal Forum* 25, 28 (1993).

44. Olmstead, "In Defense of the Indefensible," 716–718.

45. Michael Dorf, "Can the Government Limit Speech to Protect a Captive Audience?" *Findlaw Legal News and Commentary*, Apr. 26, 2006, http://writ.news.findlaw.com/dorf/20060426.html.

46. Njeri Mathis Rutledge, "A Time to Mourn: Balancing the Right of Free Speech against the Right of Privacy in Funeral Picketing," 67 *Maryland Law Review* 295, 331–332 (2008).

47. William E. Lee, "The Unwilling Listener: *Hill v. Colorado*'s Chilling Effect on Unorthodox Speech," 35 *University of California Davis Law Review* 387, 405 (Jan. 2002).

48. Mathis Rutledge, "A Time to Mourn," 330.

49. Lange, "Racist Speech on Campus," 125.

50. Johnson, "Stopping Hate Speech without Stifling Speech," 1863–1864.

51. In addition to cases cited elsewhere in this book, consider three cases discussed in John E. Matejkovic and David A. Redle, "Proceed at Your Own Risk: The Balance between Academic Freedom and Sexual Harassment," 2006 *BYU Education and Law Journal* 295, 309–315 (2006). In *Johnson v. Galen Health Institutes, Inc.*, 267 F. Supp. 2d 679 (W.D. Ky 2003), a professor began with sexual touching, then began making comments about the nursing student's "boobies" and "cha-chas" and finally made a quid pro quo offer (that was rejected). In *Wills v. Brown*, 184 F. 3d 20 (1st Cir. 1999), the court upheld university discipline—and eventually firing when the conduct was found to be persistent—for a professor found to have fondled a student who came to get his help with course materials. Also, in *Zimmer v. Ashland University*, 2001 U.S. Dist. LEXIS 15075 (N.D. Ohio, Sept. 5, 2001), the court ruled that a member of the women's swim team had sufficient basis to state a hostile environment claim based on unwelcome post-practice massages and targeted sexual comments. It should be noted that in all three cases, although the court found a legitimate complaint was made, the university was found not liable for damages since official actions exceeded the "deliberate indifference" standard for liability.

52. See, e.g., Timothy C. Shiell, "Three Conceptions of Academic Freedom," in Evan Gerstmann and Matthew Streb (eds.), *Academic Freedom at the Dawn of a New Century* (Stanford, Calif.: Stanford University Press, 2006); Todd A. DeMitchell and Vincent J. Connelly, "Academic Freedom and the Public School Teacher: An Exploratory Study of Perceptions, Policy, and the Law," 2007 *Brigham Young University Education and Law Journal* 83 (2007); Alan Chen, "Bureaucracy and Distrust: Germaneness and the Paradoxes of the Academic Freedom Doctrine," 77 *Colorado Law Review* 955 (Fall 2006); R. George Wright, "The Emergence of First Amendment Academic Freedom," 85 *Nebraska Law Review* 793 (2007); Donald J. Weidner, "Thoughts on Academic Freedom: *Urofsky* and Beyond," 33 *Toledo Law Review* 257 (Fall 2001); and Frederick Schauer, "Is There a Right to Academic Freedom?" 77 *Colorado Law Review* 907 (Fall 2006).

53. DeMitchell and Connelly, "Academic Freedom and the Public School Teacher," 83.

54. Wright, "Emergence of First Amendment Academic Freedom," 794.

55. *Bonnell* at 804.

56. *Bair v. Shippensburg University*, 280 F. Supp. 2d 357, 373 (M.D. Pa. 2003), quoting *Elrod v. Burns*, 427 U.S. 347, 373 (1976).

57. Since the university changed policies during the elapsed time, Roberts asked the court to find unconstitutional both the initial "prior" policy and the later "interim" policy. However, the court ruled that there was no unconstitutional application of the "prior policy" since Roberts was not denied an opportunity to speak, agreed to a reasonable change in venue, and in fact did not speak by his own choice. *Roberts v. Haragan*, 346 F. Supp. 2d 853, 864 (N.D. Tex. 2004).

58. *College Republicans* at 1016–1021.

59. Ibid. at 1021–1023.

60. Editorial, "Free Speech on Campus," *Washington Times* (Aug. 13, 2008), A26.

61. Avern Cohn, "Life on Campus Really Ain't So Bad," 98 *Michigan Law Review* 1549 (May 2000), 1561.

62. See, e.g., David Weiner and Marc Berley (eds.), *The Diversity Hoax* (New York: Foundation for Academic Standards and Tradition, 1999); and Jonathan Yardley, "Politically Corrected," *Washington Post* (Mar. 5, 2001), C2.

63. See, e.g., Donald A. Downs, *Restoring Free Speech and Liberty on Campus* (Cambridge: Cambridge University Press, 2006), and "Political Mobilization and Resistance to Censorship," in Gerstmann and Streb (eds.), *Academic Freedom at the Dawn of a New Century*, 61–78.

64. Downs, "Political Mobilization," 63.

65. Ibid., 66. The "standard" account is "Marcuse's Revenge," ch. 4 in Kors and Silverglate, *The Shadow University*. Stefan Braun too identifies the "progressive left" as the major culprit in the recent trend toward increased speech regulation in *Democracy off Balance*, 3.

66. Delgado and Stefancic, *Understanding Words That Wound*, 118.

67. Jon Gould, *Speak No Evil*, 173–176, and "Returning Fire," *Chronicle of Higher Education* (supp.) (Apr. 20, 2007), 1. Others, e.g., Judge Avern Cohn, have criticized Kors and Silverglate's *The Shadow University* as a "diatribe, jeremiad, philippic, and polemic." See Cohn, "Life on Campus Really Ain't So Bad," 1551.

68. See, e.g., O'Neil's response to Silverglate and Lukianoff: Robert O'Neil, "…but Litigation is the Wrong Response," *Chronicle of Higher Education Review* (Aug. 1, 2003), B9–B10.

69. See, e.g., Jon Gould, "Look Who's (Not) Talking: The Real Triumph of Hate Speech Regulation," 8 *Green Bag* 2d 367 (Summer 2005).

70. For an extensive recent analysis finding little evidence of "liberal indoctrination" at American campuses, see A. Lee Fritschler, Bruce L. R. Smith, and Jeremy D. Mayer, *Closed Minds? Politics and Ideology in American Universities* (Washington, D.C.: Brookings Institution Press, 2008)

71. Gould, *Speak No Evil*, 149–153.

72. Cohn, "Life on Campus Really Ain't So Bad," 1562–1563.

73. Sedler, "Speech Codes Are Still Dead," 103–104.

74. Anthony Lewis, *Freedom for the Thought That We Hate: A Biography of the First Amendment* (New York: Basic Books, 2007), 167.

75. See, e.g., Delgado and Stefancic, *Understanding Words That Wound*, 195–200.

76. See, e.g., Scott J. Catlin, "A Proposal for Regulating Hate Speech in the United States: Balancing Rights under the International Covenant on Civil and Political Rights," 69 *Notre Dame Law Review* 771 (1994); Stephanie Farrior, "Molding the Matrix: The Historical and Theoretical Foundations of International Law Concerning Hate Speech," 14 *Berkeley Journal of International Law* 1 (1996); Friedrich Kubler, "How Much Freedom for Racist Speech? Transnational Aspects of a Conflict of Human Rights," 27 *Hofstra Law Review* 335 (Winter 1998); Kevin Boyle, "Hate Speech—The United States versus the Rest of the World?" 53 *Maine Law Review* 485 (2001); Petal Nevella Modeste, "Race Hate Speech: The Pervasive Badge of Slavery That Mocks the Thirteenth Amendment," 44 *Howard Law Journal* 311 (Winter 2001); Judge Helen Ginger Berrigan, "'Speaking Out' About Hate Speech," 48 *Loyola Law Review* 1 (Spring 2002); Frederick Schauer, "The Exceptional First Amendment," in Michael Ignatieff (ed.), *American Exceptionalism and Human Rights* (Princeton, N.J.: Princeton University Press, 2005), 29–56; Eduardo Bertoni, "War and Freedom of Expression: Hate Speech under the American Convention on Human Rights," 12 *ILSA Journal of International and Comparative Law* 569 (Spring 2006); Robert Sedler, "An Essay on Freedom of Speech: The United States against the Rest of the World," 2006 *Michigan State Law Review* 377 (2006); and Wilhelm Brugger, "Ban On or Protection of Hate Speech?: Some Observations Based on German and American Law," 17 *Tulane European and Civil Law Forum* 1 (2002).

77. See Tsesis, *Destructive Messages*, 180; and Delgado and Stefancic, *Understanding Words That Wound*, 198–199.

78. Haupt, "Regulating Hate Speech," 300–301. Haupt cites fourteen articles (including some of those listed *supra*, n. 76), but the actual number is considerably higher.

79. Brugger, "Ban On or Protection of Hate Speech?" 3.

80. Section 130(1) states: "Whosoever, in a manner liable to disturb public peace, (1) incites hatred against parts of the population or invites violence or arbitrary acts against them, or (2) attacks the human dignity of others by insulting, maliciously degrading, or defaming parts of the population shall be punished with imprisonment of no less than three months and not exceeding five years." Brugger, "Ban On or Protection of Hate Speech?" 5. Sections 185, 186, and 187 protect the honor of all humans as humans regardless of individual accomplishments, the honor necessary for civil public discourse, and the honor of a person necessary to reputation or standing in the community. Brugger, "Ban On or Protection of Hate Speech?" 8–10.

81. Tsesis, *Destructive Messages*, 195–196 and 173.

82. Delgado and Stefancic, *Understanding Words That Wound*, 199.

83. Tsesis, *Destructive Messages*, 173.

84. Delgado and Stefancic, *Understanding Words That Wound*, 199.

85. Delgado, "Are Hate Speech Rules Constitutional Heresy? A Reply to Steven Gey," 146 *Pennsylvania Law Review* 865, 874 (1998).

86. Steven Gey, "Postmodern Censorship Revisited: A Reply to Richard Delgado," 146 *Pennsylvania Law Review* 1077, 1081–1082 (Apr. 1998).

87. Gey, "Postmodern Censorship Revisited," 1083–1086. For more examples, see Gey, "The Case against Postmodern Censorship Theory," 145 *Pennsylvania Law Review* 193 (1996).

88. Braun, *Democracy off Balance*, 105.

89. Cited in Douglas Farrow, "Kangaroo Canada," *First Things* (Aug.–Sept. 2008), 17–19.

90. Adam Liptak, "Unlike Others, U.S. Defends Freedom to Offend in Speech," *New York Times,* June 12, 2008, http://www.nytimes.com/2008/06/12/us/12hate.html.

91. Neu, *The Philosophy of Insults*, 209; Lewis, *Freedom for the Thought That We Hate*, 161.

92. Braun, *Democracy off Balance*, 97.

93. Ibid., 6.

94. "How Free Is the Canadian Press?" *National Post*, May 3, 2004, A13.

95. Haupt, "Regulating Hate Speech," 303, 316ff.

96. Ibid., 323–332.

97. James Q. Whitman, "Enforcing Civility and Respect: Three Societies," 109 *Yale Law Journal* 1279, 1282 (Apr 2000).

98. Ibid., 1307–1311.

99. Brugger, "Ban On or Protection of Hate Speech?" 1–21.

100. Kubler, "How Much Freedom for Racist Speech?" 375.

101. Boyle, "Hate Speech," 502.

102. Haupt, "Regulating Hate Speech," 301.

103. Brugger, "Ban On or Protection of Hate Speech?" 7.

104. Haupt, "Regulating Speech," 313.

105. Ibid., 314–315.

106. Ibid., 315–316.

107. Gey, "Postmodern Censorship Revisited," 1086.

108. Lewis, *Freedom for the Thought That We Hate*, 166.

109. Brugger, "Ban On or Protection of Hate Speech?" 2.

110. Whitman, "Enforcing Civility and Respect," 1353–1356.

111. Ronald J. Krotoszynski Jr., *The First Amendment in Cross Cultural Perspective* (New York: NYU Press, 2006).

112. Roger P. Alford, "Free Speech and the Case for Constitutional Exceptionalism," 106 *Michigan Law Review* 1071 (Apr. 2008), 1087.

113. Brugger, "Ban On or Protection of Hate Speech?" 14–15.

114. More than a dozen recent law review articles have been published for and against the legality of banning funeral protests; see, e.g., Rutledge, "A Time to Mourn."

# BIBLIOGRAPHY

## ARTICLES AND BOOKS

AAUP. "Academic Freedom and Sexual Harassment." *Academe*, Sept.–Oct. 1994, 64–72.

———. "On Freedom of Expression and Campus Speech Codes." *Academe*, July–Aug. 1992, 30–31.

———. "Report of the Subcommittee on Academic Freedom and Sexual Harassment." *Academe*, Sept.–Oct. 1994, 64–68.

Abel, Richard. *Speaking Respect, Respecting Speech*. Chicago: University of Chicago Press, 1998.

Adams, David M., ed. *Philosophical Problems in the Law*. Belmont, Calif.: Wadsworth, 1992.

Alexandar, William Shaun. "Regulating Speech on Campus: A Plea for Tolerance." 26 *Wake Forest Law Review* 1349 (1991).

Alexander, Larry. "Banning Hate Speech and the Sticks and Stones Defense." 13 *Constitutional Commentary* 71 (Spring 1996).

Alford, Roger P. "Free Speech and the Case for Constitutional Exceptionalism." 106 *Michigan Law Review* 1071 (April 2008).

Allport, Gordon. *The Nature of Prejudice*. Cambridge, Mass.: Addison-Wesley, 1954.

Altman, Andrew. "Liberalism and Campus Hate Speech: A Philosophical Examination." *Ethics* 103 (1993): 302–317.

Amar, Akhil R. "The Case of the Missing Amendments: *R.A.V. v. City of St. Paul.*" 106 *Harvard Law Review* 124 (1992).

Anastaplo, George. *Campus Hate-Speech Codes, Natural Rights, and Twentieth Century Atrocities*. Rev. ed. Lewiston, N.Y.: Edwin Mellen Press, 1999.

Anti-Defamation League of B'nai B'rith. *Combatting Bigotry on Campus*. 1989.

Asante, Molefi Kete. "Unraveling the Edges of Free Speech." *Phi Kappa Phi Journal*, Spring 1995, 12–15.

Attanasio, J. B. "Equal Justice under Chaos: The Developing Law of Sexual Harassment." 51 *Cincinnati Law Review* 1 (1982).

Au, Kammy. "Freedom from Fear." 15 *Lincoln Law Review* 45 (1984).

Auxier, A. H. "Tiptoeing through the Junkyard: Three Approaches to the Moral Dilemma of Racist Hate Speech." 21 *Notre Dame Journal of Law, Ethics, and Public Policy* 215 (2007).

Baker, C. Edwin. "Scope of the First Amendment Freedom of Speech." 25 *UCLA Law Review* 964 (1978).

Baker, Liva. *The Justice from Beacon Hill*. New York: HarperCollins, 1991.

Bardett, Katherine T., and Jean O'Barr. "The Chilly Climate on College Campuses: An Expansion of the 'Hate Speech' Debate." 1990 *Duke Law Journal* 574 (1990).

Bartlett, Thomas. "Chapel Hill Responded Properly to Instructor Who Harassed Student, Report Says." *Chronicle of Higher Education*, Oct. 8, 2004, A12.

Baruch, Chad. "Dangerous Liaisons: Campus Racial Harassment Policies, the First Amendment, and the Efficacy of Suppression." 11 *Whittier Law Review* 697 (1990).

Battaglia, Jack M. "Regulation of Hate Speech by Educational Institutions: A Proposed Policy." 31 *Santa Clara Law Review* 345 (1991).

Beck, Robert N. "Liberty and Equality." 10 *Idealistic Studies* 24 (1980).

Becker, Mary. "The Legitimacy of Judicial Review in Speech Cases." In *The Price We Pay*, edited by Lederer and Delgado: 208–215.

Bell, Derrick. *And We Are Not Saved: The Elusive Quest For Racial Justice*. New York: Basic Books, 1987.

Bellacosa, Joseph W. "The Regulation of Hate Speech by Academe vs. the Idea of a University: A Classic Oxymoron?" 67 *St. John's Law Review* 1 (Winter 1993).

Bellah, Robert, et al. *Habits of the Heart: Individualism and Commitment in American Life*. New York: Harper and Row, 1985.

Berns, Walter. *Freedom, Virtue, and the First Amendment*. Baton Rouge: Louisiana State University Press, 1957.

———. "Government by Lawyers and Judges." *Commentary*, June 1987, 17.

Bernstein, David E. "Anti-Discrimination Laws and the First Amendment." 68 *Missouri Law Review* 83 (2001).

———."Defending the First Amendment from Antidiscrimination Laws." 82 *North Carolina Law Review* 223 (Dec. 2003).

———. "Hostile Environment Law and the Threat to Freedom of Expression in the Workplace." 30 *Ohio Northern University Law Review* 1 (2004).

———. *You Can't Say That!: The Growing Threat to Civil Liberties from Antidiscrimination Laws*. Washington, D.C.: Cato Institute, 2003.

Berrigan, Helen Ginger. "'Speaking Out' about Hate Speech." 48 *Loyola Law Review* 1 (Spring 2002).

Bertoni, Eduardo. "War and Freedom of Expression: Hate Speech under the American Convention on Human Rights." 12 *ILSA Journal of International and Comparative Law* 569 (Spring 2006).

Bird, K. L. "Racist Speech or Free Speech? A Comparison of the Law in France and the United States." *Comparative Politics* (July 2000): 399–418.

Blanchard, Margaret. *Revolutionary Sparks: Freedom of Expression in Modern America*. New York: Oxford University Press, 1992.

Bodinger–de Uriarte, Christina. "Hate Crime." *Phi Kappa Delta Research Bulletin* 10 (Dec. 1991): 6.

Boggs, D. J. "Reining in Judges: The Case of Hate Speech." 52 *SMU Law Review* 217 (Winter 1999).

Bok, Derek. "Reflections on Free Speech: An Open Letter to the Harvard Community." *Educational Record* (Winter 1985): 4, 6.

Bollinger, Lee. "Rethinking Group Libel." In *Group Defamation and Free Speech*, edited by Freedman and Freedman: 243–251.

———. *The Tolerant Society*. New York: Oxford University Press, 1986.

Bork, Robert. *The Tempting of America: The Political Seduction of the Law*. New York: Macmillan, 1990.

———. "That Delicate Balance: Our Bill of Rights, the First Amendment, and Hate Speech." Panel Discussion at Columbia University. PBS video, 1992.

Bowman, Cynthia Grant. "Street Harassment and the Informal Ghettoization of Women." 106 *Harvard Law Review* 517 (1993).

Boyle, Kevin. "Hate Speech—the United States versus the Rest of the World?" 53 *Maine Law Review* 487 (2001).

Bracken, Harry. *Freedom of Speech: Words Are Not Deeds*. Westport, Conn.: Praeger, 1994.

Braun, Stefan. "Are Criminal Trials of Hate-Mongers Self-Defeating? Emerging Lessons from the Canadian Experience." *Jewish Spectator* 57 (Fall 1992): 26–28.

———. *Democracy off Balance: Freedom of Expression and Hate Propaganda Law in Canada*. Toronto: University of Toronto Press, 2004.

———. "Is Canada Still Tolerant and Fair? Why Jewish Speech and Hate Censorship Do Not Mix." *Jewish Magazine* (Oct. 2006). http://www.jewishmag.com/107mag/freespeech/freespeech.htm (accessed Aug. 26, 2008).

Brison, Susan J. "The Autonomy Defense of Free Speech." *Ethics* (Jan. 1998): 312–339.

Browne, Kingsley R. "Title VII as Censorship: Hostile Environment Harassment and the First Amendment." 52 *Ohio State Law Journal* 481 (1991).

———. "Zero Tolerance for the First Amendment: Title VII's Regulation of Employee Speech." 27 *Ohio Northern University Law Review* 563 (2001).

Brownstein, Alan E. "Hate Speech and Harassment: The Constitutionality of Campus Codes That Prohibit Racial Insults." 3 *William and Mary Bill of Rights Journal* 179 (Summer 1994).

———. "Hate Speech at Public Universities: The Search for an Enforcement Model." 37 *Wayne State Law Review* 1451 (1991).

Brugger, Winfried. "Ban on or Protection of Hate Speech?: Some Observations Based on German and American Law." 17 *Tulane European and Civil Law Forum* 1 (2002).

Bruns, Diana, and Jeffrey W. Bruns. "Hate Speech: Implications for Administrators." *Academic Exchange Quarterly* 16, no. 3 (2006): 229–234.

Bryne, J. Peter. "Racial Insults and Free Speech within the University." 79 *Georgetown Law Review* 399 (1991).

Buchanan, Allan. "Assessing the Communitarian Critique of Liberalism." *Ethics* 99 (1989): 852–882.

Burke, Debra D. "Workplace Harassment: A Proposal for a Bright Line Test Consistent with the First Amendment." 21 *Hofstra Labor & Employment Law Journal* 591 (Spring 2004).

Caldwell-Hill, Julie. "Campus Speech Codes: Whatever Happened to the 'Sticks and Stones' Doctrine?" 23 *Northern Kentucky Law Review* 583 (1996).

Calleros, Charles R. "Conflict, Apology, and Reconciliation at Arizona State University: A Second Case Study in Hateful Speech." 27 *Columbia Law Review* 91 (1996–1997).

———. "Paternalism, Counterspeech, and Campus Hate-Speech Codes: A Reply to Delgado and Yun." 27 *Arizona State Law Journal* 1249 (Winter 1995).

———. "Preparing for the Worst—and Striving for the Best: Training University Employees to Respond Clearly, Constructively, and Constitutionally to Hateful Speech on Campus." 25 *Journal of Law and Education* 41 (Oct. 1997).

———. "Reconciliation of Civil Rights and Civil Liberties after *R.A.V. v. City of St. Paul*:

Free Speech, Antiharassment Policies, Multicultural Education, and Political Correctness at Arizona State University." 1992 *Utah Law Review* 1205 (1992).

——. "Title VII and the First Amendment: Content Neutral Regulation, Disparate
Impact, and the 'Reasonable Person.'" 58 *Ohio State Law Journal* 1217 (1997).

——. "Title VII and Free Speech: The First Amendment Is Not Hostile to a Content
Neutral Hostile Environment Theory." 1996 *Utah Law Review* 227 (1996).

Calvert, Clay, and Robert D. Richards. "Lighting a FIRE on College Campuses: An
Inside Perspective on Free Speech, Public Policy, and Higher Education." 3 *Georgetown Journal of Law and Public Policy* 205 (Winter 2005).

Campbell, Linda. "College Debate: Free Speech vs. Freedom from Bigotry." *Chicago
Tribune*, March 18, 1991.

Candido, Amy H. "A Right to Talk Dirty? Academic Freedom Values and Sexual Harassment in the University Classroom." 4 *University of Chicago School Roundtable* 85 (1997).

Carlson, Scott. "North Carolina Instructor's Email on 'Hate Speech' Prompts Investigation." *Chronicle of Higher Education*, Apr. 9, 2004, A12.

Carnegie Fund for the Advancement of Teaching. *Campus Life*. New York: Carnegie
Fund for the Advancement of Teaching, 1990.

Carnevale, D. "Racist E-mail Floods a College Campus." *Chronicle of Higher Education*,
Apr. 26, 2002, A39.

Carr, Jeff. Memorandum to Chancellor Joseph Wyatt, April 12, 1994. Reprinted in Korwar, *War of Words*.

Carter, Stephen. *Reflections of an Affirmative Action Baby*. New York: Basic Books, 1992.

Catlin, Scott J. "A Proposal for Regulating Hate Speech in the United States: Balancing
the Rights under the International Covenant on Civil and Political Rights." 69 *Notre
Dame Law Review* 771 (1994).

Chafee, Zechariah, Jr. *Free Speech in the United States*. Cambridge, Mass.: Harvard University Press, 1941.

Chen, Alan. "Bureaucracy and Distrust: Germaneness and the Paradoxes of the Academic Freedom Doctrine." 77 *Colorado Law Review* 955 (Fall 2006).

Cleary, Edward J. *Beyond the Burning Cross: The First Amendment and the Landmark
R.A.V. Case*. New York: Random House, 1994.

Cohen, Carl. "Free Speech and Political Extremism: How Nasty Are We Free to Be?"
*Law and Philosophy* 7 (1989).

Cohen-Almagor, Raphael. "Hate in the Classroom: Free Expression, Holocaust Denial,
and Liberal Education." *American Journal of Education* 114 (Feb. 2008): 215–241.

Cohn, Avern. "Life on Campus Ain't Really So Bad." 98 *Michigan Law Review* 1549
(May 2000).

Coleman, Arthur L., and Jonathan A. Alger. "Beyond Speech Codes: Harmonizing
Rights of Free Speech and Freedom from Discrimination on University Campuses."
23 *Journal of College & University Law* 91 (1996).

Coleman, Brady. "Shame, Rage, and Freedom of Speech: Should the United States
Adopt European 'Mobbing' Laws?" 35 *Georgia Journal of International and Comparative Law* 53 (Fall 2006).

Corlett, J. Angelo, and Robert Francescotti. "Foundations of a Theory of Hate Speech."
48 *Wayne State Law Review* 1071 (Fall 2002).

Cortese, Anthony. *Opposing Hate Speech*. Westport, Conn.: Praeger, 2006.

Cowan, Gloria, Miriam Resendez, and Elizabeth Marshall. "Hate Speech and Constitutional Protection: Priming Values of Equality and Freedom." *Journal of Social Issues* (Summer 2002): 247–263.

Cox, Phil. "The Disputation of Hate: Speech Codes, Pluralism, and Academic Freedoms." *Social Theory and Practice* (Spring 1995): 113–144.

Craddock, Jeanne M. "Words that Injure, Laws that Silence: Campus Hate Speech Codes and the Threat to American Education." 22 *Florida State University Law Review* 1047 (Spring 1995).

Cram, Ian. *Contested Words: Legal Restrictions on Freedom of Speech in Liberal Democracies.* Aldershot, U.K.: Ashgate Publishing, 2006.

Crenshaw, Kimberle. "Comments of an Outsider on the First Amendment." In *The Price We Pay,* edited by Lederer and Delgado: 169–175.

Cudd, Ann. "When Sexual Harassment Is Protected Speech: Hostile Environment Sexual Harassment Policy in the University." 4 *Kansas Journal of Law and Public Policy* 69 (1994).

D'Amato, Anthony. "Harmful Speech and the Culture of Indeterminacy." 32 *William and Mary Law Review* 329 (1991).

Delgado, Richard. "About Your Masthead: A Preliminary Inquiry into the Compatibility of Civil Rights and Civil Liberties." 39 *Harvard Civil Rights–Civil Liberties Law Review* 1 (Winter 2004).

———. "Are Hate-Speech Rules Constitutional Heresy? A Reply to Steven Gey." 146 *University of Pennsylvania Law Review* 865 (Mar. 1998).

———. "Campus Antiracism Rules: Constitutional Narratives in Collision." 85 *Northwestern Law Review* 343 (1991).

———. "First Amendment Formalism Is Giving Way to First Amendment Legal Realism." 29 *Harvard Civil Rights–Civil Liberties Law Review* 169 (1994).

———. "Hate Cannot Be Tolerated." *USA Today,* March 3, 2004, 12A.

———. Rejoinder to Marjorie Heins, 18 *Harvard Civil Rights–Civil Liberties Law Review* 593 (1983).

———. "Words That Wound: A Tort Action for Racial Insults, Epithets, and Name Calling." 17 *Harvard Civil Rights–Civil Liberties Law Review* 133 (1982).

Delgado, Richard, and Jean Stefancic. "Hateful Speech, Loving Communities: Why Our Notion of a 'Just Balance' Changes So Slowly." 82 *California Law Review* 851 (1994).

———. "Images of the Outsider in American Law and Culture: Can Free Expression Remedy Systemic Social Ills?" 77 *Cornell Law Review* 1258 (1992).

———. *Must We Defend Nazis? Hate Speech, Pornography, and the New First Amendment.* New York: Basic Books, 1997.

———. "Overcoming Legal Barriers to Regulating Hate Speech on Campus." *Chronicle of Higher Education,* Aug. 11, 1993, B1–B3.

———. "Ten Arguments against Hate-Speech Regulation: How Valid?" 23 *Northern Kentucky Law Review* 475 (1996).

———. *Understanding Words That Wound.* Boulder, Colo.: Westview Press, 2004.

Delgado, Richard, and David Yun. "The Neoconservative Case against Hate-Speech Regulation—Lively, D'Souza, Gates, Carter, and the Toughlove Crowd." 47 *Vanderbilt Law Review* 1807 (1994).

———. "Pressure Valves and Bloodied Chickens: An Analysis of Paternalistic Objections to Hate Speech Regulation." 82 *California Law Review* 871 (1994).

——. "'The Speech We Hate': First Amendment Totalism, the ACLU, and the Principle of Dialogic Politics." 27 *Arizona State Law Journal* 1281 (Winter 1995).

Delgado, Richard, et al. "Overcoming Legal Barriers to Regulating Hate Speech on Campuses." *Chronicle of Higher Education*, Aug. 11, 1993, B1–B3.

De Maske, Chris. "Modern Power and the First Amendment: Reassessing Hate Speech." 9 *Communication Law and Policy* 273 (Summer 2004).

DeMitchell, Todd A., and Vincent J. Connelly. "Academic Freedom and the Public School Teacher: An Exploratory Study of Perceptions, Policy, and the Law." 2007 *Brigham Young University Education and Law Journal* 83 (2007).

Denis, Martin K. "Race Harassment Discrimination: A Problem That Won't Go Away?" 10 *Employee Relations Law Journal* 415 (1984).

Dennis, Everette E., Donald M. Gilmour, and David L. Grey, eds. *Justice Hugo Black and the First Amendment*. Ames: Iowa State University, 1978.

Desai, Anuj C. "Attacking *Brandenburg* with History: Does the Long-Term Harm of Biased Speech Justify a Criminal Statute Suppressing It?" 55 *Federal Communications Law Journal* 353 (March 2003).

Dessayer, Kathryn Marie, and Arthur J. Burke. "Leaving Them Speechless: A Critique of Speech Restrictions on Campus." 14 *Harvard Journal of Law and Public Policy* 565 (1991).

Di Domenico, Timothy E. "*Silva v. University of New Hampshire*: The Precarious Balance between Student Hostile Environment Claims and Academic Freedom." 69 *St. John's Law Review* 609 (Summer–Fall 1995).

Dodge, Susan. "Campus Codes That Ban Hate Speech Are Rarely Used to Penalize Students." *Chronicle of Higher Education*, Feb. 12, 1992, A35.

Dorf, Michael. "Can the Government Limit Speech to Protect a Captive Audience?" *Findlaw Legal News and Commentary*, Apr. 26, 2006. http://writ.news.findlaw.com/dorf/20060426.html (accessed Aug. 17, 2008).

Downey, John Pone, et al. "Hate Crimes and Violence on College and University Campuses." *Journal of College Student Development* 40 (Jan.–Feb. 1999): 3–9.

Downs, Donald A. *Nazis in Skokie: Freedom, Community, and the First Amendment*. Notre Dame, Ind.: Notre Dame University Press, 1985.

——. "Political Mobilization and Resistance to Censorship." In *Academic Freedom at the Dawn of a New Century*, edited by Gerstmann and Streb: 61–78.

——. *Restoring Free Speech and Liberty on Campus*. Cambridge and New York: Cambridge University Press, 2006.

——. "Skokie Revisited: Hate Group Speech and the First Amendment." 60 *Notre Dame Law Review* 629 (1985).

D'Souza, Dinesh, *Illiberal Education*. New York: Free Press, 1991.

——. "Illiberal Education." *Atlantic*, March 1991, 51–58.

——. Interview on MacNeil-Lehrer Newshour. In *Debating PC: The Controversy over Political Correctness on College Campuses*, edited by Paul Berman. New York: Dell, 1992.

Dworkin, Ronald. "The Coming Battles over Free Speech." *New York Review of Books*, June 11, 1992, 56.

——. *Taking Rights Seriously*. Cambridge, Mass.: Harvard University Press, 1978.

Earle, Beverly, and Anita Cava. "The Collision of Rights and a Search for Limits: Free Speech in the Academy and Freedom from Sexual Harassment on Campus." 18 *Berkeley Journal of Employment and Labor Law* 282 (1997).

Ebel, Lauri A. "University Anti-Discrimination Codes versus Free Speech." 23 *New Mexico Law Review* 169 (Winter 1993).

Eberle, Edward J. "Hate Speech, Offensive Speech, and Public Discourse in America." 29 *Wake Forest Law Review* 1135 (1994).

Editorial. "Abolish the Speech Codes." *Wall Street Journal*, June 11, 1993, A10.

Editorial. "How Free Is the Canadian Press?" *National Post*, May 3, 2004, A13.

Editorial. "Talking Dirty." *New Republic*, Nov. 4, 1991. Reprinted in *Sexual Harassment*, edited by Wall.

Ehrlich, Howard. *Campus Ethnoviolence . . . and the Policy Options*. Report no. 4. Baltimore: National Institute against Prejudice and Violence, 1990.

——. *Campus Ethnoviolence: A Research Review*. Report no. 5. Baltimore: National Institute against Prejudice and Violence, 1992.

——. "Studying Workplace Ethnoviolence." *International Journal of Group Tensions* 19 (1989): 69–80.

Ehrlich, Howard, and Joseph Scimecca. "Offensive Speech on Campus: Punitive or Educational Solutions?" 72 *Educational Record* 26 (1991).

Ehrlich, Howard, Barbara Larcom, and Robert Purvis. "The Traumatic Impact of Ethnoviolence." In *The Price We Pay*, edited by Lederer and Delgado: 62–79.

Ely, John Hart. "Flag Desecration: A Case Study in the Roles of Categorization and Balancing in First Amendment Analysis." 88 *Harvard Law Review* 1482 (1981).

Emerson, Ken. "Only Correct." *New Republic*, Feb. 18, 1991.

Emerson, Thomas I. *Toward a General Theory of the First Amendment*. New York: Random House, 1966.

Estlund, Cynthia L. "Freedom and Expression in the Workplace and the Problem of Discriminatory Harassment." 75 *Texas Law Review* 687 (Mar. 1997).

Farrior, Stephanie. "Molding the Matrix: The Historical and Theoretical Foundations of International Law Concerning Hate Speech." 14 *Berkeley Journal of International Law* 1 (1996).

Farrow, Douglas. "Kangaroo Canada." *First Things* (Aug.–Sept. 2008), 17–19.

Feinberg, Joel. "Limits to the Free Expression of Opinion." In *Philosophy of Law*, 3rd ed., edited by Joel Feinberg and Hyman Gross, Belmont, Calif., Wadsworth, 1986.

Finn, Chester E., Jr. "The Campus: 'An Island of Repression in a Sea of Freedom.'" *Commentary*, Sept. 1989, 17–23.

Fish, Stanley. *There's No Such Thing as Free Speech: And It's a Good Thing, Too*. New York: Oxford University Press, 1994.

Fisher, Linda E. "A Communitarian Compromise on Speech Codes: Restraining the Hostile Environment Concept." 44 *Catholic University Law Review* 97 (Fall 1994).

Fiss, Owen. "Groups and the Equal Protection Clause." 5 *Philosophy and Public Affairs* 107 (1976).

Fleischer, Stephen. "Campus Speech Codes: The Threat to Liberal Education." 27 *John Marshall Law Review* 709 (Spring 1994).

Foley, Tom. Interview by Laura Lederer. In *The Price We Pay*, edited by Lederer and Delgado: 194–198.

Fowler, Robert Booth. *The Dance with Community: The Contemporary Debate in America*. Lawrence: University Press of Kansas, 1991.

Frankel Paul, Ellen. "Bared Buttocks and Federal Cases." *Society* 28, 4 (1991). Reprinted in *Sexual Harassment*, edited by Wall: 151–157.

Frederickson, George. *Racism: A Short History*. Princeton, N.J.: Princeton University Press, 2002.

Freedman, Monroe H., and Eric M. Freedman, eds. *Group Defamation and Free Speech: The Relationship between Language and Violence*. Westport, Conn.: Greenwood Press, 1995.

Fried, Charles. "The New First Amendment Jurisprudence: A Threat to Liberty." 59 *University of Chicago Law Review* 225 (1992).

Friedman, Lawrence. "Regulating Hate Speech at Public Universities after *R.A.V. v. City of St. Paul*." 37 *Howard Law Journal* 1 (1993).

Friedman, Leon. "Freedom of Speech: Should It Be Available to Pornographers, Nazis, and the Klan?" In *Group Defamation and Free Speech*, edited by Freedman and Freedman: 307–319.

——. "On Curbing Racial Speech." 1 *Responsive Community* 55 (Winter 1990–1991).

Gail, R. W. "The University as an Industrial Plant: A Workplace Theory of Discriminatory Harassment Creates a 'Hostile Environment' for Free Speech in America's Universities." *Law and Contemporary Problems* 60, 4 (Autumn 1997): 203–243.

Gale, Mary Ellen. "Reimagining the First Amendment: Racist Speech and Equal Liberty." 65 *St. John's Law Review* 119 (1991).

Gard, Stephen W. "Fighting Words as Free Speech." 58 *Washington University Law Quarterly* 531 (1980).

Garry, Patrick. "Censorship by the Free Speech Generation." *Phi Kappa Phi Journal*, Spring 1995, 29–31.

Gates, Henry Louis, Jr. "Let Them Talk." *New Republic*, Sept. 20–27, 1993, 37–49.

——. "War of Words: Critical Race Theory and the First Amendment." In *Speaking of Race*, edited by Gates et al.: 17–58.

——, et al. *Speaking of Race, Speaking of Sex*. New York and London: New York University Press, 1994.

Gelber, Katharine. *Speaking Back: The Free Speech versus Hate Speech Debate*. Amsterdam and Philadelphia: John Benjamins Publishing, 2002.

Gerstmann, Evan, and Matthew Streb, eds. *Academic Freedom at the Dawn of a New Century: How Terrorism, Governments, and Culture Wars Impact Free Speech*. Stanford, Calif: Stanford University Press, 2006.

Gey, Steven G. "The Case against Postmodern Censorship Theory." 145 *Pennsylvania Law Review* 193 (Dec. 1996).

——. "Postmodern Censorship Revisited: A Reply to Richard Delgado." 146 *Pennsylvania Law Review* 1077 (Apr. 1998).

Gibbs, Annette. *Reconciling Rights and Responsibilities of Colleges and Students*. Washington, D.C.: ASHE-ERIC Higher Education Reports, vol. 21, no. 5 (1992).

Gibson, James L., and Richard D. Bingham. *Civil Liberties and Nazis: The Skokie Free Speech Controversy*. New York: Praeger, 1985.

Glaser, Steven R. "Sticks and Stones May Break My Bones, but Words Can Never Hurt Me: Regulating Speech on University Campuses." 76 *Marquette Law Review* 265 (Fall 1992).

Glasser, Ira. Introduction. *Speaking of Race*, edited by Gates et al.: 1–15.

Glenn, R. A., et al. "Campus Hate Speech and Equal Protection: Competing Constitutional Values." 6 *Widener Journal of Public Law* 349 (1997).

Goldberg, Stephanie B. "First Amendment." *ABA Journal* 80 (March 1994): 88.

Gould, Jon B. "Look Who's (Not) Talking: The Real Triumph of Hate Speech Regulation." 8 *Green Bag* 2d 367 (Summer 2005).

———. "The Precedent That Wasn't: Campus Hate Speech Codes and the Two Faces of Legal Compliance." 35 *Law and Society Review* 345 (2001).

———. *Speak No Evil: The Triumph of Hate Speech Regulation*. Chicago: University of Chicago Press, 2005.

———. "Title IX in the Classroom: Academic Freedom and the Power to Harass." 6 *Duke Journal of Gender Law and Policy* 61 (Spring 1999).

———. "The Triumph of Hate Speech Regulation: Why Gender Wins but Race Loses in America." 6 *Michigan Journal of Gender and Law* 153 (1999).

Graber, Mark A. *Transforming Free Speech*. Berkeley: University of California Press, 1990.

Graham, Hugh Davis. *The Civil Rights Era*. New York: Oxford University Press, 1990.

Greenawalt, Kent. *Fighting Words*. Princeton, N.J.: Princeton University Press, 1995.

———. "Insults and Epithets: Are They Protected Speech?" 42 *Rutgers Law Review* 287 (1990).

———. *Speech, Crime, and the Uses of Language*. New York: Oxford University Press, 1989.

Greene, Linda S. "Racial Discourse, Hate Speech, and Political Correctness." *Phi Kappa Phi Journal*, Spring 1995, 32–35.

Greenup, John S. "The First Amendment and the Right to Hate." 34 *Journal of Law Education* 605 (Oct. 2005).

Grey, Thomas C. "Civil Rights vs. Civil Liberties: The Case of Discriminatory Verbal Harassment." *Social Philosophy and Policy* 8, no. 2 (1991): 81–107.

———. "Discriminatory Harassment and Free Speech." 14 *Harvard Journal of Law and Public Policy* 157 (1991).

———. "How to Write a Speech Code without Really Trying: Reflections on the Stanford Experience." 29 *University of California Davis Law Review* 891 (Spring 1996).

Griffin, Anthony P. "The First Amendment and the Art of Storytelling." In *Speaking of Race*, edited by Gates et al.: 257–279.

Gruberg, Martin. "How Should Campuses Respond to Expressions Which Demean?" *AAUP Wisconsin Conference Newsletter*, Fall 1993, 2.

Gunther, Gerald. "Good Speech, Bad Speech—No." 42 *Stanford Lawyer* 7 (1990).

Gutmann, Amy. "Communitarian Critics of Liberalism." *Philosophy and Public Affairs* 14 (Summer 1985): 308–322.

Hacker, Andrew. *Two Nations*. New York: Charles Scribners' Sons, 1992.

Haiman, Franklyn. "The Remedy Is More Speech." *American Prospect*, Summer 1991, 30–35.

———. *Speech Acts and the First Amendment*. Carbondale, Ill.: Southern Illinois University Press, 1993.

———. *Speech and Law in a Free Society*. Chicago: University of Chicago Press, 1981.

Hajdin, Mane. *The Law of Sexual Harassment*. Selinsgrove, Pa.: Susquehanna University Press, 2002.

Hamlin, David. *Nazi-Skokie Conflict*. Boston: Beacon Press, 1980.

Harbour, William R. *The Foundations of Conservative Thought*. Notre Dame, Ind.: Notre Dame University Press, 1982.

Harel, Alon. "Bigotry, Pornography, and the First Amendment: A Theory of Unprotected Speech." 65 *Southern California Law Review* 1887 (1992).

Harrison, Jack. "Hate Speech: Power in the Marketplace." 20 *Journal of College and University Law* 461 (1994).

Hart, H. L. A. "Between Utility and Rights." 79 *Columbia Law Review* 828 (1979).

Hart, Harold, ed. *Censorship: For and Against*. New York: Hart, 1971.

Hartley, Roger C. "Cross Burning—Hate Speech as Free Speech: A Comment on *Virginia v. Black*." 54 *Catholic University Law Review* 1 (Fall 2004).

Hartman, Rhonda G. "Hateful Expression and First Amendment Values: Toward a Theory of Constitutional Constraints on Hate Speech after *R.A.V. v. St. Paul*." 19 *Journal of College and University Law* 343 (1993).

———. "Revitalizing Group Defamation as a Remedy for Hate Speech on Campus." 71 *Oregon Law Review* 853 (1993).

Haupt, Claudia. "Regulating Hate Speech—Damned If You Do and Damned If You Don't: Lessons Learned from Comparing the German and U.S. Approaches." 23 *Boston University International Law Journal* 299 (Fall 2005).

Heins, Marjorie. "Banning Words: A Comment on 'Words That Wound.'" 18 *Harvard Civil Rights–Civil Liberties Law Review* 585 (Summer 1983).

Heiser, Gregory, and Lawrence Rossow. "Hate Speech or Free Speech: Can Broad College Hate Speech Rules Survive Current Judicial Reasoning?" 22 *Journal of Law and Education* 139 (1993).

Hentoff, Nat. "Black Bigotry and Free Speech." *Progressive*, May 1994, 20–21.

———. "Campus Follies: From Free Speech . . ." *Washington Post*, Nov. 4, 1989, A23.

———. "The Different Faces of the ACLU." *Washington Post*, Mar. 31, 1990.

———. *The First Freedom—The Tumultuous History of Free Speech in America*. New York: Delacorte, 1980.

———. "Free Speech: Are There Limits?" *Progressive*, May 1993, 16–17.

———. *Free Speech for Me—But Not for Thee*. New York: HarperCollins, 1992.

———. "If a Civil Liberties Union Can't Agree on Free Speech . . ." *Washington Post*, June 2, 1990.

———. "Let All Hate Speech Be Heard." *Village Voice*, Mar. 1, 1994, 16–17.

———. "Mari Matsuda: Star of the Speech Police." *Village Voice*, Feb.18, 1992, 25.

———. "A Startling Triumph for Free Speech." *Village Voice*, July 28, 1992, 18–19.

Herron, Vince. "Increasing the Speech: Diversity, Campus Speech Codes, and the Pursuit of Truth." 67 *Southern California Law Review* 407 (Jan. 1994).

Heumann, Milton, and Thomas W. Church (eds.). *Hate Speech on Campus: Cases, Case Studies, and Commentary*. Boston: Northeastern University Press, 1997.

Heyman, Steven J. (ed.) *Hate Speech and the Constitution*. Volume 1: *The Development of the Hate Speech Debate*. Volume 2: *The Contemporary Debate*. New York: Routledge, 1996.

Hodulik, Patricia. "Prohibiting Discriminatory Harassment by Regulating Student Speech: A Balancing of First Amendment and University Interests." 16 *Journal of College and University Law* 573 (1990).

———. "Racist Speech on Campus." 37 *Wayne State Law Review* 1433 (1991).

Holmes, Stephen. "The Permanent Structure of Antiliberal Thought." In *Liberalism and the Moral Life*, edited by Rosenblum: 227–253.

Horton, Amy. "Of Supervision, Centerfolds, and Censorship: Sexual Harassment, the First Amendment, and the Contours of Title VII." 46 *University of Miami Law Review* 403 (1991).

Hughes, Art. "Large Crowd Rallies against Hate Speech at St. Thomas." Minnesota

Public Radio, Nov. 1, 2007. http://minnesota.publicradio.org/display/web/2007/11/01/antihaterally (accessed Aug. 10, 2008).

Hulshizer, Robin M. "Securing Freedom from Harassment without Reducing Freedom of Speech: *Doe v. University of Michigan.*" 76 *Iowa Law Review* 383 (1991).

Hustoles, Thomas P., and Walter B. Connolly, eds. *Regulating Racial Harassment: A Legal Compendium.* Washington, D.C.: National Association of College and University Attorneys, 1990.

Hyde, Henry J., and George M. Fishman. "The Collegiate Speech Protection Act of 1991: A Response to the New Intolerance in the Academy." 37 *Wayne State Law Review* 1469 (1991).

Ignatieff, Michael (ed.). *American Exceptionalism and Human Rights.* Princeton, N.J.: Princeton University Press, 2005.

Ingber, Stanley. "The Marketplace of Ideas: A Legitimizing Myth." 1984 *Duke Law Journal* 1 (1984).

Jaschik, Scott. "Crusade against a Crusader." *Inside Higher Education,* July 28, 2008.

———. "First Amendment Carries Most Weight in 2 Race-Harassment Rulings." *Chronicle of Higher Education,* Apr. 21, 1995, A38.

———. "First Amendment Implications of Hate Speech to Be Studied." *Chronicle of Higher Education,* Apr. 27, 1994, A24.

———. "What the Professor Said." *Inside Higher Education,* Mar. 7, 2006.

Jenifer, Franklyn G. "Hate Speech Is Still Free Speech." *New York Times,* May 13, 1994, A31, late N.Y. edition.

Johnson, Catherine B. "Stopping Hate Speech without Stifling Speech: Re-examining the Merits of Hate Speech Codes on University Campuses." 27 *Fordham Urban Law Journal* 1821 (Aug. 2000).

Johnson, Thomas S. "These Wise Restraints Which Make Us Free." *Vital Speeches of the Day,* Aug. 15, 2001, 662–664.

Jones, Charles H. "Equality, Dignity, and Harm: The Constitutionality of Regulating American Campus Ethnoviolence." 37 *Wayne State Law Review* 1383 (1991).

Kagan, A. "The Regulation of Hate Speech on College Campuses and the Library Bill of Rights." *Journal of Librarianship* 20 (Sept. 1994): 241.

Kagan, Elena. "When a Speech Code Is a Speech Code: The Stanford Policy and the Theory of Incidental Restraints." 29 *University of California Davis Law Review* 957 (Spring 1996).

Kahn, Robert B. "Cross-Burning, Holocaust Denial, and the Development of Hate Speech Law in the United States and Germany." 83 *University of Detroit Mercy Law Review* 163 (Spring 2006).

Kalven, Harry, Jr. *The Negro and the First Amendment.* Chicago: University of Chicago Press, 1966.

———. *A Worthy Tradition: Freedom of Speech in America.* New York: Harper & Row, 1988.

Kant, Immanuel. *Ethical Philosophy.* Indianapolis, Ind.: Hackett Publishing, 1983.

Kaplan, William. "A Proposed Process for Managing the First Amendment Aspects of Campus Hate Speech." *Journal of Higher Education* (Sept. 1992): 517–538.

Karst, Kenneth. *Belonging to America: Equal Citizenship and the Constitution.* New Haven, Conn: Yale University Press, 1989.

———. "Equality as a Central Principle in the First Amendment." 43 *University of Chicago Law Review* 20 (1975).

Kendall, Willmore. "The 'Open Society' and Its Fallacies." *American Political Science Review* 54 (1960): 972–979.

Kennedy, Randall L. "'Nigger!' as a Problem in the Law." 2001 *University of Illinois Law Review* 935 (2001).

Kersch, Ken I. "How Conduct Became Speech and Speech Became Conduct: A Political Development Case Study in Labor Law and the Freedom of Speech." 8 *Pennsylvania Journal of Constitutional Law* 255 (Mar 2006).

Kircher Cole, Elsa, ed. *Sexual Harassment on Campus: A Legal Compendium*. Washington D.C.: National Association of College and University Attorneys, 1990.

Kitano, Harry. *Race Relations*. Englewood Cliffs, N.J.: Prentice-Hall, 1974.

Kleven, Thomas. "Free Speech and the Struggle for Power." 315 *New York Law School Journal of Human Rights* 9 (Spring 1992).

Knectle, John C. "When to Regulate Hate Speech." 116 *Penn State Law Review* 539 (Spring 2006).

Kors, Alan Charles. "Harassment Policies in the University." *Society* 28, no. 4 (1991): 22–25, 28, 29. Reprinted in *Sexual Harassment*, edited by Wall: 41–47.

———. "It's Speech, Not Sex, the Dean Bans Now," *Wall Street Journal*, Oct. 12, 1989, sec. 1, 16.

Korwar, Arati. *War of Words: Speech Codes at Public Colleges and Universities*. Nashville, Tenn.: Freedom Forum First Amendment Center, 1994, 1995.

Kratz, A. M. "Unpopular Advocacy versus True Threat: *U.S. v. J.H.H.*" 28 *Creighton Law Review* 823 (Apr. 1995).

Kress, Ken. "Legal Indeterminacy." 77 *California Law Review* 283 (1989).

Kretzmer, David. "Freedom of Speech and Racism." 8 *Cardozo Law Review* 445 (1987).

Krotoszynski, Ronald J., Jr. "A Comparative Perspective on the First Amendment: Free Speech, Militant Democracy, and the Primacy of Dignity as a Preferred Constitutional Value in Germany." 78 *Tulane Law Review* 1549 (May 2004).

———. *The First Amendment in Cross-Cultural Perspective: A Comparative Legal Analysis of the Freedom of Speech*. New York: New York University Press, 2006.

Kübler, Frederich. "How Much Freedom for Racist Speech?: Transnational Aspects of a Conflict of Human Rights." 27 *Hofstra Law Review* 335 (1998).

Kwok, Chi Steve. "A Study in Contradiction: A Look at the Conflicting Assumptions Underlying Standard Arguments for Speech Codes and the Diversity Rationale." 4 *Pennsylvania Journal of Constitutional Law* 493 (Apr. 2002).

Ladenson, Robert. "Is the Right to Free Speech Special?" Paper presented at the Pacific Division Meeting of the American Philosophical Association, Apr. 4, 1996.

Lane, Charles. "The Urge to Outlaw Hate." *Newsweek*, Feb. 15, 1993, 33.

Lange, Ellen E. "Racist Speech on Campus: A Title VII Solution to a First Amendment Problem." 64 *Southern California Law Review* 105 (1990).

Lasson, Kenneth. "Racial Defamation as Free Speech: Abusing the First Amendment." 17 *Columbia Human Rights Law Review* 11 (1985).

———. "To Stimulate, Provoke, or Incite? Hate Speech and the First Amendment." In *Group Defamation and Free Speech*, edited by Freedman and Freedman: 267–306.

Lawrence, Charles R., III. "Acknowledging the Victim's Cry." *Academe*, Nov.–Dec. 1990, 10.

———. "Cross-Burning and the Sound of Silence: Anti-subordination Theory and the First Amendment." In *The Price We Pay*, edited by Lederer and Delgado: 114–121.

——. "The Debates over Placing Limits on Racist Speech Must Not Ignore the Damage It Does to Its Victims." *Chronicle of Higher Education*, Oct. 25, 1989, B1.

——. "Good Speech, Bad Speech—Yes." 42 *Stanford Lawyer* 6 (1990).

——. "The Id, the Ego, and Equal Protection: Reckoning with Unconscious Racism." 39 *Stanford Law Review* 317 (1987).

——. "If He Hollers Let Him Go: Regulating Racist Speech on Campus." 1990 *Duke Law Journal* 431 (1990).

Lawrence, Frederick M. "Resolving the Hate Crimes/Hate Speech Paradox: Punishing Bias Crimes and Protecting Racist Speech." 68 *Notre Dame Law Review* 673 (1993).

Leatherman, Courtney. "Court Finds College Violated First Amendment." *Chronicle of Higher Education*, Sept. 6, 1996, A16.

——. "Free Speech or Harassment?" *Chronicle of Higher Education*, Sept. 28, 1994, A22.

Lederer, Laura. "'Freedom of Hate Speech' Too Costly." *Minneapolis Star-Tribune*, May 31, 1995.

——. "The Prosecutor's Dilemma: An Interview with Tom Foley." In *The Price We Pay*, edited by Lederer and Delgado: 194–198.

——, and Richard Delgado, eds. *The Price We Pay: The Case against Racist Speech, Hate Propaganda, and Pornography*. New York: Hill and Wang, 1994.

Lederman, Doug. "Freer Speech at Georgia Tech." *Inside Higher Education*, Aug. 16, 2006.

Lee, William E. "The Unwilling Listener: *Hill v. Colorado*'s Chilling Effect on Unorthodox Speech." 35 *University of California Davis Law Review* 387 (Jan. 2002).

Leo, John. "Free Inquiry? Not on Campus." *City Journal* (Winter 2007). http://www.city-journal.org/html/17_1_free_speech.html (accessed Aug. 8, 2008).

——. "Our Misguided Speech Police." *U.S. News and World Report*, Apr. 8, 1991, 25.

Leslie, Connie. "Lessons from Bigotry 101." *Newsweek*, Sept. 25, 1989, 48–49.

Levy, Leonard. *Emergence of a Free Press*. New York: Oxford University Press, 1985.

——. *Freedom of Speech and Press in Early America: A Legacy of Suppression*. New York: Harper and Row, 1963.

Lewis, Anthony. *Freedom for the Thought That We Hate: A Biography of the First Amendment*. New York: Basic Books, 2007.

——. *Make No Law*. New York: Random House, 1991.

Lindemann, Barbara, and David D. Kadue. *Primer on Sexual Harassment*. Washington, D.C.: Bureau of National Affairs, 1992.

Liptak, Adam. "Unlike Others, U.S. Defends Freedom to Offend in Speech." *New York Times*, June 12, 2008. http://www.nytimes.com/2008/06/12/us/12hate.html (accessed June 20, 2008).

Lively, Donald. "Racial Myopia in the Age of Digital Compression." In *Speaking of Race*, edited by Gates et al.. 59–114.

——. "Reformist Myopia and the Imperative of Progress: Lessons for the Post Brown Era." 46 *Vanderbilt Law Review* 865 (1993).

Love, Jean C. "Discriminatory Speech and the Tort of Intentional Infliction of Emotional Distress." 47 *Washington & Lee Law Review* 123 (1990).

Lynch, Brendan P. "Personal Injuries or Petty Complaints? Evaluating the Case for Campus Hate Speech Codes: The Argument from Experience." 32 *Suffolk University Law Review* 613 (1999).

Ma, Alice K. "Campus Hate Speech Codes: Affirmative Action in the Allocation of Speech Rights." 83 *California Law Review* 693 (March 1995).

Machan, Tibor. "Equality's Dependence on Liberty." 2 *Equality and Freedom* 663 (1977).

MacIntyre, Alastair. *After Virtue.* 2nd ed. Notre Dame, Ind.: University of Notre Dame Press, 1984.

——. *Whose Justice? Whose Reason?* Notre Dame, Ind.: University of Notre Dame Press, 1988.

MacKinnon, Catharine. *Only Words.* Cambridge, Mass.: Harvard University Press, 1993.

——. "Pornography, Civil Rights, and Speech." 20 *Harvard Civil Rights–Civil Liberties Law Review* 1 (1985).

——. *Sexual Harassment of Working Women: A Case of Sex Discrimination.* New Haven, Conn.: Yale University Press, 1979.

Magruder, Calvert. "Mental and Emotional Disturbances in the Law of Torts." 49 *Harvard Law Review* 1033 (1936).

Mahoney, Kathleen. "The Constitutional Approach to Freedom of Expression in Hate Propaganda and Pornography." 55 *Law and Contemporary Problems* 77 (1992).

——. "Recognizing the Constitutional Significance of Harmful Speech: The Canadian View of Pornography and Hate Propaganda." In *The Price We Pay*, edited by Lederer and Delgado: 277–289.

Masler, Ross Paine. "Tolling the Final Bell: Will Public School Doors Remain Open to the First Amendment?" 14 *Mississippi Civil Liberties Review* 55 (1993).

Massaro, Toni M. "Equality and Freedom of Expression: The Hate Speech Dilemma." 32 *William and Mary Law Review* 211 (1991).

Matejkovic, John E., and David A. Redle. "Proceed at Your Own Risk: The Balance between Academic Freedom and Sexual Harassment." 2006 *BYU Education & Law Journal* 295 (2006).

Mathis Rutledge, Njeri. "A Time to Mourn: Balancing the Right of Free Speech against the Right of Privacy in Funeral Picketing." 67 *Maryland Law Review* 295 (2008).

Matsuda, Mari, ed. "Public Response to Racist Speech: Considering the Victim's Story." 87 *Michigan Law Review* 2320 (1989).

——. *Words That Wound.* Boulder, Colo.: Westview Press, 1993.

McAllister, Thomas L. "Rules and Rights Colliding: Speech Codes and the First Amendment on College Campuses." 59 *Tennessee Law Review* 409 (Winter 1992).

McArthur, Harvey K. "Golden Rule." In *Westminster Dictionary of Christian Ethics*, edited by James F. Childress and John Macquarrie. Philadelphia: Westminster Press, 1986.

McCristal Culp, Jerome. "Water Buffalo and Diversity: Naming Names and Reclaiming the Racial Discourse." 26 *Connecticut Law Review* 209 (Fall 1993).

McGee, Robert W. "Hate Speech, Free Speech, and the University." 24 *Akron Law Review* 363 (1990).

McGowan, David F., and Ragesh K. Tangri. "A Libertarian Critique of University Restrictions of Offensive Speech." 79 *California Law Review* 825 (1991).

McMasters, Paul. "Free Speech versus Civil Discourse: Where Do We Go From Here?" *Academe*, Jan.–Feb. 1994, 8–13.

McMurtrie, Beth. "War of Words." *Chronicle of Higher Education*, May 2003, A31.

Meiklejohn, Alexander. *Free Speech and Its Relation to Self-Government.* New York: Harper & Brothers, 1948.

Mendoza, Mariejoy. "Making Friends: Sexual Harassment in the Workplace, Free

Speech, and *Lyle v. Warner Bros.*" 40 *University of California Davis Law Review* 1963 (June 2007).

Michelman, Frank I. "Civil Liberties, Silencing, and Subordination." In *The Price We Pay*, edited by Lederer and Delgado: 272–276.

Mill, John Stuart. *On Liberty.* Edited with an introduction by Currin V. Shields. Indianapolis, Ind.: Bobbs-Merrill, 1956.

Minow, Martha. "Looking Ahead to the 1990's: Constitutional Law and American Colleges and Universities." In *Regulating Racial Harassment on Campus*, edited by Hustoles and Connolly: 203–235.

Modeste, Petal Nevella. "Race Hate Speech: The Pervasive Badge of Slavery that Mocks the Thirteenth Amendment." 44 *Howard Law Journal* 311 (2001).

Moon Dorsett, Dana. "Hate Speech Debate and Free Expression." 5 *Southern California Interdisciplinary Law Journal* 259 (Spring 1997).

Moore, Brooke Noel, and Richard Parker. *Critical Thinking.* 4th ed. Mountain View, Calif.: Mayfield, 1995.

Murphy, Paul L. *The Meaning of Freedom of Speech.* Westport, Conn.: Greenwood Press, 1972.

———. *World War I and the Origins of Civil Liberties in the United States.* New York: W. W. Norton, 1979.

Murray, S. Douglas. "The Demise of Campus Speech Codes." 24 *Washington State Law Review* 247 (Spring 1997).

Napier, Carol W. "Can Universities Regulate Hate-Speech after *Doe v. University of Michigan?*" 69 *Washington University Law Quarterly* 991 (1991).

Neier, Aryeh. *Defending My Enemy: American Nazis, the Skokie Case, and the Risks of Freedom.* New York: Dutton, 1979.

Neiser, J. A., et al. "Addressing Hate Speech and Hate Behavior in Codes of Conduct: A Model for Public Institutions." *NASPA Journal* (Spring 1998): 193–206.

Neu, Jerome. *Sticks and Stones: The Philosophy of Insults.* Oxford: Oxford University Press, 2008.

Nielsen, Laura Beth. "Situating Legal Consciousness: Experiences and Attitudes of Ordinary Citizens about Law and Street Harassment." *Law and Society Review* 34, no. 4 (2000): 1055–1090.

———. "Subtle, Pervasive, Harmful Racist and Sexist Remarks in Public as Hate Speech." *Journal of Social Issues* 58, no. 2 (Summer 2002): 265–280.

Nirshberg, Irina V. "Prior Restraint on Speech and Workplace Discrimination: The Clashing of Two Fundamental Rights." 34 *Suffolk University Law Review* 577 (2001).

Nockleby, John T. "Hate Speech in Context: The Case of Verbal Threats." 42 *Buffalo Law Review* 653 (Fall 1994).

Note. "A Communitarian Defense of Group Libel Laws." 101 *Harvard Law Review* 682 (1988).

Note. "A Consideration of the Massachusetts Group Libel Statute." 32 *Boston University Law Review* 414 (1952).

Note. "Hate Is Not Speech." 106 *Harvard Law Review* 1314 (1993).

Note. "Statutory Prohibition of Group Defamation." 47 *Columbia Law Review* 595 (1947).

Oberst, Thomas. "*Cornell American* Article Sparks Panel Discussion on Free Speech, Hate Speech, and Censorship." *Cornell Chronicle Online*, Oct. 31, 2005. http://www.news.cornell.edu/stories/Oct05/Censorship.cover.TO.html (accessed Oct. 27, 2008).

Olmstead, Audrey P. "Words Are Acts: Critical Race Theory as a Rhetorical Construct." *Howard Journal of Communication* 9, no. 4 (Oct.–Dec. 1998): 323–331.

Olmstead, Richard Allen. "In Defense of the Indefensible: Title VII Hostile Environment Claims Unconstitutionally Restrict Free Speech." 27 *Ohio Northern Univ. Law Review* 691 (2001).

O'Neil, Robert M. ". . . but Litigation Is the Wrong Response." *Chronicle of Higher Education Review*, Aug. 1, 2003, B9–B10.

——. "Hateful Messages that Force Free Speech to the Limit." *Chronicle of Higher Education*, Feb. 16, 1994, A52.

——. "The Pitfalls of Stifling Campus Speech." *AGB Reports*, Jan.–Feb. 1990: 12–14.

——. "A Time to Re-evaluate Speech Codes." *Chronicle of Higher Education*, July 8, 1992, A40.

Oring, Mark, and S. D. Hampton. "When Rights Collide: Hostile Work Environment vs. First Amendment Free Speech." 31 *Univ. of West Los Angeles Law Review* 135 (2000).

Ortner, William G. "Jews, African-Americans, and the Crown Heights Riots: Applying Matsuda's Proposal to Restrict Racist Speech." 73 *Boston University Law Review* 897 (Nov. 1993).

Oshige McGowan, Miranda. "Certain Illusions about Free Speech: Why the Free Speech Critique of Hostile Work Environment Harassment Is Wrong." 19 *Constitutional Commentary* 391 (Summer 2002).

Oskay, Stephen. "Students Rally against Hate at UMC." The Campus Press, Feb. 28, 2008. http://media.www.thecampuspress.com/media/storage/paper1098/news/2008/02/28/News/Students.Rally.Against.Hate.At.Umc-3240371.shtml (accessed May 20, 2008).

Page, Richard Kirk, and Kat HartWell Hunnicutt. "Freedom for the Thought That We Hate: Speech Regulation at America's Twenty Largest Public Universities." 21 *Journal of College and University Law* 1 (1994).

Pally, Marcia. *Sex and Sensibility: Reflections on Forbidden Mirrors and the Will to Censor*. Hopewell, N.J.: Ecco Press, 1994.

Palmer, C. J., et al. "Hate Speech and Hate Crimes: Campus Conduct Codes and Supreme Court Rulings." *NASPA Journal* 34 (Winter 1997): 112–122.

Patai, Daphne. "What Price Utopia?" *Chronicle of Higher Education*, Oct. 27, 1995, A56.

Peirce, Ellen R. "Reconciling Sexual Harassment Sanctions and Free Speech Rights in the Workplace." 4 *Virginia Journal of Social Policy and Law* 127 (Fall 1996).

Phillips, Derek. *Looking Backward: A Critical Appraisal of Communitarian Thought*. Princeton, N.J.: Princeton University Press, 1993.

Plato. *The Republic*. In *The Collected Dialogues of Plato*, edited by Edith Hamilton and Huntington Cairns. Princeton, N.J.: Princeton University Press, 1961.

Post, Robert C. "The Constitutional Concept of Public Discourse: Outrageous Opinion, Democratic Deliberation, and *Hustler Magazine v. Falwell*." 103 *Harvard Law Review* 601 (1990).

——. "Racist Speech, Democracy, and the First Amendment." 32 *William and Mary Law Review* 267 (1991). Reprinted in *Speaking of Race*, edited by Gates et al.: 115–180.

Powell, John A. "Worlds Apart: Reconciling Freedom of Speech and Equality." In *The Price We Pay*, edited by Lederer and Delgado: 332–342.

Prah, Erin. "Project to Shed Light on Campus Hate-Speech." *Daily Collegian Online*,

Apr. 7, 2008. http://www.collegian.psu.edu/archive/2008/04/07/project_to_shed_light_on_campu.aspx (accessed July 25, 2008).

President's Ad Hoc Committee on Racial Harassment. "Report to the President." University of Texas at Austin, Nov. 27, 1989.

Rabban, David A. "The First Amendment in Its Forgotten Years." 90 *Yale Law Journal* 516 (1981).

Rabe, Lee Ann. "Sticks and Stones: The First Amendment and Campus Speech Codes." 37 *John Marshall Law Review* 205 (Fall 2003).

Randall, Jennie. "Don't You Say That: Injunctions against Speech Found to Violate Title VII Are Not Prior Restraints." 3 *Pennsylvania Constitutional Law* 990 (May 2001).

Raphael, D. D. "Tensions between the Goals of Liberty and Equality." 2 *Equality and Liberty* 543 (1977).

Rauch, Jonathan. "In Defense of Prejudice." *Harper's Magazine*, May 1995, 37–46.

———. *Kindly Inquisitors: The New Attack on Free Thought*. Chicago: University of Chicago Press, 1993.

Rawls, John. "Justice as Fairness." 67 *Philosophical Review* 164 (1958).

———. "Justice as Fairness: Political Not Metaphysical." *Philosophy and Public Affairs* 14 (Summer 1985): 223–251.

———. *A Theory of Justice*. Cambridge, Mass.: Harvard University Press, 1971.

Raz, Joseph. "Free Expression and Personal Identification." In *Free Expression*, edited by Waluchow: 1–29.

———. *The Morality of Freedom*. Oxford: Clarendon Press, 1986.

Redish, Martin H. "The Content Distinction in First Amendment Analysis." 34 *Stanford Law Review* 113 (1981).

Rehnquist, William. "The Notion of a Living Constitution." 54 *Texas Law Review* 693 (1978).

Richards, David A. J. "Free Speech as Toleration." In *Free Expression*, edited by Waluchow: 31–57.

Richardson, Dean M. "Racism: A Tort of Outrage." 61 *Oregon Law Review* 267 (1982).

Riesman, David. Comment I. 42 *Columbia Law Review* 1085 (1942).

———. Comment II. 42 *Columbia Law Review* 1282 (1942).

———. "Democracy and Defamation: Control of Group Libel." 42 *Columbia Law Review* 727 (1942).

Roescher, R. A. "Saving Title VII: Using Intent to Distinguish Harassment from Expression." *Review of Litigation* 23, no. 2 (Spring 2004): 349–380.

Rose, Suzanna. "'Hate Speech' on Campus." *Florida International University Diversity Exchange*. Spring 2001. http://news.fiu.edu/diversity/spring2001/p18–19.html (accessed June 9, 2008).

Rosenblum, Nancy L., ed. *Liberalism and the Moral Life*. Cambridge, Mass: Harvard University Press, 1989.

Rubin, Linda J., and Sherry B. Borgers. "Sexual Harassment in Universities during the 1980's." *Sex Roles* 23, nos. 7–8 (1990). Reprinted in *Sexual Harassment*, edited by Wall: 25–40.

Rubinstein, William B. "Since When Is the Fourteenth Amendment Our Route to Equality? Some Reflections on the Construction of the 'Hate Speech' Debate from a Lesbian/Gay Perspective." In *Speaking of Race*, edited by Gates et al.: 280–299.

Rychlak, Ronald J. "Civil Rights, Confederate Flags, and Political Correctness: Free Speech and Race Relations on Campus." 66 *Tulane Law Review* (1992).

Saad, Henry W. "The Case for Prohibitions of Racial Epithets in the University Class-room." 37 *Wayne State Law Review* 1351 (1991).

Sandel, Michael. *Liberalism and the Limits of Justice*. Cambridge: Cambridge University Press, 1982.

——. "Morality and the Liberal Ideal." *New Republic*, May 7, 1984, 15–17.

Savage, David G. "Forbidden Words on Campus." *Los Angeles Times*, Feb. 12, 1991, A11.

Scanlon, Thomas. "A Theory of Freedom of Expression." *Philosophy and Public Affairs* 1, no. 2 (1972): 204–226.

Schauer, Frederick. "Categories and the First Amendment: A Play in Three Acts." 34 *Vanderbilt Law Review* 265 (1981).

——. "Commercial Speech and the Architecture of the First Amendment." 56 *Cincinnati Law Review* 1181 (1988).

——. "The Exceptional First Amendment." In *American Exceptionalism and Human Rights*, edited by Ignatieff: 29–56.

——. "The First Amendment as Ideology." 33 *William and Mary Law Review* 856 (1992).

——. *Free Speech: A Philosophical Enquiry*. New York: Cambridge University Press, 1982.

——. "Is There a Right to Academic Freedom?" 77 *Colorado Law Review* 907 (Fall 2006).

——. "Slippery Slopes." 99 *Harvard Law Review* 361 (1985).

——. "Uncoupling Free Speech." In *The Price We Pay*, edited by Lederer and Delgado: 259–265. Reprinted from 92 *Columbia Law Review* 1321 (1992).

Schimmel, David. "Are Hate Speech Codes Unconstitutional?" *West's Educational Law Reporter*, Oct. 22, 1992, 653–665.

Schlesinger, Arthur. *The Disuniting of America*. New York: W. W. Norton, 1992.

Schmidt, Benno. "Freedom of Thought: A Principle in Peril?" *Yale Alumni Magazine*, Oct. 1989.

Schnapper, Eric. "Some of Them Still Don't Get It: Hostile Work Environment Litigation in the Lower Courts." 1999 *University of Chicago Legal Forum* 277 (1999).

Schneider, Ronna G. "Sexual Harassment and Higher Education." 65 *Texas Law Review* 530 (1987).

Schweitzer, Thomas A. "Hate Speech on Campus and the First Amendment: Can They Be Reconciled?" 27 *Connecticut Law Review* 493 (Winter 1995).

Scialabba, George. "Only Words." *Nation*, Jan. 1994, 135–137.

Sedler, Robert A. "*Doe v. Michigan* and Campus Bans on 'Racist Speech': The View from Within." 37 *Wayne State Law Review* 1325 (1991).

——. "An Essay on Freedom of Speech: The United States against the Rest of the World." 2006 *Michigan State Law Review* 377 (2006).

——. "Speech Codes Are Still Dead." *Academe*, May–June 2006, 103–104.

——. "The Unconstitutionality of Campus Bans on 'Racist Speech': The View from Without and Within." 53 *University of Pittsburgh Law Review* 631 (1992).

Seebach, Linda. "Colleges Shouldn't Guarantee Right Not to Be Offended." *Los Angeles Daily News*. Reprinted in *Eau Claire Leader-Telegram*, Dec. 17, 1994, 11A.

Segal, Jonathan. "The Expressive Workplace Doctrine: Protecting the Public Discourse from Hostile Work Environment Actions." 15 *UCLA Entertainment Law Review* 1 (Winter 2008).

SeLegue, Sean M. "Campus Antislur Regulations: Speakers, Victims, and the First Amendment." 79 *California Law Review* 919 (1991).

Shapiro, John T. "The Call for Campus Conduct Policies: Censorship or Constitutionally Permissible Limitations on Speech?" 75 *Minnesota Law Review* 201 (1990).

Shea, Thomas F. "Don't Bother to Smile When You Call Me That: Fighting Words and the First Amendment." 63 *Kentucky Law Journal* 1 (1975).

Shea, Christopher. "A Sweeping New Code." *Chronicle of Higher Education*, Nov. 17, 1995, A37.

Sherry, Suzanna. "Speaking of Virtue: A Republican Approach to University Regulation of Hate Speech." 75 *Minnesota Law Review* 933 (1991).

Shiell, Timothy. "Hate Speech Codes and Hostile Environment Law." 92 *APA Newsletter on Philosophy and Law* 64 (1993).

———. "Three Conceptions of Academic Freedom." In *Academic Freedom at the Dawn of a New Century*, edited by Gerstmann and Streb: 17–40.

Shoop, Julie Gannon. "Freedom vs. Equality: Battle over Hate Speech." *Trial* 27, no. 1 (June 1991): 12–14.

Siegel, Evan G. S. "Closing the Campus Gates to Free Expression: The Regulation of Offensive Speech at Colleges and Universities." 39 *Emory Law Journal* 1351 (1990).

Silverglate, Harvey, and Greg Lukianoff. "Speech Codes: Alive and Well at Colleges . . ." *Chronicle of Higher Education Review*, Aug. 1, 2003, B8.

Silversten, Matthew. "What's Next for Wayne Dick? The Next Phase of the Debate over College Hate Speech Codes." 61 *Ohio State Law Journal* 1247 (2000).

Simon, Theodore. "Fighting Racism: Hate Speech Detours." 26 *Indiana Law Review* 411 (1993).

Singer, Marcus. "Golden Rule." In *Encyclopedia of Philosophy*, vol. 3, edited by Paul Edwards. New York: Macmillan, 1967, 365–367.

Smolla, Rodney. "Academic Freedom, Hate Speech, and the Idea of a University." 53 *Law and Contemporary Problems* 195 (1990).

———. *Free Speech in an Open Society*. New York: Knopf, 1992.

Stone, Geoffrey. "Content-Regulation and the First Amendment." 25 *William and Mary Law Review* 189 (1983).

———. "Restrictions on Speech Because of Its Content: The Peculiar Case of Subject-Matter Restrictions." 46 *University of Chicago Law Review* 81 (1978).

Strossen, Nadine. "Censuring the Censors of Free Speech." *Chicago Tribune*, Sept. 2, 1993, 27.

———. "Hate Speech and Pornography: Do We Have to Choose between Freedom of Speech and Equality?" 46 *Case Western Reserve* 449 (Winter 1996).

———. "Incitement to Hatred: Should There Be a Limit?" 25 *Southern Illinois University Law Journal* 243 (Winter 2001).

———. "Legal Scholars Who Would Limit Free Speech." *Chronicle of Higher Education*, July 7, 1993, B1–B2.

———. "Liberty, Equality, and Democracy: Three Bases for Reversing the Minnesota Supreme Court Ruling." 18 *William Mitchell Law Review* 965 (1992).

———. "Regulating Racist Speech on Campus: A Modest Proposal?" 1990 *Duke Law Journal* 484 (1990).

———. "The Tensions between Regulating Workplace Harassment and the First Amendment: No Trump." 71 *Chicago-Kent Law Review* 701 (1995).

Sunstein, Cass. *Democracy and the Problem of Free Speech*. New York: Free Press, 1993.

——. "Words, Conduct, Caste." In *The Price We Pay*, edited by Lederer and Delgado: 266–271. Reprinted from *University of Chicago Law Review* (1993).

——. "Law, Speech Codes, and Related Concerns." *Academe*, July–Aug. 1993, 14–15.

——. "Ideas, Yes; Assaults, No." *American Prospect*, Summer 1991, 35–39.

Sykes, Charles J., and Brad Miner. "Sense and Sensitivity." *National Review*, Mar. 18, 1991, 30–31.

Tanenhaus, Joseph. "Group Libel." 35 *Cornell Law Quarterly* 261 (Winter 1950).

Taslitz, Andrew E. "The Limits of Civil Society: Law's Complementary Role in Regulating Harmful Speech." 1 *Margins* 305 (2001).

Taylor, Charles. "Atomism." In *Philosophy and the Human Sciences*. Cambridge: Cambridge University Press, 1985: 187–210.

——. "Cross-Purposes: The Liberal-Communitarian Debate." In *Liberalism and the Moral Life*, edited by Rosenblum: 159–182.

Tribe, Laurence. *American Constitutional Law*. 2nd ed. Mineola, N.Y.: Foundation Press, 1988.

Tsesis, Alexander. *Destructive Messages: How Hate Speech Paves the Way for Harmful Social Movements*. New York: New York University Press, 2002.

——. "Regulating Intimidating Speech." 41 *Harvard Journal on Legislation* 389 (Summer 2004).

Tuana, Nancy. "Sexual Harassment in Academe: Issues of Power and Coercion." *College Teaching* 33, no. 2 (1985): 53–57, 61–63. Reprinted in *Sexual Harrassment*, edited by Wall: 49–60.

Turner, Ronald. "Hate Speech and the First Amendment: The Supreme Court's *R.A.V.* Decision." 61 *Tennessee Law Review* 197 (Fall 1993).

Turpin-Petrosino, C. "Hateful Sirens . . . Who Hears Their Song? An Examination of Student Attitudes toward Campus Hate Groups and Affiliation Potential." *Journal of Social Issues* 58, no. 2 (Summer 2002): 281–301.

Unger, Roberto. *Knowledge and Politics*. New York: Free Press, 1975.

——. *Politics: A Work in Constructive Social Theory*. Cambridge: Cambridge University Press, 1987.

Vacca, Richard S., and H. C. Hudgins Jr. "Student Speech and the First Amendment: The Courts Operationalize the Notion of Assaultive Speech." 89 *West's Education Law Reporter* 1 (1994).

Volokh, Eugene. "Freedom of Speech and Appellate Review in Workplace Harassment Cases." 90 *Northwestern University Law Review* 1009 (1996).

——. "Freedom of Speech and Workplace Harassment." 39 *UCLA Law Review* 1791 (August 1992).

——. "Harassment Law Flirts with Speech Suppression." *Wall Street Journal*, June 28, 1995, A19.

——. "A Hostile Environment for Free Speech." Printed under various titles in *Atlanta Journal-Constitution* and *Albany Times Union*, Apr. 12, 2000; *Las Vegas Review-Journal*, Apr. 13, 2000; *Montgomery Advertiser*, Apr. 15, 2000; *Charleston Gazette & Daily Mail*, Apr. 16, 2000; *Washington Times*, May 11, 2000; and eight other newspapers.

——. "How Harassment Law Restricts Free Speech." 47 *Rutgers Law Journal* 561 (1995).

——. "If Everything Is Harassment, Then Nothing Is." *Baltimore Sun*, Jan. 12, 1995.

——. "A National Speech Code from the EEOC." *Washington Post*, Aug. 22, 1997.

Reprinted under other titles in *Rocky Mountain News* (Denver), Aug. 31, 1997, and *Chicago Tribune*, Sept.14, 1997.

——. "Rights Trampled in Workplace." *Montgomery Advertiser*, July 4, 1997. Adapted into editorial in *Daily Oklahoman*, Aug. 6, 1997.

——. "Thinking Ahead about Freedom of Speech and 'Hostile Work Environment' Harassment." 17 *Berkeley Journal Employment & Labor Law* 305 (1996).

——. "What Speech Does 'Hostile Work Environment' Harassment Law Restrict?" 85 *Georgia Law Journal* 627 (1997).

Walker, Samuel. *Hate Speech: The History of an American Controversy*. Lincoln and London: University of Nebraska Press, 1994.

——. *In Defense of American Liberties: A History of the ACLU*. New York: Oxford University Press, 1990.

Wall, Edmund, ed. *Sexual Harassment: Confrontations and Decisions*. Buffalo, N.Y.: Prometheus Books, 1992.

Wallach, John R. "Liberals, Communitarians, and the Tasks of Political Theory." *Political Theory* 15 (Nov. 1987): 581–611.

Waluchow, W. J., ed. *Free Expression*. Oxford: Clarendon Press, 1992.

Ward, K. D. "Free Speech and the Development of Liberal Values: An Examination of the Controversies Involving Flag-burning and Hate Speech." 52 *University of Miami Law Review* 733 (Apr. 1998).

Weidner, Donald J. "Thoughts on Academic Freedom: *Urofsky* and Beyond." 33 *Toledo Law Review* 257 (Fall 2001).

Weiner, David, and Marc Berley (eds.). *The Diversity Hoax*. New York: Foundation for Academic Standards and Tradition, 1999.

Weinstein, James. "A Constitutional Roadmap to the Regulation of Campus Hate Speech." *Wayne State Law Review* 163 (1991).

Wendel, W. Bradley. "The Banality of Evil and the First Amendment." 102 *Michigan Law Review* 1404 (May 2004).

——. "Certain 'Fundamental Truths': A Dialectic on Negative and Positive Liberty in Hate-Speech Cases." 65 *Law & Contemporary Problems* 33 (Spring 2002).

——. "A Moderate Defense of Hate Speech Regulation on University Campuses." 41 *Harvard Journal on Legislation* 407 (Summer 2004).

Weng, K. "Type No Evil: The Proper Latitude of Public Education Institutions in Restricting Expression of Their Students on the Internet." 20 *Hastings Communication and Entertainment Law Journal* 751 (Summer 1998).

Wertheimer, A. O. "The First Amendment Distinction between Conduct and Content: A Conceptual Framework for Understanding Fighting Words Jurisprudence." 63 *Fordham Law Review* 739 (Dec. 1994).

White, Lawrence. "Hate Speech Codes That Will Pass Constitutional Muster." *Chronicle of Higher Education*, May 25, 1994, A48.

Whitman, James Q. "Enforcing Civility and Respect: Three Societies." 109 *Yale Law Journal* 1279 (Apr. 2000).

Wilkerson, Isabel. "Campus Blacks Feel Racism's Nuances." *New York Times*, Apr. 17, 1988, 1, 34.

Will, George. "Academic Liberals' Brand of Censorship." *San Francisco Chronicle*, Nov. 7, 1989, A22.

——. "In Praise of Censure." *Time*, July 31, 1989, 71–72.

——. "Liberal Censorship." *Washington Post*, Nov. 5, 1989, C7.

——. "The Pollution of Politics." *Newsweek*, Nov. 5, 1989, 92.

Williams, Patricia. "The Obliging Shell: An Informal Essay on Formal Equal Opportunity." 87 *Michigan Law Review* 2128 (1989).

——. "Spirit-Murdering the Messenger: The Discourse of Finger-Pointing as the Law's Response to Racism." 42 *University of Miami Law Review* 127 (1987).

Williams, Walter E. "Race, Scholarship, and Affirmative Action." *National Review*, May 5, 1989, 36–38.

Wilson, John K. *The Myth of Political Correctness: The Conservative Attack on Higher Education.* Durham, N.C., and London: Duke University Press, 1995.

Wilson, Robin. "Colleges' Anti-Harassment Policies Bring Controversy over Free Speech Issues." *Chronicle of Higher Education*, Oct. 4, 1989, Al, A38.

——. "Whose Rights Are Protected?" *Chronicle of Higher Education*, Sept. 8, 1995, A25–A26.

Wirenius, John. "Actions as Words, Words as Actions: Sexual Harassment Law, the First Amendment and Verbal Acts." 28 *Whittier Law Review* 905 (Spring 2007).

Woerner, William L., and Sharon L. Oswald. "Sexual Harassment in the Workplace: A View through the Eyes of the Courts." *Labor Law Journal* (Nov. 1990). Reprinted in *Sexual Harassment*, edited by Wall: 171–181.

Wolgast, Elizabeth H. *The Grammar of Justice.* Ithaca, N.Y.: Cornell University Press, 1987.

Woodward, Lisa. "Collision in the Classroom: Is Academic Freedom a License for Sexual Harassment?" 27 *Capital University Law Review* 667 (1999).

Wright, R. George. "Dignity and Conflicts of Constitutional Values: The Case of Free Speech and Equal Protection." 43 *San Diego Law Review* 527 (Summer 2006).

——. "The Emergence of First Amendment Academic Freedom." 85 *Nebraska Law Review* 793 (2007).

——. "Racist Speech and the First Amendment." 9 *Mississippi Law Review* 1 (1988).

Yardley, Jonathan. "Politically Corrected." *Washington Post*, Mar. 5, 2001, C2.

Young, J. R. "Stanford Officials Try to Trace Origin of Racist E-mail Messages." *Chronicle of Higher Education* June 18, 1999, A30.

## CASES

*Abrams v. United States*, 250 U.S. 616 (1919).

*Aguilar v. Avis Rent-a-Car*, 980 P.2d 846 (Cal. 1999).

*Alexander v. Yale*, 459 F. Supp. 1 (D.C. Conn. 1977).

*American Booksellers Association v. Hudnut*, 475 U.S. 1001 (1986).

*American Communications Association v. Douds*, 339 U.S. 382 (1950).

*Bair v. Shippensburg University*, 280 F. Supp. 2d 357 (M.D. Pa. 2003).

*Barnes v. Glen Theatre, Inc.*, Ill. S. Ct. 2456 (1991).

*Barnes v. Train*, 13 FEP 123 (D.C. Dist. of Col. 1974).

*Beauharnais v. Illinois*, 343 U.S. 250 (1952).

*Berger v. Battaglia*, 799 F.2d 992 (4th Cir. 1985).

*Bethel School District v. Fraser*, 478 U.S. 675 (1986).

*Bishop v. Aranov*, 926 F.2d 1066 (11th Cir. 1991).

*Bob Jones University v. United States*, 461 U.S. 574 (1983).

*Bonnell v. Lorenzo*, 241 F.3d 800 (6th Cir. 2001).
*Brandenburg v. Ohio*, 395 U.S. 444 (1969).
*Broadrick v. Oklahoma*, 413 U.S. 601 (1973).
*Brown v. Board of Education*, 347 U.S. 483 (1954).
*Brown v. Oklahoma*, 408 U.S. 914 (1972).
*Burson v. Freeman*, 504 U.S. 191 (1992).
*Burton v. Wilmington Parking Authority*, 365 U.S. 715 (1961).
*Carey v. Brown*, 447 U.S. 455 (1980).
*Carlan v. City of Cincinnati*, 416 U.S. 924 (1974).
*Chaplinsky v. New Hampshire*, 315 U.S. 568 (1942).
*City of Bellevue v. Lorang*, 992 P.2d 496 (Wash. 2000).
*City of Houston v. Hill*, 482 U.S. 451 (1987).
*Clark v. Holmes*, 474 F.2d 928 (7th Cir. 1972).
*Cockburn v. Santa Monica Community College*, 207 Cal. Rptr. 589 (Ct. App. 2d Dist. 1984).
*Cohen v. California*, 403 U.S. 15 (1971).
*College Republicans v. Reed*, 523 F. Supp. 2d 1005 (N.D. Cal. 2007).
*Collin v. Smith*, 578 F.2d 1197 (7th Cir.), *cert. denied*, 439 U.S. 916 (1978).
*Corne v. Bausch and Lomb, Inc.*, 390 F. Supp. 163, 9 EPD Par. 10,093.
*Corry et al. v. Stanford*, Santa Clara Superior Court, Case no. 740309, February 27, 1995.
*Cox v. Louisiana*, 379 U.S. 536 (1965).
*Crist v. Focus Homes, Inc.*, 122 F.3d 1107 (8th Cir. 1997).
*Dambrot v. Central Michigan University*, 839 F. Supp. 477 (E.D. Mich. 1993).
*Dambrot v. Central Michigan University*, 55 F.3d 1177 (6th Cir. 1995).
*Davis v. Monsanto Chemical Co.*, 858 F.2d 345 (6th Cir. 1989).
*Debs v. United States*, 249 U.S. 211 (1919).
*DeJohn v. Temple University*, 2008 U.S. App. LEXIS 16463 (3d Cir. Aug. 4, 2008).
*Dejonge v. Oregon*, 299 U.S. 353 (1937).
*Dennis v. United States*, 341 U.S. 494 (1951).
*Doe v. University of Michigan*, 721 F. Supp. 852 (E.D. Mich. 1989).
*Eaton v. City of Tulsa*, 415 U.S. 697 (1974).
*Edwards v. South Carolina*, 372 U.S. 229 (1963).
*EEOC v. Murphy Motor Freight Lines*, 488 F. Supp. 381 (D. Minn. 1980).
*Faragher v. City of Boca Raton*, 524 U.S. 775 (1998).
*FCC v. Pacifica Foundation*, 438 U.S. 726 (1978).
*Feiner v. New York*, 340 U.S. 315 (1951).
*Fiske v. Kansas*, 274 U.S. 380 (1927).
*Folkerson v. Circus Circus Enterprises, Inc.*, 107 F.3d 754 (9th Cir. 1997).
*Frisby v. Schultz*, 487 U.S. 474 (1980).
*Frohwerk v. United States*, 249 U.S. 204 (1919).
*Garvey v. State*, 537 S.W.2d 709 (Tenn. Crim. App. 1975).
*Gay Alliance of Students v. Matthews*, 544 F.2d 162 (4th Cir. 1976).
*Gayle v. Browder*, 352 U.S. 903 (1956).
*Gertz v. Robert Welch, Inc.*, 418 U.S. 323 (1974).
*Gitlow v. New York*, 268 U.S. 652 (1925).
*Gooding v. Wilson*, 405 U.S. 518 (1972).
*Grayned v. City of Rockford*, 408 U.S. 104 (1972).

*Gregory v. Chicago*, 394 U.S. 111 (1969).

*Grove City v. Bell*, 465 U.S. 555 (1984).

*Harris v. Forklift Systems*, 510 U.S. 17 (1993).

*Hazelwood v. Kuhlmeier*, 484 U.S. 260 (1988).

*Healy v. James*, 408 U.S. 169 (1972).

*Henson v. City of Dundee*, 682 F.2d 897 (11th Cir. 1981).

*Hess v. Indiana*, 414 U.S. 105 (1973).

*Higgins v. Gates Rubber Co.*, 578 F.2d 281 (10th Cir. 1978).

*Hill v. Colorado*, 530 U.S. 703 (2000).

*Hoffman Estates v. The Flipside*, 455 U.S. 489 (1982).

*Holmes v. City of Atlanta*, 350 U.S. 879 (1955).

*Hustler v. Falwell*, 485 U.S. 46 (1988).

*In re S.L.J.*, 263 N.W.2d 412 (Minn. 1978).

*Iota Xi Chapter of Sigma Chi Fraternity v. George Mason University*, 773 F. Supp. 792 (E.D. Va. 1991).

*James v. Board of Education*, 461 F.2d 566 (2d Cir. 1972).

*Johnson v. Galen Health Institutes, Inc.*, 267 F. Supp. 2d 679 (W.D. Ky. 2003).

*Johnson v. Virginia*, 373 U.S. 61 (1963).

*Kelly v. Ohio*, 416 U.S. 923 (1974).

*Keyishian v. Board of Regents*, 385 U.S. 589 (1967).

*Kolender v. Lawson*, 461 U.S. 352 (1983).

*Korf v. Ball State University*, 726 F.2d 1222 (7th Cir. 1984).

*Kovacs v. Cooper*, 336 U.S. 77 (1949).

*Lanzetta v. New Jersey*, 306 U.S. 451 (1939).

*Lehman v. Shaker Heights*, 418 U.S. 298 (1974).

*Levitt v. University of Texas at El Paso*, 259 F.2d 1724 (5th Cir. 1984).

*Lewis v. New Orleans*, 408 U.S. 913 (1972).

*Loftin-Boggs v. Meridian*, 633 F. Supp. 1323 (S.D. Miss. 1986).

*Lucas v. Arkansas*, 416 U.S. 919 (1974).

*Lynch v. Des Moines*, 454 N.W.2d 827 (Iowa 1990).

*Madsen v. Women's Health Center, Inc.*, 512 U.S. 753 (1994).

*Mailloux v. Kiley*, 448 F.2d 1242 (1st Cir. 1971).

*Martin v. Parrish*, 805 F.2d 583 (5th Cir. 1986).

*Matter of Welfare of R.A.V.*, 464 N.W.2d 507 (Minn. 1991).

*Mayor of Baltimore v. Dawson*, 350 U.S. 877 (1955).

*Meritor Savings Bank, FSB v. Vinson*, 477 U.S. 57 (1986).

*Miles v. Denver Public Schools*, 944 F.2d 773 (10th Cir. 1991).

*Milkovich v. Lorain Journal Co.*, 497 U.S. 1 (1990).

*Miller v. California*, 413 U.S. 15 (1973).

*Moire v. Temple School of Medicine*, 800 F.2d 1136 (3d Cir. 1986).

*Morales v. Transworld Airlines*, 504 U.S. 374 (1992).

*NAACP v. Button*, 371 U.S. 415 (1963).

*Naragon v. Wharton*, 737 F.2d 1403 (5th Cir. 1984).

*Near v. Minnesota*, 283 U.S. 697 (1931).

*New York v. Ferber*, 458 U.S. 747 (1982).

*New York Times v. Sullivan*, 376 U.S. 254 (1964).

*Northern Securities Co. v. United States*, 193 U.S. 197 (1904).

*Piarowski v. Illinois Community College*, 759 F.2d 625 (7th Cir.), *cert. denied*, 474 U.S. 1007 (1985).

*Plessy v. Ferguson*, 163 U.S. 537 (1896).

*Police Dept. of Chicago v. Mosley*, 408 U.S. 92 (1972).

*Rabidue v. Osceola Refining Co.*, 805 F.2d 611 (6th Cir. 1986), *cert. denied*, 481 U.S. 1041 (1987).

*R.A.V. v. City of St. Paul*, 505 U.S. 377 (1992).

*Regina v. Keegstra*, [1990] 3 S.C.R. 697 (1990) (Canadian case).

*Roberts v. Haragan*, 346 F. Supp. 2d 853 (N.D. Tex. 2004).

*Roberts v. U.S. Jaycees*, 468 U.S. 609 (1984).

*Rogers v. EEOC*, 454 F.2d 234 (5th Cir. 1971), *cert. denied*, 406 U.S. 957 (1972).

*Rosen v. California*, 416 U.S. 924 (1974).

*Rosenfeld v. New Jersey*, 408 U.S. 901 (1972).

*Rowan v. U.S. Post Office*, 397 U.S. 728 (1970).

*Russo v. Central School District No. 1*, 469 F.2d 623 (1972).

*Sanchez v. Texas*, 995 S.W.2d 677 (Tex. Crim. App. 1999).

*Saxe v. State College Area School District*, 240 F.3d 200 (3d Cir. 2001).

*Schenk v. United States*, 249 U.S. 47 (1919).

*Schiro v. Clark*, 963 F.2d 962 (7th Cir. 1992).

*Shelly v. Kraemer*, 334 U.S. 1 (1948).

*Shelton v. Tucker*, 364 U.S. 479 (1960).

*Smith v. Goguen*, 415 U.S. 566 (1974).

*Smith v. Metropolitan School District*, 128 F.3d 1014 (7th Cir. 1997).

*Strauder v. West Virginia*, 100 U.S. (10 Otto) 303 (1880).

*Stromberg v. California*, 283 U.S. 359 (1931).

*Sweeney v. New Hampshire*, 354 U.S. 234 (1957).

*Swentek v. US Air, Inc.*, 830 F.2d 522 (4th Cir. 1987).

*Terminiello v. Chicago*, 337 U.S. 1 (1949).

*Terry v. Adams*, 345 U.S. 461 (1953).

*Texas v. Johnson*, 491 U.S. 397 (1989).

*Tinker v. Des Moines School District*, 393 U.S. 503 (1969).

*Tomkins v. Public Service Electric and Gas Co.*, 422 F. Supp. 553 (DC NJ 1976).

*United States v. American Airlines*, 743 F.2d 1114 (5th Cir. 1984), *cert. denied*, 474 U.S. 1001 (1985).

*United States v. Eichman*, 496 U.S. 310 (1990).

*United States v. Macintosh*, 283 U.S. 605 (1931).

*United States v. O'Brien*, 391 U.S. 367 (1968).

*United States v. Schwimmer*, 279 U.S. 644 (1929).

*University of Pennsylvania v. EEOC*, 493 U.S. 182 (1990).

*UWM-Post v. Board of Regents of the University of Wisconsin*, 774 F. Supp. 1163 (E.D. Wis. 1991).

*Vance v. Judas Priest*, 1990 WL 1300920 (Nev. Dist. Ct., Aug. 24, 1990).

*Vega v. Miller*, 273 F.3d 460 (2d Cir. 2001).

*Village of Skokie v. National Socialist Party*, 373 N.E.2d 21 (1978).

*Virginia v. Black*, 538 U.S. 343 (2003).

*Watts v. United States*, 394 U.S. 705 (1969).

*West Virginia State Board of Education v. Barnette*, 319 U.S. 624 (1943).

*Whitney v. California*, 274 U.S. 357 (1927).
*Widmar v. Vincent*, 454 U.S. 263 (1981).
*Williams v. Saxbe*, 413 F. Supp. 654 (D.D.C., 1976).
*Wills v. Brown*, 184 F.3d 20 (1st Cir. 1999).
*Zimmer v. Ashland University*, 2001 U.S. Dist. LEXIS 15075 (N.D. Ohio, Sept. 5, 2001).

# INDEX